The Big Picture

The Big Picture

DIARY OF A NATION

EDITED BY MAX PRISK,
TONY STEPHENS AND
MICHAEL BOWERS

Doubleday

The Sydney Morning Herald

THE BIG PICTURE

A DOUBLEDAY BOOK

First published in Australia and New Zealand in 2005
by Doubleday

National Library of Australia
Cataloguing-in-Publication Entry

Sydney Morning Herald.
The big picture : diary of a nation.

ISBN 1 86471 098 5.

1. Sydney Morning Herald. 2. Australia — History. 3. Australia — Social life and customs. I. Title.

994

Transworld Publishers,
a division of Random House Australia Pty Ltd
20 Alfred Street, Milsons Point, NSW 2061
http://www.randomhouse.com.au

Random House New Zealand Limited
18 Poland Road, Glenfield, Auckland

Transworld Publishers,
a division of The Random House Group Ltd
61–63 Uxbridge Road, Ealing, London W5 5SA

Random House Inc
1745 Broadway, New York, New York 10036

Front cover photograph: Diving competition, Empire Games, North Sydney Pool, 1938. (Photo: B. Richards)
Endpapers: A view of Sydney "as from a balloon", by the Australian artist A. H. Fullwood, was printed in 1888 to mark the centenary of white settlement. Drawn on a wood block and cut into 112 sections for engraving, it was the largest such work produced by an Australian newspaper.
Previous pages: Sydney skyline, December 31, 2003. (Photo: Mike Bowers)
Frontispiece: Front page, first issue of *The Sydney Herald*, April 18, 1831. Government notices and classifieds held sway. News was not run on page one until April 15, 1944.

Cover design by Greg Bakes, Jemma Cummings
Text design by Greg Bakes, Bruce Nicholson, Jemma Cummings
Printed and bound by Sing Cheong Printing Co. Ltd, Hong Kong

10 9 8 7 6 5 4 3 2 1

THE SYDNEY HERALD.

"In moderation placing all my glory,
While Tories call me Whig—and Whigs a Tory."—POPE

TERMS OF SUBSCRIPTION, Sydney, per quarter 5s.—Single Numbers 7d. Country, (postage included) 6s 3d p. quarter:

VOLUME I MONDAY, APRIL 18, 1831. NUMBER I.

TERMS OF ADVERTISEMENTS. For Eight Lines and under, 2s 6d, and 1d each for every Line above Eight.

Public Notice.

Colonial Secretary's Office, Sydney, April 4, 1831.

THE undermentioned Prisoners of the Crown have obtained Tickets of Leave since the last day of publication, viz:—

SYDNEY.

Donohoe Martin, Mangles (4).

BATHURST.

Hunter Thomas, Asia (1).

MAITLAND.

Taylor James, Tottenham.

By Command of His Excellency the Governor.
ALEXANDER M'LEAY.

Government Notice.

Colonial Secretary's Office, Sydney, April 6, 1831.

HIS Excellency the Governor has been pleased to approve of the appointment of Mr. Charles Cowper, to be Clerk to the Commissioners for managing the affairs of the Church and School Estates.

By His Excellency's Command,
ALEXANDER M'LEAY.

Government Notice.

Colonial Secretary's Office, Sydney, April 6, 1831.

HIS Excellency the Governor directs it to be notified, that the following Rules and Regulations, for the conduct of business in the Supreme Court, which have been prepared by His Honor the Chief Justice, have been transmitted to England for His Majesty's confirmation and allowance, as required by the Order of the King in Council, dated the 19th day of October, 1824.

By His Excellency's Command,
ALEXANDER M'LEAY.

I, Francis Forbes, Esquire, Chief Justice of the Supreme Court of New South Wales, do hereby certify, that the several Rules and Regulations, hereunto annexed (being fifteen in number), for the conduct and despatch of business in the said Court, are truly and faithfully copied from the original Rules and Regulations made by me, in pursuance of His Majesty's Order in Council in such case made, and remaining of record in the Office of the said Court.

In Witness whereof I have hereunto set my hand and caused the Seal of the said Court to be affixed, this 17th day of February, in the First Year of the Reign of His Majesty King William, and in the Year of our Lord 1831.

FRANCIS FORBES,
Chief Justice, Supreme Court.

MARCH 7th, 1829.

Bills of Exchange and Promissory Notes.

IT IS ORDERED, that from and after the first day of next Term, in all actions upon Bills of Exchange and Promissory Notes, wherein the Defendant or defendants shall suffer judgment by default, instead of executing a Writ of Inquiry, the plaintiff or plaintiffs may apply to the Supreme Court, in Term time, or to a Judge thereof in Vacation, on an affidavit of the nature of the action, for a rule or summons, to shew cause why it should not be referred to the Master of the said Court, to see what is due for principal and interest, and to tax the plaintiff or plaintiffs, his, her, or their costs, and why final judgment should not be signed for that sum, without executing a Writ of Inquiry; and that, upon proof of service of such rule or order on the defendant or defendants, the same shall be made absolute, and the said plaintiff or plaintiffs may proceed to have principal and interest referred to the said Master, and have the same computed, and costs taxed accordingly.

Admission of Attornies.

IT IS ORDERED, that from and after the first day of next Term, every person who shall intend to apply for admission, as an Attorney or Solicitor of the Supreme Court of New South Wales, shall, for the space of one full Term previous to the Term in which he shall apply to be admitted, cause his name and place of abode, written in legible characters, to be affixed in the Office of the Supreme Court, and also on the outside door of the Court-house of the said Court; and shall also cause notice of such his intended application to be three several times published in the public newspapers of Sydney, during the Term previous to the Term in which he shall apply to be admitted.

SEPTEMBER 30th, 1829.

Division of the Profession.

IT IS ORDERED, that the business of the profession of the Law be divided in this Court in like manner as the same is divided in England, provided that this rule shall not take effect until His Majesty's pleasure shall first be made known.

That the several practitioners admitted in the Supreme Court, at the date of this rule, be allowed to elect to which branch of the profession they will adhere; such election to be made and signified to the Court within the time limited for the preceding rule to take effect.

That no other persons be admitted as Barristers in the Supreme Court, unless such persons shall have been duly admitted as Advocates or Barristers in some one or other of the King's Courts in Great Britain or Ireland.

That from and after this rule, the following persons only shall be eligible to act as Solicitors or Attornies in the Supreme Court; namely—

1st.—Persons actually admitted as Solicitors, Attornies, Proctors, or Writers to the Signet, in some one or other of the King's Supreme Courts within the United Kingdom of Great Britain or Ireland.

2d.—Persons having been articled to some practising Solicitor, or Attorney in New South Wales, and having served the term of five years of clerkship.

3d.—Persons who, having been so articled, and served for any period of time, shall complete the residue of the full term of five years of clerkship in England; or who, having been duly articled and served, as aforesaid, in England, shall complete the residue of the full term of five years of clerkship in New South Wales; or,

4th.—Persons who shall have served the term of five years as a Clerk in the Office of the Supreme Court.

Division of Business.

WHEREAS the business of the Supreme Court hath much increased, and it hath become necessary, with a view to the ease & despatch of the same, to separate the several Jurisdictions of the Court, and to define the duties of the respective Offices;—Now therefore it is ordered, that there shall be three distinct and separate Offices of the said Court, which shall be respectively styled, "The Registrar's Office," "The Master's Office," and "The Chief Clerk's Office."

That, in "The Registrar's Office," all Laws or Ordinances, Grants, Deeds, Mortgages, Wills, and other Instruments, which by any law or usage may be required to be enrolled, recorded, or registered in the Supreme Court, shall be enrolled, recorded or registered; and in the said Office all proceedings on the Ecclesiastical side of the said Court shall also be commenced and conducted.

In "The Master's Office" all proceedings on the Equity side of the Supreme Court, or which belong to the jurisdiction of the Chancellor by the common Law, shall be commenced and conducted. And to the said Office shall be referred all Bills of costs, Bills of Exchange, Promissory Notes, and all other matters and things which, by the course and practice of the said Court, shall from time to time be ordered to be referred.

In "The Chief Clerk's Office" all other proceedings of the said Court shall be commenced and conducted as heretofore used and practised.

That all records, documents, and proceedings whatsoever belonging to or deposited in the said Supreme Court, shall be transferred to the said several and respective Offices, and there deposited for safe custody and reference, according to the nature of such records, documents, and proceedings respectively, and as the same may properly belong to the business hereby assigned to such respective Offices.

DECEMBER 5th, 1829.

Jury cases.

WHEREAS by the statute 9th Geo. IV., c. 83. Sec. 8. it is among other things provided, that if either of the parties, plaintiff or defendant in any action brought in the Supreme Court of New South Wales, shall be desirous of having any issue or issues of fact joined in any such action tried by a Jury, and shall apply for that purpose to the said Supreme Court, it shall be lawful for the said Court to award or to refuse a trial by Jury, as the Justice of each particular case may seem to require:—NOW IT IS ORDERED, that such application for a Trial by Jury as aforesaid, shall be made to the said Court within the first four days of the Term next after issue or issues shall be joined in any cause in which either of the parties, plaintiff or defendant, shall be desirous of having a trial by a Jury, where such issue or issues shall have been joined in Vacation; and that where such issue or issues shall have been joined in Term time, then such application shall be made in the same Term in which such issue or issues shall have been joined in order that the same may be brought to trial on such day after Term as the Court shall from time to time especially appoint for such purpose. Provided always, that such applications respectively as aforesaid, when made, shall be made by motion in open Court on a short affidavit, setting forth the nature of the action, the grounds of the motion, and stating whether the application be for a trial by a special or by a common Jury; and if the Court see fit, a rule shall be awarded absolute in the first instance, for allowing such a mode of trial accordingly.

Entry of Jury cases for trial.

That wherever the party desiring to have any cause set down for trial as directed by the Rules of Court, shall apply for such purpose to the Clerk of the Court, he shall, at the time of such application, communicate to such Clerk whether he intends to move the Court to have such cause tried by a Jury; and in case such party shall so intend to move the Court, the Clerk shall enter such cause in the list for trial on some one of such days as shall, from time to time, be appointed for the trial of Jury cases.

That the following be the form of a general Venire Facias directed to the Sheriff for summoning Juries, in pursuance of the local Ordinance, in such case made:—

George the Fourth, &c.—To the Sheriff of New South Wales, Greeting: We command you, that you cause to come before us, at the Court-house, in King-street, Sydney, on the day of lawful men, of good fame and repute, of the said Colony, and residing within the town of Sydney, or within the distance of 22 measured miles from the said town, each of whom shall have a clear income arising out of lands, houses, or other real estate of at least thirty pounds per annum, or a clear personal estate of at least three hundred pounds, by whom the truth of the matter may be better known, to make a certain Jury of the Colony aforesaid, for the trial of all and every issue and issues of fact joined in any cause, and ordered for trial by a Jury by Our said Supreme Court, in the Term of the year , and that you have then there the names of those Jurors, and this Writ. Witness, Our trusty and well-beloved Our Chief Justice of Our said Court.

Prisoners of the Crown detained in Sydney as witnesses.

WHEREAS it sometimes happens that unassigned prisoners of the crown are detained in Sydney at the desire of parties to Civil issues depending in the Supreme Court, in order to give evidence on the trial of such issues when they shall be brought on for trial, and the crown is in such cases improperly subjected to the expense of maintaining such prisoners in idleness: IT IS THEREFORE ORDERED, that as often as it shall happen that the testimony of such persons shall be deemed necessary in such cases as aforesaid, the party or parties desiring to have the testimony of such persons for such purposes as aforesaid, shall either cause the examination of such persons to be taken *de bene esse*, or, in default of such mode of proceeding, shall enter into an undertaking to the Superintendent of Convicts to pay to the crown the expense of maintaining such prisoner or prisoners during the time he, she, or they shall be respectively detained in Sydney aforesaid, for the purpose aforesaid, which undertaking, if not complied with on demand, may be enforced by attachment.

Term Book entry of cases.

IT IS ORDERED, for the greater convenience, regularity, and despatch of the business of the Supreme Court in Term time, that there be henceforth kept in the Office of the said Court a book, to be called the "Term Book," in which shall be set down, under distinct heads, peremptory cases, new trial cases, special cases, crown cases, and equity cases, appointed for hearing on such days in Term time as are set apart for motions: that under the head of peremptory cases shall be comprehended all short motions arising collaterally out of causes which are or have been depending in the said Court; that under the head of new trial cases shall be comprehended all cases in which notices of motions for new trials, or for arresting judgment in civil causes, shall have been filed according to the rules and practice of the Court, or in which conditional rules shall have been granted; that under the head of special cases shall be comprehended all causes in which special cases shall have been granted for deliberate argument and adjudication, all issues of law, or demurrers to pleading, in which issues shall have been joined between the parties, and all special verdicts found; that under the head of crown cases shall be comprehended all cases in which the name of the King shall be used, either for form or substance; and that under the head of equity cases shall be comprehended all cases on the equity side of the said Court appointed for hearing, for final decree, upon exceptions, for further directions, or otherwise, as the case may be: AND IT IS FURTHER ORDERED, that the Chief Clerk for the time being of the said Court shall bring, or cause to be brought, the said book into open Court, on every day appointed in Term time for hearing motions; and shall, at the sitting of the Court on every such day, call on the causes set down therein under the respective heads as aforesaid, in their order as herein specified, until the whole shall be heard and determined, if the Court shall so long sit, or unless the Court shall otherwise order: AND IT IS FURTHER ORDERED, that if, when any of the cases so called on, neither of the parties thereto shall be ready to proceed therein, the same shall be forthwith struck out of the paper, and shall not be re-entered for hearing during the Term in which such default shall be made: Provided always, that if one of the parties shall appear, but not the other, the Court shall proceed *ex-parte*, and give judgment in like manner as if both had appeared and had been heard.

Special cases.

That whenever the Court shall grant a case in any civil or criminal matter depending in the said Court for solemn argument, the party applying for the same shall, upon notice to the other side, enter the said special case with the Chief Clerk of the said Court, who shall set down the same in the special paper book for hearing on the first motion day in the Term following the Term in which the special case shall have been granted, and not before: Provided that no special case shall be heard, unless a copy thereof, settled and signed by Counsel on each side, be delivered to each of the Judges of the said Court two clear days before the day appointed for the argument of such special case: AND IT IS FURTHER ORDERED, that no special verdict, demurrer to pleading, or evidence, shall be heard by the said Court, unless a copy of the special verdict, or demurrer book, settled and signed by Counsel, be delivered to each of the Judges of the said Court two clear days before the day appointed for arguing the same.

Judgment of non pros.

That judgments of *non pros* may be entered at any time after the commencement of the Term.

Judgment by default.

That in case of judgment by *nil dicit*, such judgments shall be entered, and damages shall thereupon be assessed, on the second and third days of each Term.

Trial of issues.

That all issues in fact joined before term shall be tried on any days after the third and before the twenty-fifth days of such Term; and all such issues joined during Term shall be tried on such days as the Court shall, from time to time, appoint for the trial of issues joined as last aforesaid.

Hearing arguments.

That all arguments shall be heard on some Saturday during Term, or on such other days as the Court shall, from time to time, appoint for such purpose.

Motions for new trial and in arrest of judgment.

That as often as any cause shall be tried during Term, and the plaintiff or defendant in such cause shall intend to move for a new trial, or in arrest of judgment, he shall file a notice of such motion, setting forth in a brief and compendious manner the grounds upon which such motion is intended to be made (and in case such motion shall be for a new trial, shall also, where an affidavit is required, file such affidavit in support of the same) in the Office of the Supreme Court, at least four days before the last day of term; and shall also, within the like time, deliver to the Judge who tried the cause, or at his Chambers, a copy of such notice, accompanied with a request to the Judge to bring his notes to Court on the day appointed for hearing such motion; and the Clerk of the Court shall mark on the back of every such notice and affidavit respectively, the day on which the same shall have been filed; and the filing of such notice and affidavit respectively, in manner as aforesaid, shall be of the like force and effect as the service of a rule *nisi* on the adverse party in such cause: And if the party intending to move for a new trial, or in arrest of judgment, shall neglect to file such notice and affidavit respectively, within the time, and in the manner hereby directed, then final judgment may be signed without any rule, or other notice for such purpose.

That as often as any cause shall be tried after Term, then a notice to the same effect as directed by the last rule (together with an affidavit, if the same be for a new trial) shall be filed in the Office of the Supreme Court, and a copy thereof delivered to the Judge, on or before the first day of the Term next ensuing the trial of such cause.

Bringing money into Court.

That the defendant in any cause may bring into Court, without any order or rule for such purpose, at any time, upon giving due notice thereof to the plaintiff or his attorney, and paying all costs incurred up to the time of bringing such money into Court.

Rendering defendant already in custody.

That as often as any defendant shall be in the custody of the Sheriff, at the suit of another plaintiff, the bail may, on filing the gaoler's certificate, verified by affidavit that such defendant is in his custody at such other suit, apply to the Court, or to a Judge at Chambers, for a *committitur* in any cause in which such application shall be made; and upon filing, in the Office of the said Court, a further certificate from the gaoler, verified as aforesaid, that he has the defendant in his custody by virtue of such *committitur*, an *exoneretur* shall be forthwith entered upon the bail-piece, and the bail thereby discharged, unless such bail shall fail to pay the costs incurred upon any proceedings commenced against them.

THIRD TERM, 11th, GEO. IV.

WHEREAS by the Act of Governor and Council, 10th Geo. IV. No. 8, every person summoned as a Special Juror, for the trial of issues in the Supreme Court, is entitled to be allowed the sum of fifteen shillings for his attendance;—Now it is ordered, that after the trial of any cause appointed to be tried by a Special Jury, the party or parties who had applied to have the same so tried, shall forthwith, in open Court, pay, or cause to be paid, to each and every Special Juror sworn, the said sum of fifteen shillings: And notwithstanding the plaintiff or plaintiffs shall be nonsuited therein, and no verdict actually delivered by such Jurors, as the case may be, and if the party or parties who shall have applied as aforesaid for a Special Jury, shall fail to pay the said sum as aforesaid, the same shall and may be enforced by attachment.

SATURDAY, 4th SEPTEMBER, 1830.

IT IS ORDERED, that the defended causes set down for trial during the present Term, be divided in the following manner; that is to say:—That twelve causes be set down for trial for each and every day appointed for the trial of issues before Assessors during the present Term, according to the priority in which they have been already entered in the cause book: And it is further ordered, that when a cause shall be called on, and neither party shall be ready for the trial thereof, the same shall be put at the bottom of the list of causes entered for trial during the term: And it is farther ordered and notified, that the Court will not sit for the trial of any issues before Assessors after the regular days appointed for the trial thereof, unless the said Court shall be prevented by the illness of the Judges, or other cause, from trying the whole of the cases entered for trial as aforesaid: And it is further ordered, that in future no more than twelve defended causes shall be entered for trial on any one day.

Government Notice.

Colonial Secretary's Office, Sydney, April 9, 1831.

HIS Excellency the Governor has been pleased to approve of the following alterations in the Police of the Colony, namely:—

SYDNEY.

To be Constables.

William Longhurst, came free, from the 25th February.

James Mayo, per Neptune (2), from the 25th February

Hugh Montague, per Recovery (2), from the 25th February.

James Sperin, per Mangles (2), from the 11th ultimo,

Edward Moriarty, per Countess Harcourt (2), from the 23d ultimo.

To be Water Police Boatman.

William Mitchell, came free, from the 25th February.

Constable resigned.

Patrick Fitzpatrick.

Constables dismissed.

Hugh Montague and John Turner, for highly improper conduct.

Water Police Boatmen dismissed.

Michael Garvey, for highly improper conduct and drunkenness, and

William Mitchell, for highly improper conduct.

By Command of His Excellency the Governor,
ALEXANDER M'LEAY.

Government Notice.

Colonial Secretary's Office, Sydney, April 12, 1831.

A BRICK BARREL DRAIN being required from the rear of the Military Barracks to Darling Harbour, persons disposed to contract for Building the same, are requested to transmit Tenders to this Office, by Twelve o'Clock on Monday the Second of May next, sealed and endorsed "*Tender for Drain.*"

A Plan and Specification may be seen at the Office of the Director of Public Works, from whom further particulars may also be obtained.

Security will be required for the due performance of the work.

By Command of His Excellency the Governor,
ALEXANDER M'LEAY

Contents

Previous pages Peeping through: morning fog over the city, from North Sydney, 1999. (Photo: Robert Pearce)

Right Work break: a new home for *The Sydney Morning Herald* in Hunter Street, completed 1929. In 1955 the newspaper moved to a larger building at Broadway, before making Darling Park in Sussex Street its headquarters in 1995 and setting up a separate printing division at Chullora.

Foreword

We are 175 years young, and still chronicling the life and times of the nation and of Sydney, Australia's birthplace and now its largest city. We serve a vibrant population that is proud of its past, revels in the present and is confident of its future.

As this book shows, a great newspaper like *The Sydney Morning Herald* is more than the first draft of history — it is a window on our world and a mirror on ourselves. It is a champion of our democracy: a forum for free speech, a prism for accountability, a chamber of reflection and commentary, a platform for ideas and schemes and dreams.

A great newspaper also knows that its true owners are its readers. Every day we hear from them. They feel the paper is theirs and tell us when it delights them and when it infuriates them. They, too, are proud of its history and are always ready to defend the bastion that is a free press. And they are never slow to take us to task should our journalistic frailties show through.

It has ever been thus because the *Herald* holds a unique place in our history. No nation in the world has so much of its story told in the pages of one living newspaper. There are a handful of newspapers that are older — *The Times* of London is one — but they are all in countries with much longer recorded histories.

The Sydney Herald, as it was first called, appeared just 43 years after the First Fleet dropped anchor. Sydney Town was still a convict dumping ground. Government censorship had been lifted only seven years before, and the many things we now take for granted, such as the vote for all, universal education, public hospitals, courts with an openly selected jury, a market-driven system of land sales and a properly financed immigration program, were yet to come.

Today we live in a federated nation, our population has grown to 20 million, our standard of living is among the world's highest — and we are fighting to stay the lucky country in a world that can be shaken in an instant by the actions of a handful of terrorists.

As important as our words are, our photographs are indelible. The *Herald* has the greatest photojournalism library in the southern hemisphere, with 2 million images, some going back more than 100 years. Those chosen for this book capture the scenes and faces of our collective memory, and depict a world that changes constantly.

We celebrate, we endure, we commemorate, we chronicle, we connect. After 175 years we are in business and in touch. A legacy is entrusted to our successors and to tomorrow's readers.

Illustration by Michael Fitzjames.

Mark Scott
Editor-in-chief
The Sydney Morning Herald

A note from the editors

Above At its birth in 1831 *The Sydney Herald* was printed on a hand-operated Columbian press. An original sits in the foyer of the *Herald's* present-day headquarters in Sussex Street, Sydney.

Despite all manner of obstacles — fire and flood, strikes and epidemics, wartime alerts and censorship, even a lack of suitable paper to print on — *The Sydney Morning Herald* has never missed an issue. For 175 years since Monday, April 18, 1831, the newspaper has hit the streets, or the dirt tracks that served Sydney Town. It was born at a time when explorers were showing the way; the country was opening up and the steady stream of free settlers was widening. Sydney's population was about 15,000; Parramatta, with hopes of becoming the seat of government, had 2000; and the known world radiated to Windsor, Richmond, Penrith, Liverpool and Campbelltown, as well as the outposts of Port Macquarie, Newcastle, Port Stephens, Bathurst, Goulburn and Yass. The emerging

colony's population of Europeans was about 50,000, including at least 20,000 convicts.

Getting the paper to outlying districts in good time was a problem for more than a century, but advances in printing processes and improved transport brought more and more *Herald* readers into the breakfast circle. By the four-page issue on May 3, 1831, *The Sydney Herald*, as it was then known, had enlisted 750 subscribers and took all night to print on its hand-operated Columbian press.

Today's multi-section *Herald* with full-colour illustrations and advertisements is produced from a separate printing plant at Chullora, and the presses can run at up to 80,000 copies an hour. On a normal day the *Herald* produces four editions, updating

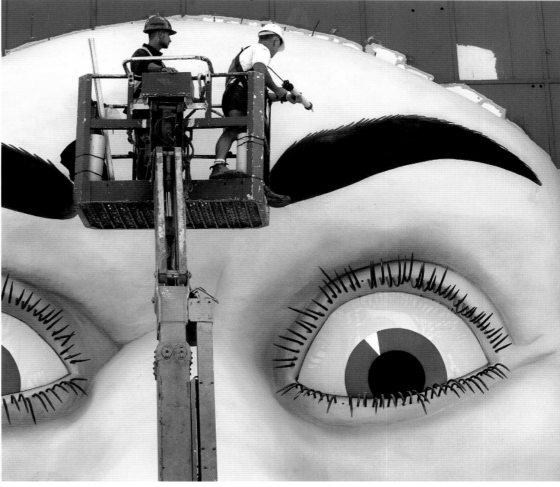

Centre The drowned river valley that forms Sydney Harbour, with a growing city wrapping around every twist and turn. (Photo: Robert Pearce)

Above Workmen touch up the face of fun at Luna Park, North Sydney, 2004. (Photo: Robert Pearce)

the news and making changes as new information becomes available. With major news events, such as the terrorist attacks of September 11, 2001, or the tsunami of Boxing Day 2004, those editions can extend through the night and into the day. The *Herald's* computer website also plays a key role in keeping readers informed. The website — www. smh.com.au — has become the electronic newspaper dreamt of when it began in 1995.

A book such as this can only sample the hundreds of bound volumes of the *Herald* in our archives, which constitute a diary of the nation. When the newspaper began, convicts were still being hanged and flogged within walking distance of the *Herald's* printing works in Lower George Street,

and windmills were our skyscrapers. Today Australia plays a part on the world stage and, instead of rushing to collect papers from sailing ships, the *Herald* maintains a team of correspondents around the globe. The very complexity of events means the need has never been greater for trustworthy information that a quality newspaper like the *Herald* can provide.

That's why 175 years on is a good time to take stock. Having decided against publishing a text book or anything encyclopedic, we set out to produce a sampler that would both inform and entertain. We asked some of our best-known writers to record their impressions of the events and issues that have shaped the nation and its people, using the *Herald* as a reference point.

Sometimes the views from those yellowing old copies can shock: the paper was slow to condemn the slaughter, disease and indifference that all but exterminated Aborigines and their culture; it was reluctant to recognise that convicts could reform and play their part in building a new country; and while it always advocated benevolence for the poor, the *Herald* failed at first to challenge the underlying causes of poverty. Those early views were shaken off with the realisation that there was a bigger, more important picture beyond vested interests and popular acclaim. If the colonies were to be a democratic nation, they had to act the part.

From the 1840s, during the long reign of the Fairfax family, the newspaper began to look at nation-building from the grassroots. It called for, and won, a long-term plan for Sydney's water and sewerage system. The "rorting" of the land sales system and lack of housing standards were assailed. Conditions in the asylums were exposed and corrected. Street-by-street exposés of vice and degradation drove reform and fuelled

slum-clearance campaigns. All these stories have modern equivalents: exposure of the evils of deep-sleep therapy; the alienation of land and funds meant for the wider benefit of Aboriginal communities; the rugby league salary cap "rorts".

In this digital age of "instant information", the *Herald* offers relentless questioning and investigation to get to the truth. The results are recorded permanently in print so that history can judge. The people of a democracy have a right to know if governments, public organisations and businesses are acting in their best interests. The *Herald* has pursued that right since 1831.

Within this sampling of the Australian story is stitched an outline of the *Herald* story, a little of the work of our artists and photographers, and something of the other trappings of a newspaper, from crosswords to classifieds. Our road map for this part of the journey has largely been the work of historian and former *Herald* journalist Gavin Souter, whose book, *A Company of Heralds*, remains probably

the best Australian company history ever written.

We have chosen images that cover major news events, those that capture the changing and growing nation and those that engage or arrest. Many pictures are from the lifetimes of our parents and grandparents — a period little covered in general histories, despite the burgeoning use of newspaper photography.

A newspaper is the work of many beyond editorial, from first-contact telephonists to the people from advertising, clerical, circulation, marketing, pre-press and press, workplace and corporate management and not forgetting our hard-working newsagents. Direct helpers are acknowledged elsewhere but we should give special credit here to our front-line team: Harriet Alexander, a trainee journalist with a great eye for detail; Malcolm Brown, who provided an extensive collection of crime and disaster stories, many of which he had covered; Peter Morris, who did much to boost the photographic collection, in some cases tracking down long-

retired photographers for help; Judy Prisk, the *Herald's* managing chief subeditor, who provided the skills of the newspaper's unsung heroes — the subeditors, who cut, polish, check and write headlines that sing; Andrew Stevenson, whose versatility made him an extra editor; and Felicity Walsh, who did key in-house design and imaging work, as well as keeping the project somewhere near the publisher's deadlines. And a special thanks to the publishing team at Random House.

The *Herald* is on the path to its double century. We believe it continues to meet its pledge from the first issue: "Our editorial management shall be conducted upon principles of candour, honesty and honour. Respect and deference shall be paid to all classes. Freedom of thinking shall be conceded and demanded." Although the views of our writers do not necessarily reflect the editorial view of the *Herald*, they do reflect that original goal: providing a forum for diverse opinions in the belief that debate is a sign that democracy is alive and well.

Centre To be the best: surf lifesaving carnival on Bondi beach, 1935. (Photo: H. H. Fishwick)

Above A Fairfax reporter and photographer on overnight police rounds, Sydney, 1965.

A NOTE FROM THE EDITORS **13**

CHAPTER ONE

Shaping a Nation

Australia's great adventure

BY TONY STEPHENS

History rarely looks like history to people living through it. It looks confusing and messy. Yet we live through history all the time. Sometimes, as on September 11, 2001, the history becomes shockingly and fearfully obvious. Sometimes the confusing clouds blow away, lighting up the land and its people with faith in their potential.

Edmund Barton, who was to be Australia's first prime minister, saw the clouds blow away on a summer's day in London in 1900. He linked hands with Alfred Deakin, the first attorney-general, and Charles Kingston, the first minister for trade, and danced around the Colonial Office. The colonies were to become the Australian nation.

The benefits of hindsight give history a certain inevitability, but federation was a close-run campaign. It is hard today to imagine Australia as a collection of nation states with checkpoints on the borders and separate defence policies but, for some time in the 1890s, moves towards federation appeared doomed. John Robertson, the former premier of NSW who believed the state would become a nation in its own right, said in 1891: "Federation is as dead as Julius Caesar."

As far back as 1856, *The Sydney Morning Herald* had said: "The necessity for some federal system has been demonstrated so clearly by recent events that we presume no reasonable man will deny it any longer." But it took nearly half a century before Barton, Deakin and Kingston presented a draft of Australia's constitution to London for approval. The men had left a land tortured by the longest drought on record and just emerging from one of the two worst economic depressions in its history to meet the colonial secretary, Joseph Chamberlain, in March 1900. They were still negotiating nearly two months later. Finally the parties compromised over appeals from the High Court to the British Privy Council, providing the "golden bridge" to federation. Deakin, Barton and Kingston had helped shape the nation; some say they fathered it.

Forty-one years later, prime minister

Above Two fathers of Federation: Edmund Barton, Australia's first prime minister (left), and Alfred Deakin, the first attorney-general.

Right Sunrise over Fort Denison, or Pinchgut, in Sydney Harbour. (Photo: Kate Geraghty)

Far right After Charles Sturt explored the inland river system, Major Thomas Mitchell, the NSW surveyor-general, began in 1831 four exploratory patrols which led to the spread of settlement. This lithograph shows early settlers on the Darling, with Aboriginal people on the far bank. (Lithograph: G. Barnard)

Previous pages The Endeavour replica heads up the coast off Sydney in 2005, 235 years after James Cook's Endeavour sailed the same seas. (Photo: Robert Pearce)

John Curtin was shaping the nation. In less than two months he created two defining moments in history. He said in December 1941: "I make it quite clear that Australia looks to America, free of any pangs as to our traditional links or kinship with the United Kingdom." The *Herald* saw the logic behind the announcement that Australia's security now rested with the United States. After all, with British forces tied down in Europe, a correspondent had written two days previously: "Australia must continue looking mainly towards America for assistance."

Then, in February 1942, Curtin defied Winston Churchill and Franklin D. Roosevelt by insisting that Australian troops come home from the Middle East to defend

Australia, rather than go to Burma. It is often said that Australia came of age at Gallipoli, but the Anzacs were fighting Britain's war on that sorry peninsula. Curtin's decision to bring the 7th Division home was the act of an independent nation. Some of the returned men joined the New Guinea campaign, the most important battle fought by Australians for the nation's direct security, helping to throw the Japanese back at Kokoda.

After Singapore fell to the Japanese, Frank Green, the clerk of the House of Representatives, found Curtin pacing around the Lodge in Canberra after midnight, smoking. Green asked: "Anything wrong?"

Curtin: "Can't sleep."

Green: "Can you tell me why?"

Above Colonials pack streets around Circular Quay to farewell troops bound for Sudan in 1885, urged on by a *Herald* editorial: "Talk as we may of the blessings of peace, there is nothing that half the world like better than a fight of one sort or another."

The silence lasted more than a minute until Curtin said: "How can I sleep while our transports are in the Indian Ocean with the Japanese submarines looking for them?" Curtin knew he was living through history.

Yet the prime minister and his fellow citizens had little idea of the history of the continent on which they lived, back beyond the 41 years to the federation jig in London, beyond the birth of the *Herald* in 1831,

when the colony was still a jail more than a society, and beyond the arrival of the first white settlers and Arthur Phillip's raising the flag on January 26, 1788. January 26 is the one day of the year that speaks of all that has happened in Australian history: the good, the bad, the inspiring and the shameful. The First Fleet brought cruelty to convicts and the indigenous people but it also brought good ideas, such as the need for

parliament to check the powers of executive government, an independent judiciary and the common law.

Australians think of themselves as citizens of a young country, but their system of democratic government is old by international standards. They had secret ballots, universal male suffrage (for all but indigenous Australians) and votes for women before most of the rest of the world.

The land, of course, is much older, ancient. In the broad pages of history, 104 years of nationhood, 175 years of the *Herald* or 218 years of white settlement is little more than a heartbeat. This becomes strikingly clear to visitors to Lake Mungo, in south-western NSW. Aborigines who lived there 40,000 years ago had water views. To drive across the long dried-out lake bed and to walk around the elevated shoreline and the sand dunes called the Walls of China, over the shells and bones, sharing the quiet with the kangaroos, emus, pink cockatoos and weird shingleback lizards, is to capture the vast, ancient lake in the mind's eye and to feel the enduring nature of humankind.

The first boatpeople to arrive in Australia and to stay came tens of thousands of years after Mungo Man and Mungo Woman lived by their lake, but only one year before the French Revolution and the inauguration of

Above Dan Witter, archaeologist (left), and Badger Bates, site liaison officer, at Lake Mungo National Park in 1991, long dry, in south-western NSW. The remains of Mungo Man and Mungo Woman demonstrated that indigenous Australians had lived there 40,000 years ago. (Photo: Rick Stevens)

George Washington, ushering in the modern democratic era.

Whichever way you look at 175 years as a period of time, however, the view is exciting. Look around Lake Mungo or Uluru and feel the presence of the world's oldest surviving culture. Look around Circular Quay and feel the sense of adventure in the early settlers, or over the top of the Blue Mountains for a sense of the wonder the explorers felt on first glimpsing the sunlit plains extended; see the adventure in how a scruffy garrison town transformed itself into an international city with the help of a famous bridge and an even more famous opera house; see and hear the adventure in the marvellous motley that has become the Australian people.

1838. In fact, the hangings were the first sign of reconciliation between the original Australians and those who followed; they showed that decency could prevail, through the justice system, over racial hostility. The *Herald* recanted soon after.

The discovery of gold took the Australian adventure to the world. The Reverend William Branwhite Clarke, who wrote for the *Herald*, had discovered gold particles near Hartley in 1841; but the finds by Edward Hargraves and John Lister near Bathurst in 1851 brought the first wave of immigration to NSW and Victoria. Yet the *Herald* warned readers against gold fever — "the ordinary pursuits of industry are the safest and the best" — and felt vindicated by the Eureka Stockade in 1854 when more than 30 goldminers and soldiers were killed after the miners revolted against a licence fee imposed by the Victorian government.

The stockade and the Southern Cross flag flown over it are revered in the labour movement as symbols of workers defending their rights; but the *Herald* saw it differently: "An armed resistance to the British Government must involve, under any circumstances, the sacrifice of the lives and property of many peaceable people."

Responsible government came to NSW in 1856, with the election of the first Legislative Assembly. The seeds of Australian

Top Governors of the colonies, with colonial officials from New Zealand and Fiji, at celebrations marking the centenary in 1888 of European settlement. New Zealand and Fiji both considered joining a federated commonwealth.

Above Harold Thomas, designer of the Aboriginal flag, at his home in Humpty Doo, Northern Territory. (Photo: Craig Golding)

Indigenous Australians were the country's first shapers, of course, although other Australians were either slow to recognise the fact or did their best to wipe it from their collective conscience. The *Herald* called the Aborigines savages and campaigned against the trial, and subsequent hanging, of seven men who massacred 28 Aboriginal women, children and old men at Myall Creek in

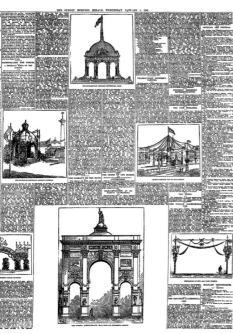

democracy were sprouting. The *Herald* applauded, while resisting the democratic ideal of one man — women's rights were not much considered in those days — one vote, one value. The paper's proprietors believed that property should qualify a man to vote.

Charles Fitzroy, the NSW governor, had written to Earl Grey in the Colonial Office in 1844, suggesting a "superior functionary" with power to review the legislation of all colonies. Deas Thomson, the NSW colonial secretary, first raised federation in the NSW Legislative Council in September, 1846. The *Herald* gave support, powerfully, in 1856. But the movement went nowhere until fears of German intentions towards New Guinea and French ambitions in the Pacific prompted the formation of the Federal Council in 1885. NSW, the mother colony, did not join. New Zealand decided against it and Fiji dropped out after one meeting.

Sir Henry Parkes stepped off a train at Tenterfield on October 24, 1889, and delivered a speech at the local school of arts about the desirability of the six colonies joining in federation. The speech was to take on the grand title of the Tenterfield Oration. The town in northern NSW has its share of history. Major J. F. Thomas, who defended Breaker Morant in the Boer War, is buried here; the rocky hideout of

bushranger Frederick "Thunderbolt" Ward is nearby, and the saddlery immortalised by singer-songwriter Peter Allen, born Peter Woolnough, is in town.

However, the *Herald* was the only newspaper to report on Tenterfield's most famous day. It did so at length, while appearing almost as interested in the train journey itself. The railway was the great cargo cult of the Australian bush. The countryfolk would put their produce on the citybound train and the train would bring back their rewards, with new people, new plans, new prosperity. Henry Lawson wrote:

> *The flaunting flag of progress*
> *Is in the West unfurled,*
> *The mighty Bush with iron rails*
> *Is tethered to the world.*

It was the year in which Banjo Paterson's *Clancy of the Overflow* was published and Tom Roberts painted *Shearing the Rams*. The total white population was estimated at 3,062,477. Aborigines were not counted.

Parkes based much of his speech on a report by a British major-general, Sir James Bevan Edwards, that the colonies offered foreign powers a "tempting prize". He called for national greatness and a convention to devise a federal constitution.

The *Herald* report, "by telegraph", appeared next morning, with an opinion piece beginning, "Is Australia ripe for federation?" The paper said in an editorial: "Great things may spring from the Premier's 'Dominion Parliament' policy, and something also may come of this fast journey

Above The first Federal cabinet is sworn in at the inauguration of the Commonwealth of Australia, in Centennial Park in 1901.

Left Sir Henry Parkes, often called the Father of Federation, gave the push for federation new impetus with his "oration" at Tenterfield, northern NSW, in 1889.

Right Many nations joined the Federation celebrations in 1901. This was the French Arch in Pitt Street.

[14 hours, 18 minutes] from Tenterfield to Redfern." Parkes became known as the Father of Federation.

Success has many fathers, and historians challenge the Parkes title, putting forward the names of Barton, Deakin, Samuel Griffith, George Reid and Andrew Inglis Clark. There is no doubt, however, that Parkes set the federation ball rolling. Forty-five delegates assembled on March 2, 1891, in Sydney for the first session of the National Australasian Convention. With Parkes president, Griffith, Barton, Clark and Kingston drafted an Australian constitution. Griffith, the Queensland premier who was to become Australia's first chief justice, polished the document during a cruise in the SS Lucinda, the Queensland government's yacht, on the Hawkesbury River and Broken Bay. Residents of the area say the Federation founders showered under a waterfall in Refuge Bay.

Although Victorians voted for federation in 1898, the people of NSW failed to pass the first referendum. Those in Queensland and Western Australia did not vote at all.

A second referendum in 1899 won the day. The act giving effect to federation passed the House of Commons on July 5, 1900, and Queen Victoria gave assent on July 9. The dates are forgotten, unlike July 4 in the United States or July 14 in France. The Australian constitution was established by peaceful development, not by war or revolution. Federation was inaugurated in Centennial Park, Sydney, on January 1, 1901. And every January 1 is a day for celebrating the start of one year, without sparing a thought for Federation. Among national days, January 1 ranks well below April 25, January 26, and the first Tuesday in November when the Melbourne Cup is run.

Newly federated Australians had defied the longest drought in recorded history, a drought that made the landscape so alien to transplanted Europeans that many wondered whether the land was cursed. They defied a great depression, with banks collapsing and workers striking, to unify in federation the previously selfish and independent colonies. As it does, the tide turned, and by the early years of the 20th century Australia enjoyed the highest per capita income in the world. Boldness was the new nation's friend.

Yet boldness has often been touched by folly. It was at Eureka. It was with Burke and Wills, who died trying to cross Australia (Australians know more of them than they do of John McDouall Stuart, who succeeded in the same task); it was with Ned Kelly, and with Gallipoli. The Anzacs turned defeat into heroism at Gallipoli, but only after political and military folly landed them there.

The perception of Gallipoli is now

more important to the Australian identity than what the men achieved there. As the historian Patsy Adam-Smith says, Australians are born with a legend, like it or not. They share a fond perception of John Simpson — a saviour who died — and his donkey. They know less about Albert Jacka, a shy youth who landed at Gallipoli on April 26, leapt into a Turkish trench at Courtney's Post, shot five Turks and bayoneted two, as the others fled. "I managed to get the beggars, sir," he reportedly told an officer. He won the AIF's first VC of the war. He won the Military Cross for gallantry at Pozieres in France, when he led a counterattack to take 50 German prisoners and retake the line. He won a bar to his MC by capturing two Germans and saving Anzac units near

Top US President Theodore Roosevelt's "Great White Fleet", on a goodwill cruise around the world, visited Sydney in 1908. The *Herald* published photographs for the first time and circulation reached 100,000.

Above New wallpaper and a touch-up on the paintwork at Sydney's Government House in 1930.

Bullecourt before being badly gassed at Villers-Bretonneux. And he came home.

Australians know more about Gallipoli, a defeat, than they do about Villers-Bretonneux, a famously bold victory which General Sir John Monash described as "the finest thing yet done in the war by Australians or any other troops". Australians have probably never had such an influence on world affairs as they had at Villers-Bretonneux, where they played a major part in halting the German push. They know even less about Fromelles, the battle fought by many Gallipoli veterans as their introduction to the savagery of the Western Front. Australia lost 5533 men, including 1719 killed, in 27 hours in the 1916 battle. It might have been the most calamitous day in Australian history. Leadership folly crippled boldness at Fromelles.

For a peace-loving people, Australians have been involved in much warlike activity. Historians such as Henry Reynolds regard some of the conflict between whites and Aborigines as frontier war. The *Herald* reported in 1841 that Sydney's "two grand points of defence, Bradleys Head and Pinchgut Island, would soon be ready in the event of war with the French or anyone else". The wars in New Zealand attracted 1475 volunteers from NSW, under the banner of the Waikato Militia, in 1863.

Reporting news of General Gordon's death at Khartoum in 1885, the *Herald* added an editorial, "The brave heart is still in death", and a letter from Sir Edward Strickland, a retired British army officer. Strickland had said privately that New South Welshmen should volunteer, and the acting premier William Bede Dalley suggested

Strickland write to the *Herald*. Strickland's letter urged that a regiment of 1000 be "placed at the service of Her Majesty the Queen". The writer thought an Australian presence necessary to maintain the integrity of the nation, and the ascendancy of Christianity. The editorial noted: "Even the Churches have caught the war fever … Men are essentially combative creatures … Romantic natures tire of the arts of peace …"

At the turn of the 20th century, Australians went to the Boxer Rebellion in China, although they arrived when it was all over, and to the Boer War, where they died fighting to help the British keep control over the freedom-seeking Boers. Arthur Conan Doyle wrote: "In all the scattered nations which came from the same home, there is not one with a more fiery courage and a

higher sense of martial duty than the men from the great island continent." Those old wars were fought for the British Empire and on the side of the established power. They seemed like good ideas at the time, much less so now. They were different from Australia's peacekeeping involvement in East Timor, where Peter Cosgrove made his name before becoming head of the Australian Defence Force. Australians stood alongside rebellious East Timorese against the authority of Indonesia. Yet Australia's culture of war can be traced from those old wars to East Timor, Afghanistan and Iraq. Cosgrove's grandfather, Bob Henries, was wounded at Villers-Bretonneux and came home with German shrapnel under the skin near the temple.

The Labor prime minister Andrew Fisher committed Australia to the last man and the last shilling in support of Britain's war effort when hostilities were declared in August 1914. "For good or ill we are engaged with the mother country in fighting for liberty and peace," the *Herald* said. "It is our baptism of fire." About 60,000 Australians were killed in the baptism.

Charles Bean, a *Herald* journalist who became Australia's official war correspondent, was a shaper of the Australian nation, a reporter who helped foster the sense of Australian nationhood.

Top King George VI unveils the Anzac memorial to World War I at Villers-Bretonneux in 1938, a year before World War II broke out.

Above Albert Jacka won the AIF's first VC of World War I, at Gallipoli. He went on to win a Military Cross and a bar to his MC in France.

Without Bean there probably would not have been an Anzac tradition. The Australian War Memorial was Bean's idea, as were the Commonwealth Archives.

World War I shaped Australian character. Gavin Souter wrote in *Lion and Kangaroo* of the returning soldiers: "They were not the same men who had embarked from Australia a few years before, bound happily for Armageddon; nor were their kinsfolk in Australia quite the same. As the heat of summer hardens a cicada newly emerged from dark years in the ground, so the heat of war might be said to have hardened the Australian sense of identity." The historian Michael McKernan says the generation was thrown into war and then into the poverty of the Depression. Their children were thrown into World War II.

To Hitler's boast, "No power on earth can stop us," the *Herald* responded: "We shall see." Ralph Honner shared those sentiments. A soldier and scholar, he fought Hitler in Libya, Greece and Crete before joining the New Guinea campaign against the Japanese and, at the Battle of Isurava on the Kokoda, he led a band of men, most of whom were too young to vote but old enough to die.

Honner's men, with an average age of 18½ years, were mocked as "chocolate soldiers" until, at Isurava, they won the admiration of AIF veterans newly arrived from the Middle East. They exhausted the attackers and their supplies while other Australians beat the Japanese at Milne Bay, the first defeat of the Japanese on land. The Australians retook Kokoda soon after. Australia was a safer place.

Just as Australians recall Simpson rather than Jacka, they know more of Edward "Weary" Dunlop than any other World War II hero, such as Diver Derrick. Derrick left school at 14, worked at odd jobs through the Depression and toiled in a vineyard before enlisting. He fought with distinction at Tobruk, won a Distinguished Conduct Medal at Tel el Eisa and the VC in New Guinea for single-handedly wiping out

Above The two men who did most to turn the exploits of the Anzacs at Gallipoli into the stuff of legend. English poet John Masefield, on the left, said: "The finest body of young men ever brought together in modern times.For physical beauty and nobility of bearing they surpassed any men I have ever seen; they walked and looked like the kings in old poems ..." With him is Charles Bean, a *Herald* journalist who became Australia's official war correspondent. He wrote: "Their story rises, as it will always rise, above the mists of ages, a monument to great hearted men and, for their nation, a possession forever."

10 enemy machine-gun posts in previously impenetrable jungle. Shot in Borneo, he continued directing his troops before dying. He had said, when ordered to withdraw: "Bugger the CO."

It might be that we are more comfortable with surgeon soldiers than with killer soldiers. But Australians do not count many true heroes and Weary Dunlop is one. His courage and tireless work made him a hero, along with other doctors, on the Burma-Thailand "death railway". Yet he was one of the first Australians to recognise we had to build bridges immediately after the war, and

he actively promoted friendship between Australia and Asian nations, including Japan. When some of Dunlop's ashes were scattered in Hellfire Pass, Thailand, in 1994, Michael Costello, the secretary of the Department of Foreign Affairs and Trade, said Weary had shown "that the truest evil men can do will never overcome the best that men can do".

John Curtin, a reformed alcoholic, died six weeks before the end of the war he had waged so valiantly.

The effort he put into the war helped kill him, although his daughter, Elsie Macleod, told the *Herald*: "I think, underneath it all,

it was the effects of the smoking. It would probably have been better for him if he could have got rid of the cigarettes and just had the odd beer." His psychological problems were such that it is unlikely he would reach the political top today.

While much of Australia rejoiced, and many wept, over the dropping of the atomic bomb on Hiroshima, the *Herald* warned: "It [the bomb] has shaken civilisation to its foundations. The impulse to rejoice over the prospective shortening of the Pacific war is tempered at once by consciousness of what this epochal and affrighting discovery

Above Early morning over North Beach at Gallipoli on Anzac Day, 2005, the 90th anniversary of the invasion of Gallipoli. Searchlights probe the sky before the dawn commemoration service, with HMAS Anzac at anchor offshore. (Photo: Mike Bowers)

Top The body of John Curtin lies in state in Kings Hall, Parliament House.

Above *Herald* journalist and war historian Charles Bean took this picture of photographer Phillip Schuler on a pyramid at Giza, overlooking Mena camp, before the Gallipoli invasion.

must mean to the future of mankind. If the invention of gunpowder revolutionised the art of war, the release of atomic power may well, in time, spell the end of war itself; either that or the human family is doomed to perish by its own hand …"

Australians went to other wars and troubled places — Korea, the Malayan Emergency and confrontation with Indonesia. The Australian government asked South Vietnam for an invitation to the Vietnam War, which divided Australians and temporarily robbed Anzac Day of its popularity. By the time our men and women were serving in Iraq, Afghanistan and East Timor, however, record crowds were attending marches and services. In recent times, Australian defence personnel have been working in peace to help deal with the disaster wrought by the 2004 Boxing Day tsunami and, in 2005, to help keep peace in Sudan.

The historian Don Watson says there are two ways of living in and looking at Australia. One is to take the big-picture view, to look at the potential of the land and its people to bring exciting change, to be bold. The other is to sit back and admire the view, an approach which others might call pragmatic. The Federation fathers

successfully took the big-picture view; the men of Gallipoli aimed for the big picture from the heights of the peninsula, lost, but created the Anzac story. The historian Graham Seal says Anzac is a myth of essential facts and certain distortions, but a necessary myth with which all Australians have a relationship, positive or negative. Anzac, he says, commemorates the dead and celebrates the living, but has manipulated the symbolism of national cohesion to help defuse disruptive forces.

Douglas Mawson took the big-picture view. Mawson studied engineering and science at Sydney University, went to the Antarctic with Ernest Shackleton and was first, with Edgeworth David, to the South Magnetic Pole. He led two major expeditions there, enduring heroically in 1911–14. He was largely responsible for Britain ceding part of her Antarctic claim to Australia. He said, about falling into a crevasse: "It was … a rare temptation to pass from the petty exploration of a planet to the contemplation of vaster worlds beyond."

Other explorers before Mawson had travelled beyond the known boundaries, minds brimming with imagination. Burke and Wills, of course; Charles Sturt, who mapped the river system and determined that the hoped-for inland sea did not exist; Thomas Mitchell, who wrote in 1836 of the "champagne country" of NSW; Edward John Eyre, who came from England to drive sheep across the Great Australian Bight in search of grazing land, championed the Aborigines and died in the year of Federation; and the Prussian-born Ludwig Leichhardt.

Leichhardt trekked to Port Essington, near present-day Darwin, after which the *Herald*, with the sunburnt, drought-ridden country far from the writer's mind, reported in 1846 that he had "established the broad fact that our continent possesses an Australia Felix to the north as well as to the south … a land of mingled sublimity and beauty; a land of majestic rivers and graceful streams … of wheat and barley, and vines and fig trees,

and pomegranates; a land of olive oil, and honey; a land wherein thou shalt eat bread without scarceness; a land whose stones are iron, and out of whose hills thou mayest dig brass!" Leichhardt disappeared in 1848 while trying to cross Australia from east to west, leaving inspiration — including the theme for Patrick White's novel *Voss* — in his wake.

Pioneers of the wheat and wool industries, those foundation stones of Australia's early prosperity, boldly saw the potential and became part of the great adventure. The miners joined in. It wasn't until 1992, in fact, that Australia's exports of manufactured goods exceeded the value of commodity exports for the first time. Total world exports had achieved this crossover in 1957, described by Paul Kennedy in *The Rise and Fall of the Great Powers* as a turning point in world economic history.

Of the pastoral pioneers, Elizabeth Macarthur, born in England in 1790, was the first woman of education and sensitivity to reach NSW. During John Macarthur's long absences from the colony, first for a court martial after having wounded his senior officer in a duel, then after his involvement in the Rum Rebellion, Elizabeth successfully managed the merino flocks, winning widespread admiration and helping to establish the colony's reputation as a quality wool-growing centre. She carried on as John sank into madness and then death. Later, William Farrer came from England to establish a wheat suitable for local conditions, crossing hundreds of different breeds every year.

The development of Australian sport reflected the growth of colonial confidence. Between the gold rushes and Federation, Australian rowers and cricketers did more than anyone else, apart from soprano Nellie Melba who won recognition as Gilda in *Rigoletto* in Brussels in 1887, to foster the idea of nationhood. When Ned Trickett became Australia's first sculling champion by defeating Englishman Joseph Henry Sadler on the Thames in 1876, it was >34

Above A typical mushroom cloud rises over the atomic testing range at Maralinga in South Australia in 1956. Many Aboriginal people who lived near the site knew nothing of the tests or their dangers.

Left Security was tight at Maralinga but it did not prevent health problems for those who witnessed the tests.

Speeding up the news

News was a relative term on Monday, April 18, 1831, when the *Herald* was first published. Colonial matters interested readers well enough, but with only 48,000 people in the entire colony, there was a certain sameness about the hangings, floggings and drunken revelry as the convicts and their military jailers ground against each other. The doings of the tiny privileged class — the governor and his senior aides, merchants and bigger landowners — somehow lacked gravitas amid the alien gum trees and the gritty dust blowing from the Botany sandhills.

The real appetite in Sydney was for Home news (home with a capital H, meaning news from England in particular), and from the rest of Europe and the Americas; from anywhere other than Australia, in fact.

The First Fleet had taken eight months to reach Botany Bay after setting out from Portsmouth in May 1787. By 1831, however, the ships were taking half that time. And in newspapers then, as now, getting the news first was everything — even if the mail and the English papers they carried were months old. Competition was cut-throat and good money was paid to lookouts for spotting an incoming ship before the other newspapers did. To get its man aboard first to bargain for the newspapers, the *Herald* kept its own boat with six strong rowers — shown here in a painting by John Allcot. Couriers on racehorses galloped with the papers back to the *Herald* printing office.

In the young colony, excitement about big stories like the Crimean War or Queen Victoria's accession to the throne was as

intense as if the events had just happened. Time brought change, however, and the reports of the ending of the American Civil War and the assassination of Abraham Lincoln were the last major world news stories to first reach Australia by ship. Lincoln was assassinated on April 14, 1865; the *Herald* first reported the event on June 24.

The completion of the cable link to London in 1872 dramatically sped up arrival of the news. The time lag on getting news from the Boer War, for example, was limited chiefly by how long it took a runner to take despatches from the *Herald's* correspondent, A.B. (Banjo) Paterson, on the front line to the nearest telegraph office. In Sydney huge crowds would gather outside the *Herald* offices waiting for the latest news. It was all a far cry from today's satellite-linked phones and instant desktop and laptop messaging.

Above left Delivery lorries outside the old Fairfax building on Hunter and O'Connell Streets, before the publishing company moved to Broadway in 1955.

Above From 1995, when journalists moved to Sussex Street, the pages were transmitted electronically for printing at Chullora, with a new generation of delivery trucks in the loading dock.

Top Douglas Mawson, a knight of great endurance in woollen armour, led two major expeditions to the Antarctic.

Above *The Great Australian Exploration Race*, a cartoon from *Punch* in 1860, depicting Burke and Wills, who died trying to cross the continent.

a proud time for colonials. When England teams first played colonials at cricket, the England XI allowed the colonials 22 men, judging the latter to be half as good. When a Combined Eleven of New South Welshmen and Victorians finally beat the All-England Eleven at Melbourne in 1877 by 45 runs, the *Herald* concluded: "There was great excitement at the close, and vociferous cheering." Two years later, as Fred "Demon" Spofforth bowled the first hat-trick in Test cricket and led Australia to victory over England, the newspaper said: "Cricket, as a national pastime, is of more importance than the issue of any particular game."

The national pastime became an international problem during the Bodyline series between England and Australia in 1932–33. Australia was loosening the old ties with the mother country.

In 1931 (100 years after publication of the first *Herald*) the prime minister, James Scullin, against the express wishes of King George V, insisted that an Australian, Isaac Isaacs, become governor-general. Three years later, the Statute of Westminster was to recognise that the dominions had equal status with Britain. Between these years and with unemployment reaching 35 per cent, the English cricket team arrived with a plan to nullify Don Bradman's brilliance by bowling fast, short-pitched balls at his body, with fieldsmen packing the leg side waiting for a catch as he strove to defend himself. Australia's cricket officials believed the tactics dangerous and against the spirit of the game. The hostility threatened diplomatic relations between the countries. "No politics ever caused me so much trouble as this damn bodyline bowling," J. H. Thomas, secretary of state for the dominions, complained.

Yet the Bodyline row pointed to another of those bold, big-picture moments in Australian history — the postwar immigration program from 1947 which helped set the nation on a sound economic footing. This began the move to a multicultural society which may prove to be

one of Australia's great human achievements — despite the recent harsh treatment dealt to asylum seekers — and which built, among other things, the Snowy Mountains hydro-electric scheme. Harold Larwood had struck fear and loathing into Australian hearts during the summer of 1932–33, taking 33 wickets, curbing Bradman and helping England to victory. Yet when he hit 98 runs in the Sydney Test, the crowd's boos turned to cheers. "I thought they were cheering because I was out," he said later, "but, cor blimey, they were cheering me. I realised Australians like a fighter." Larwood migrated to Sydney with his wife, Lois, and five daughters. Ben Chifley, the prime minister of the country that had been enemy territory, anonymously paid half the family's board for a period out of his own pocket.

Bradman's boldness had lifted spirits during the Depression. So, too, did pioneering aviator Charles Kingsford Smith, until he disappeared while flying from England to Australia in 1935. "Smithy" had served at Gallipoli and won the Military Cross in France. He flew across the Pacific in 1928. In 1934 he made the first Australia-to-America flight in a single-engine plane.

If horses can help shape a nation, they did so through Banjo Paterson's poem *The Man from Snowy River*, which appeared during the depression of the 1890s; through the Light Horse in World War I; and through Phar Lap, who raced during the 1930s Depression. Phar Lap won the Melbourne Cup famously in 1930 at 11–8 on after being shot at, and lost famously in 1931 after being asked to carry an impossible weight. The poet Peter Porter brought his own quality to the race legend: "A horse with a nation's soul upon his back — Australia's Ark of the Covenant, set before the people, perfect, loved like God."

The 2000 Olympic Games opening ceremony in Sydney set out to tell the Australian story, rejoicing in the nation's diverse culture without bending a colonial knee to the old British Empire or to the new Pax Americana. And sport has always been part of the Australian adventure: the players are far more securely in the national spotlight than are our great doctors, engineers, artists, captains of industry or scientists.

While Bradman's 90th birthday was celebrated nationally in 1998, the

Top Sir Charles Kingsford Smith's Southern Cross in the skies over Sydney. "Smithy" lifted Australian spirits with his long-distance aeronautical feats during the Depression.

Above "Smithy" in 1930 with Mary Powell, later Lady Kingsford Smith. His records included the first Australia-America flight in a single-engine plane.

Right The stuffed Phar Lap under wraps after his death in the United States. The great racehorse's heart, hide and skeleton are in museums in Canberra, Melbourne and Wellington, New Zealand, respectively.

Below Dame Nellie Melba, the great soprano who, with colonial cricketers and rowers, helped foster the notion of nationhood before Federation.

Top centre The prime minister, Ben Chifley, watches the Australia-England Test at the SCG in 1947 with Syd Smith, president of the NSW Cricket Association.

Top far right Harold Larwood, the English fast bowler, struck fear and loathing into Australian hearts during the summer of 1932-33, when he curbed Don Bradman's brilliance and was largely responsible for England's win in the Bodyline series.

Bottom right Larwood arrives in Sydney in 1950, with his wife Lois and five daughters.

centenary of Howard Florey's birth in the same year passed virtually without public recognition in his own country. Gough Whitlam described Florey as "easily the most important man born in Australia". Barry Jones listed him among the 10 most influential figures of the 20th century, with Mao, Freud, Hitler, Gandhi, F. D. Roosevelt, Einstein, Picasso, Henry Ford and Stalin. While Alexander Fleming had discovered the therapeutic qualities of penicillin, Florey brought the miracle drug to the world. Health experts estimate that penicillin saved the lives of about 50 million people. Florey and Fleming shared the Nobel prize for physiology and medicine in 1945. Rupert Murdoch is the only Australian, although now a United States citizen, to rival Florey's influence on world affairs. Murdoch turned News Corporation into a major international media empire with operations in Australia, Asia, Europe and the Americas.

The centenary of the birth of Frank Macfarlane Burnet, the pre-eminent virologist and immunologist, was scarcely noticed in 1999. Burnet developed theories on "acquired immunological tolerance" and "clonal selection" that provided bases for modern biotechnology and genetic engineering. He won the Nobel prize for medicine in 1960. In fact, Australians won 10 Nobel prizes in the 20th century, with nine going to scientists and Patrick White's the exception. Who remembers William Henry and William Lawrence Bragg, the father-and-son team of physicists who laid the foundation for X-ray technology and won the Nobel prize for physics in 1915?

About the time Florey was accepting his Nobel prize in 1945, Jessie Street was

an Australian delegate to the conference that established the United Nations in San Francisco. Australia had been, and was to remain for many years, a patriarchal society. Yet Street secured the insertion of the word "sex" in the clause "without distinction as to race, sex, language or religion" wherever that clause occurs in the UN Charter. Race, sex and religion have been three of the ongoing issues in Australian life. The White Australia policy was the first major piece of legislation enacted by the federal parliament, an act of independence from Britain, which opposed the policy. Harold Holt, who succeeded Robert Menzies as prime minister, moved the nation away from White Australia, but its remnants were not discarded until the Whitlam government ratified the 1966 UN Convention on the Elimination of All Forms of Racial Discrimination in 1975.

Religion divided Australians into the 1960s, mainly along a Catholic/Protestant divide. An understanding existed in NSW that Catholics and Freemasons would take turns to be police commissioner. The 1956 Anzac Day march ended in bitterness and confusion when marchers separated to attend two different commemorative services. Sex reared its head in the 1970s, particularly after publication of Germaine Greer's *The Female Eunuch*. Despite Jessie Street's best efforts, women found it necessary to burn their bras and chain

themselves to bars in pubs. The Whitlam government found it necessary to work towards equal pay for women.

The great unresolved issue in Australia is that of reconciliation between the first Australians and the rest. If the sentence for the Myall Creek massacre was the first step towards reconciliation, subsequent

steps have been stumbling and infrequent. The *Herald* reported on the first day of the sesquicentenary in 1938, 100 years after the massacre, that Aborigines had planned a "Day of Mourning" for January 26, "the 150th anniversary of the white man's seizure of our country". The Aborigines appealed for a new policy to raise their people to full citizen status and equality. Indigenous Australians appeared neither in melancholy footnote nor in the index of Gordon Greenwood's *Australia: A Social and Political History*, written to commemorate 50 years of Federation. Jessie Street, Faith Bandler and others took the bold, big-picture view of Australia and campaigned for change, leading to the 1967 referendum that included indigenous Australians in the census and allowed the Federal government to legislate for Aborigines. The High Court's Mabo judgement in 1992, upholding Eddie Koiki Mabo's claim for native title to the Murray Islands, overturned the doctrine of terra nullius, the legal fiction that Australia was unoccupied before European settlement.

Reconciliation with old enemies proved easier to achieve. John Crawford was one of a formidable line of public servants who, like the nation's scientists, are unrecognised by most Australians. As the trade department secretary, he worked with the Country Party's John McEwen to secure the 1957 Japan-Australia trade agreement, the foundation of Australia's postwar economic success. It was a bold, nation-shaping move by the Menzies-McEwen government,

sometimes seen as an administration content to sit back and admire the view. Crawford said: "Menzies and McEwen's decision to begin talking [to Japan] was very courageous and I … advised them to." The agreement ranks alongside Menzies' building of the education system as a major achievement of his government.

The Whitlam government's recognition of communist China produced the next major foreign policy initiative. Whitlam rewrote Labor policies before coming to power in 1972, ending 23 years of conservative rule. Although his government grew chaotic and lasted only three years, he stirred Australians out of political apathy, introduced overdue reforms, particularly in health and education, and turned upside down a hitherto inward-looking nation. The governments of Malcolm Fraser, Bob

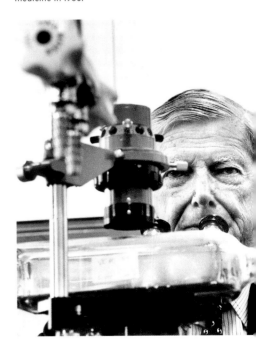

Hawke and Paul Keating continued to look north as well as towards their great and powerful friends in the United States and Britain. Keating incurred the critics' wrath for saying that, over time, Australia would become more of an Asian country, that Australians should accept that they were not an Anglo-American outpost in the southern hemisphere. He urged a foreign policy of "security in Asia rather than from Asia".

One positive aspect to emerge from the Bali bombings and the 2004 tsunami was that Australia's proper place in the world had become clearer. Australia and Asia were inextricably linked, for economic, security and now emotional reasons. John Howard's response to the tsunami was well ahead of those of America's George Bush and Britain's Tony Blair. By 2005 he was seeking new trade deals with Japan and China.

A century earlier, the White Australia policy had been one of the five pillars of what writer Paul Kelly calls the Australian Settlement. The other four were: wage arbitration to ensure a "fair go" for workers, tariff barriers to protect industry, state paternalism that brought faith in government authority, and dependence upon a great power, first Britain, then the United States. Sydney welcomed the American Fleet in 1908, when the *Herald* used photographs for the first time, but it wasn't until Curtin and General Douglas MacArthur in World War II that the strategic link with the US was sealed. Harold Holt saluted President Lyndon B. Johnson during the Vietnam War, vowing: "All the way with LBJ." And, particularly after September 11, 2001, John Howard appeared just as close to George Bush. By 2005, the only pillar of the Australian Settlement

Above The crowd wins over the Queen and Prince Philip during the closing of the Commonwealth Games in Brisbane in 1982.

left standing or not threatened with final demolition was this dependence upon a great power.

By the end of 2007, unless something completely unexpected were to occur, anti-Labor parties will have held federal power for about 74.5 of the 107 years since Federation; Labor for only 32.5. Coalition forces have captured the national mood, usually conservative, more often than Labor. The *Herald* has been cooler towards Labor than have the people at large. The first time it directly advocated support for Labor federally was in 1961. In NSW, the paper backed coalition forces even when Labor clearly looked the better alternative; Bob Carr's Labor was the first to win *Herald* approval, in 2003.

Yet the remarkable changes over the century were fashioned by politicians from all sides and by parties of changing beliefs. Deakin, generally regarded as one of the great Liberal leaders, was largely responsible for the protectionism in the Australian Settlement. Curtin began the restructure of the economy by taking income tax from the states. Howard led debate about economic deregulation in the late 1970s, but Hawke and Keating floated the dollar, abandoned centralised wage-fixing, slashed tariffs, let in foreign banks and put the Commonwealth Bank and Qantas on the market. Keating warned in 1986 of the dangers of Australia becoming a banana republic. His response to a complaint in 1987 about the slow pace of economic reform was that it was possible "to walk into any pet shop and find a galah which could parrot on about micro-economic reform".

Keating's banana-republic warning came

in the same year as the Australia Act, which cut most of the last ties to Britain, including avenues of appeal from Australian courts to the Privy Council. But the final move to a republic was taking longer than economic change. Opinion polls consistently show that Australians favour becoming a republic, a move supported by the *Herald* in 1994. Yet the 1999 referendum kept the monarchy because the various republican forces could not decide what kind of republic they wanted.

Pragmatism, perhaps even timidity, had replaced the boldness of the Federation fathers. When Princess Mary of Denmark and Prince Charles visited Australia at the same time in February 2005, it was the Australian-born princess who attracted the most interest by far. She is, after all, "one of us".

Above The Australian Parliament moved from Melbourne to Canberra in 1927. The prime minister's residence, The Lodge, was first occupied in the same year by Stanley Bruce. This photograph shows it near the end of construction.

POLITICS Trials and triumphs

Australia was a politics-free zone for 36 years after the First Fleet dropped anchor in Sydney Cove, at least as far as newspapers were concerned. But in 1824, with the lifting of government censorship under governor Sir Thomas Brisbane, the floodgates were opened. Instead of the government boosterism of *The Sydney Gazette*, new publications appeared ready to brawl over the causes of their private owners, and to take on the governor or anyone else who got in their way.

Governor Ralph Darling took over from Brisbane in 1825, and the enduring love-hate relationship between politicians and the press got under way in earnest. Darling was an old-mould autocrat and clashed hard with the notion of a free press. He tried desperately to turn back the clock by proposing new legislation — "the gagging act" — requiring newspapers to be licensed on his say-so, and trying to introduce a crippling stamp duty of four pence a copy. This brought on one of the most significant setbacks for executive power in our early history; Sir Francis Forbes, the colony's first chief justice, knocked back both measures as unconstitutional. Darling then clogged the courts with libel actions. Edward Smith Hall, who was proprietor, editor, printer and publisher of *The Monitor*, spent about three years in jail for various convictions, but his railing about the treatment of convicts and the conduct of officialdom continued unabated. Political reporting and debate was here to stay.

The *Herald* saw six months of Darling's rule before he was recalled in September 1831, and preferred the more measured view, hoping that the arrival of Bourke, the new governor, might relieve "the darkness of our horizon at present". Being all for decorum, the *Herald* did think "disgraceful" the antics of a boatload of celebrating colonists who rowed out to Darling's ship as it awaited departure to jeer him.

The *Herald's* natural home base was conservatism, but its early "sworn to no Master, of no Sect am I" motto drove it to seek balance and to analyse on merit the policy of all parties, citing in its defence the "de facto opposition" role of a newspaper. And in politics, if you are not for us you are against us. Clashes with government have not been as raw as in Darling's day, but more modern skirmishes, including a state tax on newspapers threatened in the 1920s, the withdrawal of government advertising and, during World War II, an armed confrontation with federal authorities over censorship, not to mention the forced break-up of media groups in the 1980s, still carry the lesson that newspapers take on politicians at their own risk.

For the newspapers of today, there is still no free ride. But politics now is more robust. Past excesses have led governments to complement the vigorous press scrutiny with strict compliance rules and watchdog organisations. The pictorial essay on these pages tells a familiar story across the years.

There are politicians in power today who will go down in the history books as nation builders. And there are those who will flare briefly across the sky, or will rise full of promise only to bring themselves down with some silly act or be brought down by outside events or by others impatient for their own turn in the spotlight of history.

Above John Howard, prime minister since 1996, overtook Bob Hawke's record in 2004 to become the second longest-serving prime minister, after Robert Menzies. Peter Costello (top) was usually seen as Howard's successor. Speculation about when he might succeed became perennial. (Photo: Penny Bradfield)

Left Howard is congratulated by his wife, Janette, after winning Liberal Party preselection for the Bennelong electorate in 1973. (Photo: Kevin Berry)

Right Waterside workers refused in 1938 to
load scrap metal, on the grounds that it would
be used to make munitions for the Japanese
war against China. The dispute led to Robert
Menzies being called "Pig Iron Bob". When
Menzies went to Wollongong in 1939, police
called on communist union leaders to help
him through a crowd of hostile workers.
(Photo: Norman Brown)

Above A Communist Party meeting in the Sydney Domain in 1949.

Left Liberals Billy McMahon and Harold Holt oppose Labor's Doc Evatt and Arthur Calwell in a 1958 Channel Seven television debate. The moderator was Angus Maude, the *Herald* editor who had been a Tory MP in England and was to return to the Commons. (Photo: Frank Burke)

Top far left The former prime minister Billy Hughes advised Australians that they should populate or perish. He visited Crown Street Women's Hospital in 1938 to witness his policy in action. (Photo: Gordon Short)

Bottom far left Labor electioneering from the back of a truck in Sydney's eastern suburbs in 1935. (Photo: Harry Martin)

Bottom centre Bertram Stevens, the NSW premier, delivers a policy speech via radio in 1935. (Photo: Thos Fisher)

Top right Enemies turned allies; Malcolm Fraser and Gough Whitlam, whose political struggle led to Whitlam's sacking by the governor-general, Sir John Kerr, in 1975, joined forces in 1991 to oppose the sale of the Fairfax group to Conrad Black's consortium.

Below Pauline Hanson doorknocks in Ipswich in 1999. She had formed her own One Nation party in the 1990s. (Photo: Dean Sewell)

Right Natasha Stott Despoja launches the Australian Democrats' vision for the information society in 1999. Women play an increasing role in Australian politics but only the Democrats have elected women as federal leaders: Janine Haines, Janet Powell, Cheryl Kernot, Meg Lees, Stott Despoja and Lyn Allison. (Photo: Robert Pearce)

Far right Bob Hawke and Paul Keating led Labor governments from 1983 to 1996. But the relationship between Hawke and his treasurer wore thin and Keating defeated Hawke for the leadership in 1991. Here they are attending the premiers' conference in May 1991, about six months before Keating took over. (Photos: Peter Morris)

Top The prime minister John Gorton swam and rowed a surfboat after opening North Bondi Surf Lifesaving Club extensions in 1968. (Photo: John O'Gready)

Above The former prime minister Billy McMahon takes to the waves on a surfboard. (Photo: Rick Stevens)

Top right Prime minister Harold Holt with his stepdaughters-in-law, (from left) Amanda, Caroline and Paulette. Holt disappeared while swimming off Cheviot beach, Portsea, in 1967.

Right Juni Morosi and Jim Cairns, deputy prime minister in the Whitlam government, take it easy in 1977. The couple formed one of the most controversial liaisons in Australian political history. They brought defamation actions over suggestions they were having an affair, but Cairns admitted as much in 2002.

Left Doug Anthony, then acting prime minister, at his caravan in the northern NSW town of New Brighton in December 1981. Anthony regularly "ran" the country from his caravan during the summer holiday period while Malcolm Fraser was on vacation.

Bottom left Bob Hawke and Blanche d'Alpuget married in 1995 and bared their feet, and some of their souls, to *Good Weekend* in 1998.

Bottom right Bob Carr, then premier of NSW, bared most of his body for the January 2004 issue of *the (sydney) magazine*, which named him Man of the Year.

CAMEL WAGGON CONVEYING PRISONERS AND PATIENTS FROM MOUNT BROWNE.

The first newspaper pictures of momentous and mundane events came from the hand of the artist. In the early days of the colony, when there were no cameras and printing techniques were primitive, the engraver was the go-between. He transformed everything — from grand paintings to simple drawings of products for sale in the shops of Sydney Town — into a series of etched lines. The finished product was inked and put in place under the old Columbian press and, presto, Mrs Hordern's fine high-brimmed bonnets were there for the world to admire.

The golden period for illustrators was between 1870 and 1890, when there was a huge demand for illustrations of major news events. The capture of Captain Moonlight, the Kelly Gang's last stand, the burning of the Garden Palace and portraits of notable visitors, including Anthony Trollope and Sarah Bernhardt, featured in the *Herald's* weekly, *The Sydney Mail*. A. H. Fullwood's magnificent view of Sydney "as from a balloon" — the largest wood engraving that had been produced in any newspaper in Australia — was made for the centenary celebrations of 1888 and is reproduced on the endpapers of this book.

Photography brought stiff competition, particularly from the 1890s, as Australia caught up with new printing techniques — but the illustrators fought back. Their weapon was to show what a photograph could not: the world through the artist's eye. The caricature, perfected by *Punch* and other satirical weeklies, became a stock-in-trade, so much so that it seemed to many that the more an artist parodied the looks and foibles of public figures, the more the real person came to resemble the fictitious one.

Today the illustrator also tackles the task of visual commentary, giving a take on events great and small that come under the notice of a daily newspaper. Complicated issues are summed up in one powerful image, fads and fixations are skewered, and we are invited to see the funny or ridiculous sides of our daily lives.

Each new breakthrough in technology, particularly in the area of computer-generated images, widens the opportunities. As the illustrations on these pages show, the *Herald* has embraced the gamut but continues to let shine the work of the artist who begins in the time-honoured way: with pen poised over a blank piece of paper.

Above Amanda Upton's *Opera and the Muse* for a Spectrum story by David Malouf on the role of the librettist.

Top centre Camels used to pull a coach during a drought near Wilcannia in the 1880s – a typical *Sydney Mail* illustration of the time.

Top far left A simple bonnet in an advertisement in 1834 – the first illustration used in the *Herald*.

Bottom far left A mask ringed by human skulls, brought back to Sydney from a Pacific island, was the first news illustration in the editorial pages – in 1836.

Left *Odd Mum Out* by Richard Collins illustrated a Spectrum story on mothers and the hierarchy of the schoolyard.

Above Rocco Fazzari's *Some are More Equal than Others* – on the fate of animals, for Insight.

Right John Shakespeare's *Kiwi Kong*, for a Spectrum story on filmmaker Peter Jackson.

Below Rocco Fazzari depicted Billy Hughes for a centenary of Federation special.

Below right John Shakespeare's *Fat Cat and Mere Mouse* illustrated a story on asking for more money in My Career.

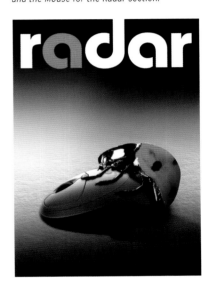

Above Jojin Kang's *Greening Sydney* for News Review.

Top far right *Plant Life* by Kerrie Leishman for Domain.

Right *A Word in Your Ear* by Michael Fitzjames.

Above Simon Letch's illustration *Karaoke King*.

Left *Cat Stroke* by Simon Letch.

CHAPTER TWO

Settlement

The rise of a city

BY DAVID MARR

By the 1830s not much remained of Sydney's early picaresque charm. The windmills were gone. The tank stream was a squalid ditch. Governor Macquarie's dream of a great colonial city — another Calcutta or Dublin — had been abandoned. A few fine buildings stood incongruously among shops, dilapidated cottages and crowded wharves. The streets were mud and dust.

Yet the city was booming — dirty, mean, bursting at the seams, hell-bent on profit, arrogant, uglier by the day and thriving. Then and now, Sydney is most itself and most rackety when the going is good. Once the early governors' high hopes were set aside, Sydney was left to grow like a lanky adolescent, all of its own accord. The real genius of the town was and is for making money and making do.

Sydney has been a city of contradictions from day one: a great place to anchor ships but a damned difficult place to build a city. The only words anyone remembers Captain Arthur Phillip uttering are his little rhapsody on a harbour "in which a thousand sail of the line may ride in most perfect security". But what was there onshore? How were they to house and feed 1500 convicts and their keepers with another fleet on the way? All they had at Sydney Cove was a single stream, lousy soil and a lot of fish.

But what was meant to be a dumping house for British convicts flourished through lucky break after lucky break to become a great port, then a great city. Nothing much was planned. The prevailing instincts of government have always been to scrimp and save. In this town, luck has been everything. They were lucky to find good soil upriver, clay for bricks close at hand and, over the water in Pyrmont, cliffs of superb golden stone. That's still the colour of Sydney.

Those who really love this town never stop complaining about its failings. Pride and despair — pride in its beauty and despair at the botched job we've made of the place over a couple of centuries — are two sides of the same coin. The rule seems to be that the more passionate you are about Sydney, the more you complain about the waste, the filth, the crowds, the expense, the heat, the trains, the politicians, the preachers, the crime and corruption, the roads, the buildings, and what makes the city most obviously itself: the sprawling suburbs.

That Sydney would be more civilised — somehow more European — if only it were more compact is an idea that never dies. Yet every attempt to contain Sydney has failed from the beginning.

The neat little settlement Phillip had in mind spread south as soon as he sailed away. Governor Bligh's determination to tidy up the city by taking back land seized by army officers, helped bring him undone. Macquarie's courts and bridges were condemned by London as evidence of hubris

Left Recycling the city: in 2000, 35 years after the photograph on pages 58–59 was taken, foreman Lex Rollason takes the place of Lance Shelton on the latest building to occupy the site in Bent Street. He is working on the curved top to Aurora Place, designed by Renzo Piano. (Photo: Andrew Taylor)

Below The two buildings that took earlier turns on the Aurora Place site: the State Office Block – dubbed the Black Stump – demolished in 1998 (Photo: Sahlan Hayes); and the old public library, which occupied the site from 1845. (Image: State Library of NSW)

and waste. After he departed in 1822, Sydney became the makeshift capital of a makeshift but booming colony.

Bringing order to the city has been one of the great causes of Sydney and *The Sydney Morning Herald* for 175 years. Civic debate on wharves, sewers, markets and roads has been a staple of the paper from the beginning, and in its pages citizens have debated big ideas for bridges, plazas, opera houses, harbour crossings, slum clearance, boulevards, cathedrals, sports grounds and parliament houses.

Few of these ideas ever come to anything and for the most part we should be grateful. So much of what we love about Sydney today — Centennial Park, old Macquarie Street, The Rocks and Paddington — were all to be swept away to make room for one scheme

Half a century was spent never quite
coming to grips with the growing need
to link the north and south sides of the
harbour. Only when it couldn't be avoided
any longer was the Sydney Harbour Bridge
finally built — and then it was built with
magnificent panache. Part of the immense
excitement around the building of the
bridge in the 1920s — even its cult status as
a subject for painting — was the hope that
this was a sign in steel and stone that the
sprawling incoherence of Sydney could
be tamed.

The true story of Sydney is its own
unstoppable, uncontrolled growth. In the
decade before *The Sydney Herald* began
publication in 1831, the population of the
town doubled to about 16,000. For a few
decades after that, the population just kept
doubling, levelled off for a while from the
1860s, when Melbourne was booming,
and picked up the pace again after
federation, adding nearly 200,000 every
decade until Sydney passed the million mark
early in the 1920s.

Sydney was — and remains — the city
where fresh arrivals most want to live. Sydney
is Australia for them and for much of the
world. New people pouring in from Europe
saw the city's population double again by the
mid-1950s. These were the years of Nissen
huts in the suburbs. Children growing up on
the north shore in the 1950s remember those
rows of mysterious, round-roofed, corrugated
iron sheds at the back of Killara with lines of
washing flapping in the bush.

The 3 million mark was reached in the
late 1980s and now the population is over
4 million, lapping the mountains, crowding
the coast, nosing into the Hunter Valley, as
hungry as ever for land. It's the sprawl that
never ended.

Something deep in the city's soul
shaped that sprawl. Travellers to the early
colony were curious about how Sydney and
its people were turning out. Early visitors
found these men and women — who called
themselves Australians, so the name stuck

or another. On the other hand, there was the
Garden Palace exhibition pavilion, which
briefly occupied a huge swathe of the Botanic
Gardens. Fortunately, in 1882, it burnt down
— unfortunately taking most of the early
colonial archive with it.

Though we debate great civic gestures
endlessly, they rarely happen unless they're
forced on us. The Opera House is the one
sublime exception to the rule, a dream that
somehow got built. It's changed the way we
feel about this town and all that's possible
here. We bask in the world's praise for having
built it, even as we baulk at putting the
money into finishing Joern Utzon's interiors.
For the outside world, the Opera House has
become the symbol of Sydney. But if you
live here, you know the real thing is still
the bridge.

to the country — as exotic as Aborigines and kangaroos. Visitors were dismayed or delighted by their bearing, manners, clothes, intelligence, education, modesty — and their way of living, even in the middle of the city, in cottages with gardens.

Most of these city cottages had disappeared by the 1820s, but not the taste for living in them. Citizens who could afford a horse were moving to the outskirts of the town to build new cottages there. Though the town was straggling out into the surrounding countryside by the 1850s and 1860s, Sydney remained quite compact until the 1870s, when steam trams and then suburban trains democratised commuting. That's when the city burst outwards.

Sydney's new suburbs of cottages and gardens clung to tram tracks and railway lines

Above Sign in a lift at the Commonwealth Bank, 1930s.

Top right Sydney by night in 1933. Brightly lit Martin Place is in the centre. The old *Sun* newspaper building in the foreground on Castlereagh Street was soon to come down to allow the plaza's final extension.

Right Until the Argyle Cut was completed, The Rocks area of Sydney was split by a sandstone ridge, with the only link a steep set of stairs cut into the rock. Convicts in chain gangs began the cut in 1843 and it was completed by Sydney Municipal Council using explosives in 1859. The rubble was used to fill the mouth of the Tank Stream as part of the reshaping of Sydney Cove into today's Circular Quay. The bridges were built for Gloucester Street, Cumberland Street and Princes Street in the 1860s – the last later disappearing to make way for the Harbour Bridge.

for the next 70 or 80 years. Sydney was still a walking town. Commuters reached their stop out in the suburbs, folded their evening paper and walked home. Then, in the 1950s, came cars for the masses. They changed the way we lived and built. They transformed the map of Sydney, first filling in between the lines, then throwing the boundaries of the city further and further out.

Once we had cars, there was no stopping the Sydney sprawl.

Those who despair about this and tell horror stories of the new suburbs encircling — indeed throttling — the city, should look at old photographs of Vaucluse when it was first cut up into building blocks. The result was as ugly in its way as the McMansion territory of the city's fringe is today. The march of raw suburbs through the bush, deplored from the moment it began, softens after a decade or so. Trees grow and houses settle into the landscape. Time does good work even in the suburbs.

Sydney is now so huge we have only the faintest idea where its edges are. Once it could be photographed from a light plane, but now we can only capture its full expanse from space.

Wherever we live in the town — Liverpool or Surry Hills — we have only a rough idea where new suburbs with very English names are springing up. We know our own Sydney intimately: the city where we grew up, work, live, shop and swim. Then there is the Sydney we half know, which still feels like our town. But beyond these >68

Above The Astor, Sydney's first high-rise apartment block, was the city's premier address until height restrictions were lifted, allowing super-size blocks with penthouses and sub-penthouses — and spectacular views to the mountains and to the sea.

Lost in time

The signal for half a million spectators to begin a procession through the streets of Sydney to celebrate the federation of the Australian colonies on January 1, 1901, was given at precisely 10am. It came from Great Parkes, the mighty 5-ton bell, which was positioned in the General Post Office (GPO) tower in 1891.

In another nation this would have lifted it to the status of an icon — an Australian liberty bell. But the bell went into storage during World War II and stayed there for 22 years. In 1942 authorities feared that the tower might provide a beacon for Japanese bombers, and its collapse would destroy the city's communication centre. So the stones were pieced away, bells and clock stowed in the telephone exchange building.

The GPO was then the colony's grandest public building, designed in Italian Renaissance style by colonial architect James Barnet and completed at considerable expense in 1874. The bell was inscribed with the initials "H. P.", honouring Sir Henry Parkes, five times premier of NSW and often called the father of federation.

The main bell had mini counterparts, which chimed out the quarter hours, and each bell bore a line of the Tennyson poem *Memoriam*: "Ring out the false, ring in the true"; "Ring out the old, ring in the new"; "Ring out the feud of rich and poor"; "Ring out false pride in place and blood"; "Ring in the common love of good".

They were known as the most reliable timekeepers in the city. When a pendulum snapped and the clock stopped for a day in January 1930, *The Sydney Morning Herald* reported that morning commuters panicked: "Many deserted the trams and fled desperately to their offices. Others were not calmed until hasty conferences among watch-owners convinced them that their alarm clocks had not failed in their duty. The 'town clock' had stopped."

When the tower failed to reappear after the end of the war, *Herald* letter-writers and editorials staged a campaign for its return. The government stalled, citing cost; at one stage it was suggested that it be rebuilt in Hyde Park. Debate in parliament resulted in the tower's reassembly atop the GPO in 1964, with a few of the stones, so carefully numbered in the dismantling, found spare on completion.

The next threat to the bells was not until 1999, when the building opened as a five-star hotel and shopping complex, the GPO having closed in 1990. Hotel management wanted to end the ringing of the bells, which they feared would disturb their jet-lagged guests. Hotels, hospitals, clubs and residents had been making the same complaint as early as the 1920s, and the chimes had been suspended between 11pm and 6am from 1927.

This time, conservationists and management reached a compromise, and the bells now chime out the hours between 9am and 9pm.

Top Detail from the facade of the General Post Office, Sydney, the city's crowning architectural achievement when it opened in 1874. (Photo: James Alcock)

Above We are not amused: electricians Tom Dixon and Ian Hatton help to freshen up Queen Victoria after a 15-year refurbishment concluded in 1999. (Photo: Andrew Taylor)

Above Rainy day, Hyde Park, 1938. The city was experiencing unseasonal rains – parts of Narrabeen were isolated and wharfies stopped unloading goods because of the lack of shelter. Enough rain fell in three days to supply Sydney with water for two months. (Photo: K. Rainsford)

Top right The sandstone ramparts of South Head in the 1930s, looking over Diamond Bay to Vaucluse, Rose Bay and the broad harbour beyond.

personal maps lies a shapeless, barely known metropolis sprawling over the horizon. The sprawl is Sydney.

The centre of the city is now fixed in the middle of that sprawl somewhere near Parramatta, but the city's heart is still the harbour. That hasn't shifted since Phillip dropped anchor at the edge of Sydney Cove in 1788.

The harbour is the reason the city exists and the source of its prosperity for most of the past two centuries. And despite the fact that we all come and go by air these days, the Heads and the harbour remain the true gateway to Australia.

Families living hard in suburbs on the outer rim of the city have every reason to resent the privileges of the harbour. But that's not how it works. All Sydney feels it owns the

harbour. Outnumbering the backpackers at Circular Quay on weekends are Sydney people in for the day to see their city. This is where the whole town celebrates New Year and Australia Day. It's our Opera House even if we never go to the opera. And along the walkways of the Quay and the Botanic Gardens we exercise a right no Australian questions: to get to the water's edge.

The harbour is a territory with its own rules and its own politics, where the prevailing weather is greed. It's a place of hidden towns, neighbourhood wars, deserted beaches, sublime beauty, evil visions, looting and pillage, bribery and sacrifice. There are few places on earth where there is such pressure from money.

Harbour views are a badge of money, power and corruption in this city. In the

plays of David Williamson and Patrick White, men and women sell their souls for a view of the water. A whole language has been developed by real estate agents to rate every type of water view, from a mere glimpse through a back window to having the stuff lapping at the bottom of the garden. The code translates to money and the big one is Absolute Deep Water Frontage.

Yet this is also a landscape of the spirit. Sydney Harbour was the earliest and remains the most potent subject of European art on this continent. You can navigate the harbour by paintings: come in through the Heads with Eugene von Guerard, along the bush shore painted by Tom Roberts, past Conrad Martens's Elizabeth Bay and Lloyd Rees's Opera House; then — with Grace Cossington Smith's bridge dead ahead and Brett Whiteley's Lavender Bay in the distance — swing into the bay painted and photographed endlessly since William Bradley's first, awkward attempt: *Sydney Cove: Port Jackson 1788*.

Lloyd Rees painted the harbour until he was almost blind. He saw it first from the deck of a coastal steamer at the age of 21.

"In that first long look, Sydney cast her spell and it has remained with me ever since, in spite of her brashness and disorder, the crimes she has committed against herself, and, above all, the opportunities she has allowed to pass — opportunities that could have made her more worthy of her setting." That lament goes back about 200 years. One of the great Australian puzzles is why that's so; why Sydney is so dazzling and yet always falls short.

From the earliest days, the harbour was also a war machine. Phillip set up the first guns on Dawes Point above The Rocks. Later the army occupied the Heads and the navy took bays and islands. All these precious hectares of bush passed to the Commonwealth at Federation. They were beyond the reach of real estate agents, safe in the hands of a foreign power: Canberra. Now the old war machine has nearly all been broken up. The bush has been turned into parks. The navy at Garden Island is still hanging on, but the inexorable dislodging of Australia's armed forces from this sublime landscape is the saddest defeat they have ever suffered.

Above Tin Hat Day began after World War I to raise money for returned soldiers. Sellers near the Cenotaph in Martin Place did brisk business.

Right Clydesdale horses move sacks of raw sugar from the wharves at Pyrmont to the nearby CSR refinery. The sugar was from the canefields of Queensland and the NSW North Coast.

Far right The feminist and anti-conscription campaigner Adela Pankhurst Walsh, taking her message to Sydney's streets in 1941. Walsh was the daughter of the famous British suffragette Emmeline Pankhurst and the younger sister of Christabel and Sylvia Pankhurst, who formed the Women's Social and Political Union.

Below The interior of the Sydney Fish Market in Woolloomooloo, 1892. Each man's catch is marked by chalk on the floor.

The harbour is more beautiful — but less dramatic — now it's no longer a busy working port.

Trucks have triumphed over trains in Australia, and trucks find it easier to reach Botany Bay. So the working port has relocated, by supreme irony, to the windswept bay Phillip abandoned in 1788. Not that we entirely forget the dirty, smoky port photographed by Cazneaux and Max Dupain and David Moore. Cities are built of memories as well as bricks and mortar, memories of what was once here but is now gone. Details of this vanished Sydney lodge in our imaginations and make sense of the city today.

Some of those memories are very deep indeed. When Phillip arrived, there was a rough division among the Eora between the warrior lands to the north and the women's country to the south. Later it was orchards and suburban hill stations to the north and the "real" city to the south. Industry and slums didn't cross the harbour. Until

the bridge was built, you needed time and money to live over the water.

The bridge was supposed to end this division, but the harbour still splits Sydney. Fierce loyalties are involved here. To grow up on the north shore rather than the eastern suburbs means different schools with different friends and perhaps even different accents. The southern suburbs of the shire have their own stand-offish pride. Out west they thumb their noses at the snobs who never visit their suburbs. But the north and east are locked in old rivalry. The CBD is a kind of commercial no-man's-land where they bury their differences to get on with their work.

Coming to town was once one of the great rituals of Sydney. Men wore suits. Women wore gloves. In every old photo album in Sydney are snaps of well-dressed women rounding the corner into Martin Place where footpath photographers were waiting in ambush. There is something very Sydney about these sunny pictures of women

in their best rig on their way to David Jones, Macquarie Street and lunch — with the off-chance of finding themselves in the women's page of *The Sydney Morning Herald* the next day, eating at Romano's.

Most reasons for coming to town — unless you work there — have moved out to the suburbs. But not quite all. There

Following pages Railway Square, 1935 (left), then as now, a busy transport hub. In the 1920s the city boasted one of the world's largest tram fleets. By 1961 they were gone. Double-decker buses (top right) had their heyday from the war years to the late 1960s, but the real nostalgia is saved for Sydney's lost trams (bottom right).

Above Macleay Street, Kings Cross, 1933. The home of Sydney's red light district, the Cross was also Sydney's bohemian heart for decades.

Top right The 43-storey Horizon apartment building, designed by Harry Seidler, soars over Darlinghurst and its living museum of architectural styles, including medium-rise apartment blocks and terrace houses. (Photo: Peter Morris)

Bottom right Skyscrapers surround Macquarie Place on land that was under the high-tide line of Sydney Cove when the First Fleet arrived in 1788. Gradually the cove was reshaped into Circular Quay, with much of the fill coming from stone quarried to open up the Argyle Cut to The Rocks. (Photo: Greg White)

are still shops, galleries, theatres, music and parades — on the harbour and in the streets. Summer is the season for parades, starting with fireworks and ferry races on the harbour at New Year and ending with the Anzac Day ceremonies in April. And somewhere in between, hundreds of thousands have been turning out from the early 1980s to watch gay and lesbian Sydney on parade in Oxford Street.

The crowds are there to enjoy something that goes beyond sexual politics: the ruthless Australian humour of Mardi Gras at its best. Patrick White was not alone in fearing a respectable backlash if homosexuals went round "swinging their handbags" in public. But in the end they won over Sydney by taking off their clothes and marching down Oxford Street.

The sexy glitz of Mardi Gras has managed to achieve what brave politicians and civil libertarians had tried and failed

to win after decades of campaigning: the affection of the city. For Sydney's preachers, however, the annual parade is evidence, every year more damning, that Sydney is the Gomorrah of the South Pacific. The parliamentarian and preacher Fred Nile once said: "If Jesus wept over Jerusalem, He must be heartbroken over Sydney."

Few monuments to the city's convict past survive, but Sydney still has the same brand of preachers sent out by London and Rome to save the worst souls in the world: criminals and redcoats. That one of the most relaxed cities on earth has such hardline preachers is another of Sydney's magnificent contradictions.

The preachers kept citizens out of the surf in daylight hours until the early 20th century and thus played a role in the strange, late development of the beach suburbs of Sydney. Palm Beach was a playground for the rich, but suburbs along the beaches closest

to the city were built for working families. Although bathing was no longer thought immoral when Bondi was being built in the 1920s, there were other odd prejudices to be overcome: for living in salt air and living at the end of the tram tracks. It took a long time for the town to realise we could actually "live" on a surf beach.

And the preachers fought to keep this a Sabbatarian town. In London and New York the fat papers are Sunday papers, but in Sydney these appear on Saturday because for a very long time respectable proprietors didn't publish, respectable folk didn't read and newsagents were forbidden by law to deliver papers on Sunday. That was the day for worship. Dragooning people to go to church is one of the longest traditions of the town, ever since Phillip ordered convicts and soldiers to bulk up the scant congregations gathering in the first days of the colony to pray under a fig tree.

Above Parade of homes. An early home show in Pennant Hills, 1960.

Right When the houses grow faster than the trees. From the 1870s to 1995 Blair Athol House, near Campbelltown, was aloof from suburbia; by 2002 it was just another roof.

Even after the battles for Sunday cricket and football were won, racing on Sundays was still banned until the early 1990s. Then the NSW government came up with a splendid device to beat the preachers: Sunday race meetings were introduced as a "temporary" measure to fund Sydney's $23 million bid for the 2000 Olympics. We won the Olympics and, of course, we kept the racing.

In the Olympic fortnight of 2000, Sydney lost its old, protective cynicism about itself. This is a city that loves hits and winners — horses, painters, football teams, politicians, lovers, even crooks. But the long haul of loyalty isn't for Sydney. The city watched with only half an eye the stadiums go up at Homebush out in the suburbs. But in September 2000 Sydney discovered it was sitting on a winner. The Games suddenly had our full attention. We lapped up the world's flattery and decided, unambiguously, that we love this town.

The capital city of the botched job showed it could plan, build, spend a fortune and get something right. The Olympics have changed the way Sydney feels about Sydney, perhaps permanently.

But they haven't changed our foundation instincts. We're still making money and making do, scrimping and saving in the face of endless good fortune. The triumphs are spectacular, the failures inexcusable. The mix barely changes over time. Sydney seems still to be what it's always been: the contradictory city.

Above Sydney's tallest structure, Sydney Tower, overlooking Hyde Park, where thousands gather at a peace rally in February 2003. (Photo: Ben Rushton)

Right Hollie Jones, 10, and her mother, Lilly, glow in the flame at Carols by Candlelight in the Domain. (Photo: Jacky Ghossein)

Centre Glitter on parade in the 1997 Sydney Mardi Gras: the festival sprang from a protest march for gay rights in 1978 in which 53 people were arrested. It is now one of the city's key tourist drawcards. (Photo: Paul Jones)

Far right *The Sun-Herald* City to Surf on William Street, Sydney, in 2004. It began with 2000 entrants in 1971, and is now the world's largest timed fun run. (Photo: James Alcock)

Above Narcissus could not have seen his reflection in the surf: no matter where in Sydney, the beach has always been home to the cult of physical perfection.

SYDNEYSIDE On the waterfront

Captain Arthur Phillip was not alone in waxing lyrical about the beauty of Sydney Harbour. Sailing in with the First Fleet, assistant surgeon Arthur Smyth found the scene "like an enchantment", the totality of which "beggared all description".

Beyond the attraction of safety, beauty became increasingly paramount. More than a ship's port, the harbour is now the spiritual anchor of a city. In the place of wharves and industry, flats and houses now hug its shores, with only scattered harbourside parks saving us from loving it to death.

For the city's first century the water affair was conducted from the safety of beaches, picnic spots or boats to skim across its surface. Those who live by the harbour shores know it in all its moods and beauty, wrote a *Herald* correspondent in 1899, but in

one day, for the annual regatta on January 26, a visitor had been given a taste of the waterway at its best: "He saw the crowded sails, the flying white wings as they flashed down the bay in the sun, the ships gay with flags, the people on the water and along the shoreline …"

But water meant danger, and drownings were frequent — until we learnt to swim. Then a new claim was staked to the harbour and, beyond its craggy heads, we took full possession of the remarkable run of sand and headlands that stretch from Palm Beach to Cronulla. We developed the Australian crawl and refined it with a turn of the head for breath — and the world embraced it and renamed it the freestyle.

No longer limited to admiring the scenery, we threw ourselves into the

water, replacing Victorian decorum with antipodean exuberance, cloth with flesh. Surf captured the city's imagination. Beyond the harbour's calm embrace, the foamy waters were wild, sensual and dangerous and held us in thrall.

Several Australian capitals can claim beaches, others safe harbours. Completed by warm, clean water in the heart of the city, Sydney has the trifecta.

Swimming led to bodysurfing, surf clubs and the bronzed lifesaver. Surfboard riding owes its origins to Duke Kahanamoku's first foray at Manly in 1915, and it became a cultural force from the 1960s. Zippy boogie boards captured the attention of children and, despite decades of warnings about skin cancer, spreading out the towel never goes out of fashion.

Right Surf city: When swells reach 5 metres along the coast, it's time to wax up inside the harbour. Surfers enjoy the action off Nielsen Park in February 2004. (Photo: David Moir)

Bottom centre Surf lifesavers' carnival at Bondi, 1936. (Photo: Harry Martin)

Below Manly girls-made-good: Pam Burridge (centre) and later Layne Beachley became world champion surfers. (Photo: Martin Brannan)

Bottom From the Hawaiian Kahanamoku brothers we learnt to surf.

Top On water as it is on land, Friday night
is prime time for the city's water taxis.
(Photo: Narelle Autio)

Above Plunge time: swimmers eye the
water at Hermit Bay in Sydney Harbour.
(Photo: Dean Sewell)

Right Police shout at onlookers to move away as massive swells pound the north end of Bondi beach. One man was already missing. A surf lifesaver can be seen, at right. (Photo: Nick Moir)

Below A crew from Avoca racing a surfboat. (Photo: Tim Clayton)

Top Spinnakers unfurled, the Morna and Norn race down Sydney Harbour in 1932. (Photo: H. H. Fishwick)

Above Schoolgirls shriek as the Manly ferry gets wet and wild. The ferry service began in 1854 and remains a vital commuter service as well as a magnet for tourists. (Photo: Dean Sewell)

Left Said to be the last working square-rigger to sail from Sydney, the Pamir prepares to head for New Zealand in March 1947.

Above Will they, won't they? Sydney people wondered how the two arches could eventually come together. The final 10-day long operation brought rejoicing and sighs of relief from everywhere.

Above This could be the start of something big: Joern Utzon inspects the Opera House site in August 1957. (Photo: Noel Herfort)

Above centre Begun in 1959, the Opera House remained a work in progress for more than a decade. The tiles were going on in 1966. (Photo: Bob Donaldson)

Top far right With fewer farewells than Nellie Melba, Dame Joan Sutherland takes her leave after her final performance at the Opera House in October 1990. (Photo: Rick Stevens)

The Opera House

The cold westerly wind could not dampen Danish architect Joern Utzon's first sighting of Bennelong Point in 1957. The vista from the point, named for the first Aborigine to be geographically honoured after Captain Arthur Phillip's muse on the "manly'" natives on the other side of the harbour, struck east, west and north across the deep water. As Utzon said, "It's absolutely breathtaking. There's no opera house site in the world to compare with it."

Utzon inspected the site, then occupied by the Fort Macquarie tram depot, with his partner Erik Andersson and an upbeat premier, Joe Cahill, who had resolved to build an opera house after a long campaign from Sir Eugene Goossens, the chief conductor of the Sydney Symphony Orchestra. It was pathetic optimism in light of what was to follow.

Utzon's design, the winner of a worldwide competition, had been unveiled in *The Sydney Morning Herald* six months previously, on January 30. Readers variously likened it to "a disintegrating circus tent in a gale", "a piece of Danish pastry", "some gargantuan monster which may have wandered over the land millions of years ago", "some large and lovely ship of the imagination" and "some 25th century Bluebeard's lair, its ominous vanes pointed skywards apparently only for the purpose of discharging guided missiles".

Others sensed its historical significance. "We must soar into the unimaginable future," wrote Lynd Nathan, from Killara. "And if the result might seem to some of us like something out of the lunar world, Mars, science fiction or the Missile Age, what is wrong with that?"

Utzon's competition entry was famously retrieved from the rejection pile by judge Eero Saarinen (although this account is contested). The original $3.5 million quote quickly blew out. When Robert Askin's Liberal government took power in 1965, Utzon was increasingly stymied by the minister for public works, Davis Hughes, and resigned in 1966. He left Australia and never returned, despite support from the architectural community and public rallies. A team of local architects completed the Opera House and it opened in 1973. It cost $102 million.

In 1998 the NSW government invited Utzon to oversee a major upgrade. He agreed to advise from a distance: he would not come to Australia. However, the government continues to baulk at the expense and a start date had not been confirmed late in 2005.

Above Highlights: the sails come to life at night. (Photo: Peter Morris)

CHAPTER THREE

The Bush

Reaping what we sow

BY ANDREW STEVENSON

Apart from the Noah's Ark collection of plants and animals they brought with them, the world of Australia's first European settlers was unsettling and strange. They left meadows and soft pastures and found sandstone cliffs and unforgiving soil that resisted their efforts. Beyond the rough roads and first buildings was an enigmatic other world; instead of a middle distance made up of a protective patchwork of farmlands, towns and villages, Sydney had a strict dividing line between European form and order and antipodean madness and mystery. The choice was clear: it was Sydney or the bush.

Two centuries later — centuries during which the bush was discovered and incorporated into the nation's psyche and soul — the spirit of mutual incomprehension between urban and rural residents remains a vibrant force in the nation's affairs.

The pattern of urban development — evident in every other continent — of farms leading to villages leading to towns and then to cities was turned on its head in Australia. Despite 50,000 years of Aboriginal occupation, there was no systematic agriculture nor any established towns. Initially, settlers had no idea how to farm a strange land in a climate that teased and tormented them. The early settlers, and most farmers ever since, saw themselves locked in a struggle for survival.

To the east the ocean represented, ironically, the known world. The frontiers lay to the north, south and west, and every year from the beginning of European settlement people spilled forth into the bush, attempting to know it and bring it to heel. Their numbers were small but their impact profound and indelible.

In 1813 there were 12,173 whites in the colony of New South Wales. Only seven — Blaxland, Wentworth, Lawson and four servants — had crossed the Blue Mountains. But it was from this crossing that the scale and opportunity of the land they were settling became apparent. With ever-increasing

Above Claiming land against the express wishes of the Crown, squatters never let go. Tenacity was their byword, helping them overcome adversity on their way to unparalleled wealth and social respectability.

Previous pages Watching the weather can become an obsession when your livelihood depends on it. Mostly, Australian farmers look to the sky in hope and expectation. But the heavens can also unleash violence and unrestrained power – as witnessed by this shelf cloud passing over farmlands near Temora. (Photo: Nick Moir)

confidence, small bands of explorers and settlers followed them westwards.

The first Great Australian Dream was not the quarter-acre block. Land was the object of desire but it was sought on a much grander scale and its pursuit defied the established power of the Crown, which had claimed the eastern part of the continent for itself in 1770. "Certain bold and lawless spirits occupied extensive lands with their sheep … in defiance of authority," recalled the *NSW Official Year Book* in 1925.

The age of the squatters had begun; within a few years a relative handful flouting every regulation the governor put in their way had staked claim to huge sections of the colony. Much of the next hundred years would be spent trying to wrest it back from their control. The squatters' influence on

our culture would be harder to shake. As the historian Michael Cannon observed, the shadow of those who mastered the land — inflexible, ultra-conservative — fell heavily across Australia.

In 1821, 80 per cent of the continent's white population (of 36,968) were clustered in and around Sydney. But the next four decades were a time of massive internal migration, the scale of which would never be seen again. By 1861 Sydney's population had virtually doubled to 56,000; in contrast, the population of the rest of the colony of NSW had reached 292,000. More than 210,000 of them lived in rural areas. Sydney remained the seat of political power but the colony's citizens had left the harbour behind as they beat a track over the mountains and spilled out onto the western plains. Many went in

Above The scale of farming – and harvesting – underwent a transformation in the space of several decades. Humping bags of wheat by hand, as these men did at the railway station at Boggabri in 1933, is finished.
(Photo: H. H. Fishwick)

search of gold and, after 1851, stayed to work the land.

Early Sydney was no doubt a rough town, but the frontier proved a brutal and often degrading place for the early squatters. One, Neil Black, wrote: "Bachelors live half-savage, half-mad … half-dressed, half-not, unshaven, unshorn." The diet was already fixed, sitting like a stone in one's stomach: mutton, damper and black tea. The absence of wire fencing before the 1850s meant squatters could hold their sheep only with a ready workforce. Their shepherds, mainly discharged convicts, often lived for years under canvas remote from even their bosses' rough huts. With no prospect of any financial windfalls these men could not quit or walk off, or else, under the strictures of the Masters and Servants Act of 1845, they would wind up back in jail. Severe limitations on transport and communication magnified the sense of isolation. The *Herald* journalist C. E. W. Bean, after a tour of far-western NSW in the early 1900s, summed it up succinctly: "Only there happened nothing … no one came. Nothing happened. That was all."

The squatter, in his lust for land, held out against whatever demands were made upon him by reforming city politicians, dispossessed Aborigines, escaped convicts or anyone else. Judith Wright, in her family

memoir *The Generations of Men*, wrote: "The Ten Commandments did not hold where niggers were concerned … Massacres, drives, the taking of women, traffic in grog and opium were matters of everyday among the men who had pushed farthest with their cattle." More tellingly, perhaps, was that "an unwritten law made men keep silence on such happenings". In 1922 the chief inspector of Aboriginal stations in NSW told the *Herald* that white society had not, "to put it mildly, treated the blacks with that measure of kindly consideration that we are, in their last days, endeavouring to show them".

Add to this harsh world convicts, both freed and in chains, and bushranging

was hardly a surprising outcome. "It is a truly deplorable state of affairs when three bushrangers can strike terror into a whole district and rob numerous drays," commented *The Sydney Herald* in 1840 on the efforts of one gang, Jewboy's mob, which ranged over the Hunter Valley flaunting ribbons and watches. They robbed the police magistrate, Mr Dunlop, as he sat down to dinner with a landowner at Wollombi, and would proudly enter the valley's many inns, shake hands with the bullock drivers and labourers and even treat them to brandy, behaving in such a manner as to suggest "an understanding" existed between the parties.

That understanding became a feature of rural life for decades. Those living on

Left Australia rode for years on the sheep's back but getting the wool away was often a challenge. In 1925, after 80,000 sheep were shorn on Mossgiel station, floods turned the road across Willandra Creek into a quagmire. But the wagons still went on. Bearing 8 tons of wool each, the first wagon bogged three times. Three times it was dug free. The second, pulled by a team of 24 horses, made it through. The third was not so lucky, capsizing in more than three feet of mud. On hand to record the travails was young jackeroo Reg Sharpless, whose iconic photograph was first published to a wide audience in *The Sydney Mail*. Sharpless, who came to Australia hoping to find a cure for asthma, spent three years in the state's far west earning a pound a week and amassing a collection of more than 600 photographs. None were as famous as *The Bog*, which came to symbolise the struggles of outback transportation.

Above When it really rains, bitumen roads and semitrailers meet the same fate as horse-drawn carts, as Jim Pianto found out near Moree in 1995. (Photo: Peter Rae)

Above A triumph of vision and technology over distance and adversity, the Royal Flying Doctor Service made rural Australia a safer place to live. Here, doctor, pilot and station hands help refuel for the return to Broken Hill. (Photo: Len Drummond)

the margins of the law and the economy would have to protect each other against the forces of authority, and those who dared "to peach [inform against] would not live 24 hours afterwards". Ultimately, whatever understanding may have been in place was not sufficient to sustain Jewboy, Edward Davis, 26, nor his mates, all transported felons from the mother country. Six of this gang, having placed the district in such "a

shocking confusion", forfeited their lives on the gallows at the rear of Sydney Gaol before a large and unruly crowd in March 1841.

In an economy in which rum was the first currency, it is no surprise that work and drink were so closely intertwined in the bush. A settler, in a letter to the *Herald* in December 1840, feared for the consequences when a good season in Mudgee was enjoyed by "a great number of free men of most

dissipated habits employed on very high terms, nearly the whole of which is spent at the public house, over which there is not the slightest control".

Of course, the bush wasn't the only place where people drank to excess; they just did it differently there than in the city. Most squatters kept their runs dry, forbade shepherds to leave and paid their workers with cheques that couldn't be cashed other than for drink at grog shops. A good spree was reckoned at £2 a day so a year's pay might last a fortnight. For a shepherd's annual holiday, the "generous" publican would throw in board and lodgings of the same standard the shepherd was accustomed to all year round. Fleecing the farm labourer until he crawled away broke or mad with delirium tremens was a well-oiled practice and, even in the early 1900s, itinerant farm

Above Once a year the shearing shed took pride of place on every farm, filled with the life of an itinerant workforce. Although squatters and shearers shared a common purpose they were frequently in conflict over pay and conditions.

Top right Heading off to school often meant a long trip to the city, such as the one begun by these children from Cashmere station, near Caragabal, in 1942.

Bottom right Every town gazetted dreamt of one day becoming a city, but many withered or died. Blackman's Swamp made it. Named for an early explorer in 1817, it became Orange in 1846 and profited from the discovery of gold nearby at Lewis Ponds Creek. By the 1980s it was well placed to cash in on the rise of the sponge cities – with other regional centres like Dubbo, Tamworth and Albury – which drew further vigour from the smaller towns and villages that surrounded them. With success comes a new crop of problems: Summer Street, Orange, is no stranger to traffic jams Sydney would be proud of. (Photo: Peter Morris)

workers were arguing about which pub was the most notorious "lambing down" joint in the inland. Prostitution was never far from the interests of those running inns designed to part single men and their money.

Edward Curr, a Victorian squatter, saw 30 men in one pub ranging in intoxication "from maudlin imbecility to that of the maddened bacchanal", and Henry Lawson wrote that "most men who have been in the bush for any length of time are more or less mad". The solution, according to Lawson, was simple: "Shepherds and boundary riders, who are alone for months, must have their periodical spree, at the nearest shanty, else they'd go raving mad. Drink is the only break in the awful monotony."

Westward, the settlers followed the merinos. Rarely bothering to farm anything at all, they lived off the sheep's back and cheap imported flour. The spinning mills of Britain consumed whatever they could grow; sheep numbers in NSW rose from 650,000 in 1830 to 7.4 million by 1850, and kept rising until there were 47 million sheep in the colony

by 1887, earning half of all export proceeds. There was money in cattle, too; profits that stood in stark contrast to a city worker's wage. As Judith Wright's grandfather vowed before heading north towards Rockhampton: "We're going to where fortunes are to be made … All one needs to set oneself up for life is a little enterprise and a good mob of cattle."

The new Australians ate meat in phenomenal quantities. Often there were no vegetables; sometimes only the hardy pumpkin or the potato. For many years the new colonists were called cornstalkers, a nod to the plant's soaring growth. But while the colony grew more corn than wheat, at least until the 1890s, it was avoided if at all possible as it carried the convict stain, having frequently been used to supplement prison rations when flour ran short.

The shadow of penal servitude also remained in the rations system. Workers, and even swagmen in the bush until the early 1900s, were given 10, 10, two and a quarter: 10 pounds of flour, 10 pounds of meat, two pounds of sugar, one-quarter pound of

tea and some salt. Was this not a worker's paradise? Australians ate twice as much meat as the English and those in the bush ate more meat than their city cousins. The result was an impressive physique, evident in a 1913–15 survey of schoolchildren, which found country lads one inch taller and four pounds heavier than city boys at the age of 12.

Land was the great political question of the day and repeated attempts were made to break down the great squatting runs, to replace sheep grazing with farming and to create a yeoman class of small landowners. New laws, such as the Robertson Land Act of 1861 in NSW, supposedly opened up Crown land and squatters' leases to selectors who could choose the land they wanted, pay down one-quarter of its value and obtain freehold by paying the balance in three years.

Virtually every attempt ended in failure, however, thwarted and rorted by squatters who used fake bidders at auctions, nominated dummy selectors to hold the land for them, barred access to watercourses or peacocked the best pieces of land. By the

end of World War I, 131,000 selections had been made in NSW but only half remained in existence, the rest having been either sold or combined. But the fight continued with compulsory acquisition of large holdings and a punitive Commonwealth land tax.

Above Ever since rabbits were first set free on Australian soil in 1859 farmers, scientists and governments have fought an endless war with them. Hundreds of millions have been killed in traps, by bullets and by poison. Even more have died at the hands of science, first by the introduction of myxomatosis (in the 1950s) and then by the calicivirus (introduced in 1995). At their worst, rabbits lived in such numbers they could make the landscape move. Here, rabbits gather at a waterhole in 1938.

Left The comparative stability of the Australian environment ended suddenly with the onset of European settlement. Set free in a new land, many plants and animals ran riot, producing plagues of biblical proportions. Plague locusts and kangaroos are both indigenous creatures, although their numbers and distribution have been dramatically affected by the spread of farming and the increased availability of feed and water. Numbers of kangaroos have been estimated as high as 60 million but several years of drought in the early years of the new millennium is thought to have had a severe impact. At first it produced huge concentrations of kangaroos around remaining food and water, such as shown above on Oxley Station near the Macquarie Marshes in 2002. When rains still did not come, starvation was the end of many. (Photo: Dallas Kilponen)

Bottom far left Prickly pear was introduced as a garden plant but ended up colonising huge swathes of country. At its worst, in 1925, it covered 62 million acres in NSW and Queensland, forcing many people off their farms. Prickly Pear Acts were written and the Prickly Pear Destruction Commission established but the plant defeated all mechanical and chemical assaults. It was only mastered by another introduced species – the cactoblastis caterpillar, released in 1926.

Bottom left Locusts can form swarms covering up to 25 square kilometres and travel 500 kilometres a day in search of food. The only viable means of control is spraying the locusts in the first four weeks of life before they take to the wing. (Photo: Nick Moir)

Above Getting out to vote takes on a new context in the far west, with a mobile polling booth making its way around remote properties. Bill O'Conner marks his ballot paper on his 165,000-hectare property Narriearra, about 60 kilometres from Tibooburra. (Photo: Steven Siewert)

Millions of pounds of government revenue were spent acquiring land and encouraging farming through all manner of schemes. The objective was not economic advantage, as a NSW Government Review of Marketing and Agricultural Economics somewhat coyly noted in 1949: "The criterion seems largely to have been, under the pressure of public opinion, how to settle the largest number of people on the land." In 1922 a former NSW premier, Sir Joseph Carruthers, was urging support for his

Million Farms proposal, arguing a million new settlers could be established in 20 years if only the idle lands would come under profitable management.

There were drives for closer settlement, and soldier-settler schemes. The World War I scheme in NSW cost £45 million and 25 years later fewer than half of the 10,000 soldier-farmers remained on the land. Invariably such schemes failed because, after paying for the land, farmers had nothing left to stock it or tide them over through tough seasons.

But what did they own? In many cases, the land so bitterly fought over gave up the ghost, misunderstood and overstocked. Long years of drought dried up any illusions of permanent prosperity. On their heels came floods or bushfires. Getting to know the country proved an enduring challenge.

By then the fauna of Australia was familiar. What was strange was the way introduced plants, animals and insects behaved in a new land. Prickly pear, Paterson's curse, Scotch thistle, Bathurst burr and blackberry wreaked their havoc. One disaster often followed another. When caterpillars were destroying crops across the eastern states, sparrows were introduced to curb their numbers. Instead, the sparrows joined the grubs and together they attacked grain and fruit harvests. Worst, of course, were rabbits, set free in 1859. The colonial governments tried to halt their spread with fencing, building enough to encircle the world eight times over. But their efforts failed, as did those of the trappers, although they managed to kill 25 million rabbits in NSW in one year. Shoved aside for sheep and

Above Beginning in the 1960s, cotton became the boom crop wherever irrigation water could be found – but chipping the weeds out was backbreaking work. A group of Aboriginal workers, accompanied by Paul Kahl, one of the industry's pioneers, finish up after another hot day in Wee Waa. (Photo: Peter Moxham)

The blocks were also frequently too small to generate a living income. The settlers and selectors and their children often had little choice but to work for the squatter, and if not the squatter then the bank or pastoral company. The squatters had won the fight for the best land but, in victory, many sowed the seeds of their own downfall, borrowing too much to freehold their runs. By 1884 squatters accounted for nearly 80 per cent of the money on bank overdrafts. Foreclosures saw the rate of company ownership skyrocket.

Above Drought has been the nation's close companion, its impact profound and its return inevitable. "The worst drought in Australia's history" is a call that's been made too many times. For those caught in their grip, all droughts are the worst and, in reality, scarcely a decade has passed without a drought worthy of the title. The consequences for farmers, communities, land and animals is inevitably dire. Here, sheep are shot at Nyngan in 1991 when there is nothing left for them to eat. (Photo: Peter Morris)

Right Eventually, the drought can become a burden too great. This home near Ivanhoe was abandoned to the dust storms in 2004. (Photo: Nick Moir)

Above left Drought had become a way of life for Ron Hoare on Tin Tin station, north of Balranald. This shot shows one of many dry dams. (Photo: Rick Stevens)

Left In December 1944 the *Herald* sent the reporter Keith Newman and the artist Russell Drysdale westwards, across "the country in which there are no bushfires. There is nothing to burn." Their journey to Wentworth, where the Murray and Darling meet, was "one long tragedy-track over scorched earth", the monotony broken by massive dust storms. Dead trees "loom through the hot murk in a variety of fantastic shapes … as though tortured by thirst". Worse than dead trees were the skeletons of dead animals. And worse than them, the skeletons of homes. "Here and there gaunt houses appear with empty sockets where the windows were, doors flapping on rusted hinges, the spidery skeletons of windmills from which the iron wind vanes have blown or rusted away." (Illustration: Russell Drysdale)

cattle, 1.7 million kangaroos also met their maker in NSW in 1886.

The push to the bush had two main motivations: patriotic duty and social redemption. Under the British Crown the Aborigines had been dispossessed, an act justified, at least in part, by the claim that they made no use of the soil. We must confirm our own title by user, cautioned the *Herald* in 1922. "Populate or perish" was first articulated by Billy Hughes in 1937 but the idea had informed public debate almost from the arrival of the First Fleet, with anxious eyes cast in every direction in fear of occupation.

Farming was a moral crusade, offering the perfect antidote to the perfidy of the industrialising cities. Contributors to the *Herald* argued that settlement remained work for patriots, noting it "is idle lands which make idle hands". Bean observed that "a new country with a new civilisation should be able to look forward to a good thousand years or so of vigorous existence";

so would Australia if her people were a country people.

The sad reality was that by 1907 in Sydney one could see the "luxury and refinement and vice of the old world gnawing at the heart of the new". The theme was taken up all over. John Flynn, founder of the Royal Flying Doctor Service, wrote that the bush was producing not just wool and wheat but "distinctive character in the Spirit

of Man". As the historian Graeme Davison has argued, the city and the country were established as separate moral universes by city poets who saw their better country selves on permanent holiday, sharing pleasures that townsfolk never know.

As ever, the pleasure of poets involved selective memory and fantasy. For many in the bush, life was a brutal affair, frequently ending in premature death. According to

official figures for 1887, violence was a major cause of death in country NSW. Of males who survived childhood, one in five went on to die violently.

Another outstanding feature was that Sydney was for sheilas, while the bush was a man's world. In 1861 there were more women than men in Sydney, a remarkable demographic fact for an old convict town. But beyond the city, men outnumbered

Above When playgroup is an impossible dream, a trip across the paddock can be a major outing. Rose Cameron, pictured with son Hamish in 1988, said her cure for isolation was to drive 30 kilometres to Jerilderie once a week, 150 kilometres to Wagga Wagga once a month and to visit Sydney or Melbourne several times a year. (Photo: John Nobley)

women by a ratio of 1.5:1. In the rural areas of Queensland and Victoria there were twice as many men as women. Even by Federation, the bush was still a man's world in fact, as well as in the cultural imagination being created by an earnest generation of writers and painters, including Henry Lawson, Banjo Paterson, Tom Roberts and Frederick McCubbin. Women made the edge of the page, if they were mentioned at all; Lawson best captured their enduring struggle with poor land and poor men in sketches such as *The Drover's Wife* and *Water Them Geraniums*.

The nationalists and bush poets invented a version of Australia; they themselves didn't know the soil but they saw a world that was different and wrote it down. Why did they ignore the cities and revere the bush? Sydney had much in common with the rest of the world; the bush remained the other world, an unploughed field of dreams. The squatters, sheep and swagmen had shifted the continent's centre of gravity: Sydney was usurped as an economic force, as the engine room of a new cultural identity and as the home for most of its people. It took more than 60 years for the city to regain its numerical pre-eminence, with Sydney reaching a majority of the NSW population only in 1924.

Ever since, in terms of influence and national identity, the bush has been in decline. Agriculture, forestry and fisheries' contribution to the economy has fallen from a high of 30 per cent during World War I to only 3 per cent in 2003. Mechanisation cut demand for rural workers at the same time as factories dominated the city fringes; when manufacturing began to decline, the slack was taken up by the services sector. At the turn of the century no farm could survive without a substantial permanent workforce, including general farmhands, tradespeople and their families.

After World War II came several decades of prosperous family farms, many still with a worker's cottage for an employee. But the constant revolution in the scale of

Above The country pub – a public bar topped by a wide verandah – is an enduring main street staple. Typical is the Tattersalls in Baradine on the edge of the Pilliga Scrub. (Photo: Andrew Meares)

Left Inside, the local pub is a community centre for blokes such as Jim Day (right), who enjoys a beer with friends in Warren's Club House Hotel. (Photo: Narelle Autio)

Above far left A great rural social institution struggling to survive in the 21st century is the debutantes ball, the official entry of young women into their society. Stacey Edmondson and friends celebrated their debut together in Gunnedah in 2002. (Photo: Steven Siewert)

Below far left Late at night black tie can turn to black humour at the ever-popular bachelors and spinsters balls. Here, mud larks revel at Goondiwindi in 1993. (Photo: Steven Siewert)

Above Before the multicultural food revolution, almost every country town had a Chinese restaurant and a Greek cafe. For more than three decades, Peter and Angela Mouhtouris ran the Elysian cafe in Mendooran – a long way from the island of Lesbos they left in 1953. (Photo: Greg White)

farming swept all that away. What was a family property in the 1950s looks more like a hobby farm today and, rather than employing labourers, most rural enterprises are dependent on someone having a job in town: the ubiquitous off-farm income needed to subsidise the rural dream. The bush was slowly leaching away people and power, a process that continues apace, despite thriving rural industries driven by a perpetual revolution of the range and scale of farming practices; and despite resentment

of a city that views and treats itself as the heart and head of the nation.

Heart and head perhaps, but not soul. It is almost as if the nation lived through its formative years exploring the great backyard, sleeping under canvas, rolling up its belongings and heading out down the track looking for work and a feed. No one does it any more, except as part of a paid holiday. But enough did — taking pleasure not just from the riches earned but from the journey — for that period when the bush ruled the

Below Meat remains a staple. In 1997 Baradine butcher Neil Hammond still made half a tonne of sausages a week. (Photo: Quentin Jones)

Bottom Two decades of remorseless economic rationalisation saw banks close branches, schools shut their doors and medical services decline in regional Australia. Everywhere, communities fought back. In Cooma, in 1996, they saved the jail. (Photo: Peter Rae)

affairs of the nation to be bathed in golden hues.

The loss of prestige is bitterly resented. "The reason for the diminishing population in many country towns was the financial starvation of rural districts," argued Mr Thorby, president of the Farmers and Settlers Association in 1924, as he bemoaned money set aside to build the Sydney Harbour Bridge. The Opera House received similar treatment. In 1974 the *Herald* reported that the gloom in the bush was now long term,

Above Tamworth has been home to the annual country music festival since 1973. It now draws a crowd of 50,000 visitors from around the nation. A fan checks out festival options in the main street. (Photo: Paul Harris)

Right One man's energy is spent, even as the festival's opening concert begins. (Photo: Penny Bradfield)

"fed by the belief that the importance of the primary sector has been kicked down the ladder of national priorities".

In the 30 years since, the story has only worsened. In country areas, banks have closed, followed by hospitals and other essential services. Patients wait weeks to see a doctor and towns that lose their doctor can wait years or in vain for a new medic to open a surgery. Occasionally the wave of discontent breaks its banks — witness the One Nation party — and those in Sydney are reminded, again, of the communities that exist on the other side of the Great Dividing Range.

Only two generations ago, practically every city person had a relative with their hands in the soil. That is no longer true.

Sydney has lost contact with the bush. The world beyond the city limits has been cut up into holiday farms, fenced off as wilderness or national park or turned into a holiday-land backdrop for postcards and television, and is in danger of becoming scenery to drive through rather than a place to live. When people leave Sydney it is no longer to farm or make their fortunes; they leave with spiritual yearnings, labelled and packaged as hippies, sea-changers or tree-changers. Once outside the metropolis they stand beside those farmers and townsfolk who have never wavered in their love of the land. Together, they are the custodians of the bush, of a distinctive vein of the nation's history and of an alternative vision of its future.

Above Tougher economic conditions, particularly from the 1970s onwards, triggered a major rethink. Farmers were forced to find new crops, such as this harvest of golden canola, and every town is keen to find its tourist niche. Hot air balloons help keep the tills ticking over in Canowindra.
(Photo: Andrew Taylor)

Left Breaking out of the supermarket, city and bush have taken pleasure from direct contact at food markets. Les Langlands of Windy Hill shows his wares at the Good Living Pyrmont Growers' Market.
(Photo: Fiona Morris)

Showing off

Years before the "best Olympic Games ever", Sydney hosted "the greatest show in the history of the Commonwealth". In 1922, the Royal Easter Show celebrated its centenary year. When it ended Sydney's longest running crowd-pleaser had set records in field events, ticket sales and exhibits.

Even before the 1922 show began, there had been predictions of unprecedented greatness and a sense that the show's success reflected that of the nation. "The history of the society is largely the history of the state, for it is a far cry back to the first show at historic Parramatta," the *Herald* reported.

In 1822, the Agricultural Society of NSW was formed by a group of citizens keen to raise the young colony's standard of agriculture through competition, and the first show was held a year later in Parramatta. In the early days the livestock consisted of cattle, poultry, stallions, hacks, ponies, sheep and dogs, and there were prizes awarded to servants who had shown the best conduct.

In 1869 the show moved to Prince Alfred Park, near the heart of Sydney, where it encompassed a much larger scope, including prizes for wine, horticulture,

machinery, fine arts and "items of colonial
manufacture".

The society caught the great exhibition
fever that had spread from Europe and
was gripping Sydney on the centenary of
Captain Cook's voyage up the eastern coast.
The Exhibition Building, built by the City
Council in Prince Alfred Park in 1870,
became the society's excuse to show the
world Australia's bounty in a grand setting:
the largest hall in the country. But the
society was struggling financially. When it
moved to Moore Park in 1881 it was down
to its last pound and did not recoup much

more in gate receipts. But by the time of the
centenary, sideshow alley, mechanical rides,
fireworks, showbags, woodchopping and the
grand parade were regular features.

The show was suspended for World
War II but returned in 1947 — still at
Moore Park — with 1.2 million visitors, an
extraordinary turnout given that the city's
population was less than 1.6 million. That
record remained until 1998, when the show
moved to Homebush. The new showground,
which cost $300 million, also hosted
competitions for the Sydney 2000 Olympic
and Paralympic Games.

Above The show in 1911, in the days before sideshow alley. The stalwarts of the show were the grand parade, woodchop, showbags and agricultural displays. That same year a plane piloted by William Hart flew from Penrith to land at Moore Park.

Right A prize pig, about 1920.

Top left Red Indians, Russian Cossacks and American cowboys on their way to perform at the show in 1936.

Above The newest carnival show ride in 2005 was the Hard Rock. The first mechanical ride at the show was brought in as part of the automobile exhibition in 1901. The ferris wheel did not arrive until 1943.

Centre left World champion axeman David Foster from Tasmania, competing in the standing block event in 1995. Australia produced the world's hardest wood and thus the best woodcutters, *The Sydney Morning Herald* reported.

Bottom left Duck judging. Poultry was included in the show's displays from the 1820s, when it was exhibited among pigs, dogs, cattle, horses and sheep, to the present day at Homebush, now rubbing shoulders with alpacas, cats, rats and mice.

LATE EDITION

GRANVILLE DEAD—Page 3

The Sydney Morning Herald

Thursday, January 20, 1977

FORECASTS (for today): Metropolitan: Mild to warm. NSW: Dry inland, mild to warm on coast. Max temps: City 25, Liverpool 28. (Weather, sun, moon, tides and fire warnings, P. 18.)

No 43,398 Telephone 2 0944 First published 1831 24 PAGES 12c*

80 dead as wreck cleared

Inquiries begin on worst Aust rail crash

After 31 hours of heart-breaking toil rescue workers made the final count yesterday in the Granville railway disaster—80 dead and 83 injured.

Some of the 36 injured still in hospitals are in a critical condition.

The rescuers took 20 hours to cut away part of the 200-tonne concrete slab which had entombed the bodies of more than 60 of the victims.

Now the workmen are breaking up the rest of the Bold Street bridge and clearing debris from the five lines to get trains moving through again to the West.

Public Transport Commission officials hope the line will be reopened late today or early tomorrow. Meanwhile, emergency bus services are linking stations on both sides of Granville.

Investigations into the disaster, Australia's worst railway accident, have already begun by PTC experts and police.

Judge visits scene

Judge Staunton, appointed to head the State Government's judicial inquiry, visited the crash scene for about 45 minutes yesterday.

He said later that the full impact of the disaster had not hit him until he was at the scene.

Two independent assessors have yet to be named but the first sittings of the inquiry are expected next week.

The Premier, Mr Wran, announced that the inquiry would not only look at the Granville crash but would use this as a guide to the State's railway operations.

"I don't think anyone who saw the results of the Granville accident could fail to suffer a loss of confidence in the railways system," he said.

He condemned the "ramshackle" state of the railways and said the dead and maimed emphasised neglect that should have been obvious years ago.

Asked to guarantee the safety of people using NSW railways he said: "I don't think anyone can guarantee anything." **(Report at right.)**

A pledge

Mr Wran, a Queen's Counsel, advised anyone injured in the crash to take immediate steps to sue the Public Transport Commission.

He also pledged that the Government would pay all reasonable funeral expenses for the victims.

But insurance companies warned yesterday that families of the victims may have to wait up to seven months to receive life insurance because of the length of time for probate to be granted in NSW.

Yesterday, as the rescue efforts tapered down, the stories of good and bad luck, of tragedy and sympathy and the efforts of rescuers began to emerge.

Mr Trevor King, Salvation Army officer and former boxer, spent Tuesday night at the temporary morgue with police trying to identify the mangled victims.

He had to console a man who lost two teenage daughters in the crash and a mother whose 11-year-old son was on the train.

Another family had two sons on the train. Only one survived.

Other passengers, treated at hospitals and discharged, remembered their luck and the escapes they had from death or more serious injury.

Doctors told how an ambulanceman spent nearly 10 hours with the last person taken alive from the wreckage, talking to him quietly throughout his ordeal and bathing his forehead with iced water.

Five young people from the ANZ banking organisation working at branches around the city died in the crash. Some other employees were injured.

Mr John Maddock, of Warrimoo, was in the third carriage of the fatal train on Tuesday but escaped unharmed. Yesterday, he repeated his journey, sitting in the same carriage as he did the previous day.

31 hours

Sergeant Joe Beecroft, the head of the Police Rescue Squad, stopped after 31 hours work and described the scene as the worst he had witnessed.

Then he joined the other policemen for a brief parade to receive congratulations from the Police Commissioner, Mr Mervyn Wood.

At Katoomba messages of sympathy poured into the offices of the Blue Mountains City Council.

Darwin, the city devastated by Cyclone Tracy two years ago, is setting up a relief fund to help the train victims.

An ecumenical service was broadcast over 2KA, the local radio station. Cardinal Freeman will say Mass today at St Mary's Cathedral and at the same time an Anglican Holy Communion memorial service will be held at St James's Church, King Street.

PAGE 3: Mammoth police and medical effort ends; train driver's ordeal; one son lived, one died.

PAGE 4: Why trains are derailed; five dead from one bank group; wait for insurance payments.

THE HEART OF A DISASTER LIES BARE

A mass of flattened seats was all that remained of a railway carriage when the last of the concrete slab that covered it was removed.

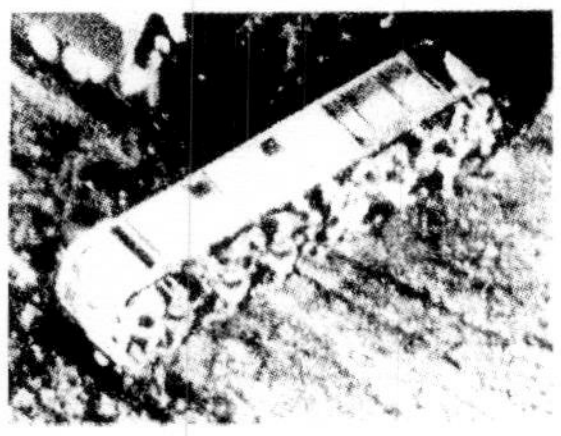

Wentworth Falls, 1965

2nd smash for loco

Granville, 1977

Electric locomotive 4620, the engine in the Granville rail disaster, was involved in a 160 km/h derailment at Wentworth Falls in 1965, a union official said yesterday.

The president of the NSW branch of the Australian Federated Union of Locomotive Enginemen, Mr J. Booth, said a braking failure was the cause of the Wentworth Falls crash on June 17, 1965.

Locomotive 4620, running from Lithgow to Enfield with a 37-truck goods train loaded with coal and cement, lost its brakes just after it left Katoomba, on the steepest section of the track.

The train jack-knifed off the tracks just outside Wentworth Falls station. The three railwaymen aboard escaped with minor injuries.

The 110-tonne, 16.5 metre long engine is one of 40 built at Stockton-on-Tees in England to NSW specifications between 1955 and 1957 by Metropolitan Vickers Ltd. It entered service on March 27, 1957.

Mr Booth — himself an engine driver — said he had driven 4620 many times.

He said it was no better and no worse than any of the other 46-Series engines.

"Drivers like the 46-Series because of their power, cleanliness and quietness of operation," he said.

The engines were regularly serviced and overhauled.

Confidence in railways shaken, says Wran

The Premier, Mr Wran, said yesterday that he thought the Granville disaster would cause a loss of confidence in the railway system.

Answering questions after announcing the appointment of the Chief Judge of the NSW District Court, Judge Staunton, to head a three-man public inquiry into the disaster, the Premier said:

"I don't think anyone who saw the results of the Granville accident could fail to suffer a loss of confidence in the railway system."

He condemned the "ramshackle" state of the railways and said the dead and maimed emphasised neglect that should have been obvious 10 years ago.

"This is a tragedy of monumental proportions not seen before," he said. "What this awful tragedy emphasises is the need for us to be more diligent than ever."

But Mr Wran said that the accident had to be seen in perspective.

It involved a terrible set of coincidences.

"For it to happen there had to be a derailment.

"The loco had to run off the line, it had to do it on a bend, and at that bend there had to be a bridge supported by a stanchion and it had to hit that support and bring it down."

Asked to guarantee the safety of people using the State's railways, Mr Wran said: "I don't think anyone can guarantee anything.

"What happened has made the Public Transport Commission more anxious than ever to see that what's on the tracks is in good order and condition.

"But," he said, "I don't contemplate anyone will ever be able to guarantee that installations or anything of a mechanical order will always work.

"I can say that enormous efforts are being made within the limitations of the railways system to make things as safe as they can be.

"It is not my role to point the finger or engage in political mud slinging, but I don't think there is any doubt we took over a very ramshackle railways system," Mr Wran said.

"It should be remembered that before the election we said the railways were in bad condition and that it would take five years of intensive efforts and many hundreds of millions of dollars to modernise the system.

"We are in the process of doing that.

"It's a pity so many people should be killed and injured and maimed to emphasise what should have been obvious 10 years ago."

Mr Wran said he was no further advanced as to the cause of the accident than anyone else.

However, the black box recorder had revealed the train's speed, and other information, and there had been a complete check of the track only a few weeks earlier.

Mining under dams backed

Fears that coal mining under Sydney's water supply reservoir's could bring a danger of catastrophic flooding of the coastal plain are dismissed as "quite unrealistic" in a 118-page report issued yesterday.

The report on an inquiry conducted by Mr Justice Reynolds, Judge of Appeal, Supreme Court of NSW, says that the valuable resource of coal reserves in the reservoir area may be mined without endangering the security of the stored waters if mining is carried out with proper safeguards.

The report is being considered by the NSW Government.

The setting up of the inquiry followed a 70-year-old dispute between the Metropolitan Water Sewerage and Drainage Board and the Department of Mines over mining in the reservoir area.

Details, Page 17.

$1,000m indexation tax cut

From MIKE STEKETEE

CANBERRA, Wednesday. — Tax indexation would give Australians income-tax cuts worth well over $1,000 million from July 1 this year, the Federal Treasurer, Mr Lynch, said today.

In an 11-page statement, he said that Cabinet had rejected calls for further tax reductions proposed by trade-unions, employers and the Labor Party.

The cuts from the middle of the year referred to by Mr Lynch apply automatically under tax indexation, introduced at the start of 1976-77.

The income brackets used to assess the amount of tax people pay will be adjusted upwards by the inflation rate during 1976-77, expected to be about 14 per cent.

Income earners who have moved into higher brackets during the year because of inflation will receive tax reductions.

Mr Lynch issued his unusually long statement soon after his return from Japan, where he attended ministerial talks, and immediately before taking a two-week holiday.

It is aimed at ending speculation that the Government will cut income or sales taxes soon to boost the economy and help fight inflation.

Mr Lynch said last Friday's Cabinet meeting had considered the series of proposals made recently and decided that tax cuts would be "quite inappropriate" at this stage.

But the Government was deeply committed to tax reform and, as circumstances permitted, to reducing the real burden of taxation.

"Inherent in the calls that have been made for reductions in taxation are both a complete misreading of economic developments and a complete lack of analysis of the implications of what is being proposed," the Treasurer said.

There had been a significant improvement in economic performance during 1976, he said.

There had been a sharp moderation in the underlying rate of inflation and an increase of more than 7 per cent in real gross non-farm product over the nine months to last September, compared to a fall of 4 per cent in the 12 years leading up to the end of 1975.

There were two fundamental reasons why the Government had decided firmly against further tax cuts, he said.

The first was that they would add to the Budget deficit, which would only increase the underlying problems of the economy.

The second was that tax reductions, like policies such as full wage indexation, would negate the benefits of devaluation.

A record for AMP

Australian Mutual Provident Society wrote a record $5,800 million in new business in 1976.

However, because of a substantial decline in New Zealand superannuation policies and an increase in the proportion of term insurance written, new premium income fell 3.4 per cent to $116 million.

Details, Page 17.

Tito seeks new PM

BELGRADE, Wednesday. —President Tito faces the problem today of choosing a new Prime Minister, following the death of Mr Dzemal Bijedic in a plane crash.

Mr Bijedic, his wife and six other people were killed yesterday when their Government executive jet crashed into a snow-clad mountain near Sarajevo, central Yugoslavia. There were no survivors.

The Prime Minister boarded the plane less than an hour after seeing President Tito off for Tripoli at the start of a nine-day Middle East tour.

The Prime Minister was viewed as a highly efficient administrator. He left no heir apparent in the Government, which has four equally ranked deputy premiers.

(AAP-Reuter)

LATE NEWS

Fighting in Japan

TOKYO, Wednesday. — Fighting broke out today when more than 3,000 riot police moved in to break up a demonstration at Narita, near here, in protest at the siting there of the Japanese capital's new international airport. —AAP.

Boy charged with murder

ADELAIDE, Wednesday.— A 12-year-old boy was charged tonight with the murder of Christopher Robin Dato, 7, at a YMCA youth camp last week.

The boy charged is one of 73 children who attended the camp. He was charged after an inquiry by a team of detectives who interviewed all the children who had been at the camp.

Christopher Dato's body was found after a search by more than 200 police and volunteers. He had been bashed to death with half a brick.

COLUMN 8

TOM Uren, the Deputy Federal Opposition Leader, didn't sleep well on Tuesday night. He lives in his electorate, Reid, in a home unit on the ninth floor of Granville Towers — overlooking the scene of the rail disaster.

. . . **AND** the condolences stream in. The Herald received this telegram from the United States yesterday: "We send our deepest sympathies to the families of the Mount Victoria train crash. Former Glenbrook residents and commuters. Terry and Barbara Stegner, Montana. USA."

EVER-interested in the broad trends of fashion, Column 8 can tell you that thin ties for men are on the way back. And so are narrow-legged trousers. Terrible news, isn't it?

MR Justice Woodward, of the Supreme Court, refused to begin a hearing on Tuesday until the air-conditioning was turned on. For two weeks he is filling in during the Law Vacation, holding court in the old Divorce Courts building in 50 Phillip Street. Courts in this building are being transferred to the new building up the street and, in the rush, officials disconnected the air flow, provoking a quick ultimatum from the judge. Yesterday justice proceeded breezily.

HOW the times have changed. Once upon a time it was cheaper to see the film version of a book than buy the book itself. Not any more. Today you can read the book for little more than half the price of the movie. David Seltzer's novel, The Omen, is an example. The paperback version sells in the City for $1.95. But to see the film you'll pay $3.50 at night.

THEY grow 'em bigger in the west. Our reports on the bonsai fig sprouting from the stone column in Centennial Park reminded W. D. Saxon, of Lindfield, of a tree in the Porongorup Range National Park, Western Australia. It's no miniature, but a karri some 50 metres tall. A tourist attraction, it grows from the centre of a large boulder 10 metres high. Well, give Sydney's midget another 200 or so years . . .

On other pages

Printed and published by John Fairfax & Sons Limited of Jones Street, Broadway. Postal-address, Box 506, G.P.O., Sydney, 2001. Registered for posting as a newspaper — Category C. *Recommended and maximum price only. Interstate by air extra.

When disaster strikes

TRAIN SMASHES When the 6.09am from the Blue Mountains left the tracks near Granville station on January 18, 1977, the train suffered relatively minor damage. But it had hit a stanchion of the Bond Street bridge (shown above). A huge segment of the bridge tilted, then slid away, landing flat on top of two carriages, killing 83 passengers. Inquiries revealed that the track was in a poor state, with termite-ridden sleepers and inadequate maintenance. Though the works program was enhanced, accidents continued. At Cowan, on May 6, 1990, six died; at Glenbrook on December 2, 1999, poor signals information led to a commuter train colliding with the Indian Pacific, killing seven (right); and at Waterfall on January 31, 2003, a deadman pedal defect that should have been fixed played a deadly role. Seven died.

Right Dogged by bad luck, HMAS Melbourne sank two friendly ships in the space of five years. Here, a crewman looks through her damaged bow in June 1969 after the aircraft carrier collided with a US warship.

Below A survivor is carried to safety after the ferry Rodney capsized in Sydney Harbour in 1938.

Bottom The ferry Greycliffe goes down after colliding with the Tahiti in Sydney Harbour in late 1927.

SEA DISASTERS

The sea has always held an edge of danger. Lieutenant James Cook was lucky to survive when the Endeavour smashed into coral on the Great Barrier Reef in 1770. Those on board the Dunbar were not so fortunate: approaching Sydney Heads in rough weather on August 20, 1857, the ship hit a reef and went down. Only one of the 121 on board survived.

On Sydney Harbour, on November 3, 1927, the ferry Greycliffe, carrying 150 people to Watsons Bay in misty conditions, collided with a steamer, Tahiti. The ferry sank and at least 37 died. A decade later, on February 13, 1938, passengers on the ferry Rodney rushed to one side of the top deck for a better view of the departing American warship, USS Louisville. The ferry capsized, killing 19.

The aircraft carrier HMAS Melbourne and destroyer HMAS Voyager collided at

Below Immigrants sailing to the Antipodes faced great risk. Many died when the Cospatrick caught fire in 1874.

Bottom Two crewmen died when the Sydney to Hobart yacht Business Post Naiad, shown at dock in Eden, rolled in the 1998 storm. (Photo: Mike Bowers)

sea off Jervis Bay at night on February 11, 1964. The Voyager, caught amidships, was sunk and a total of 82 men died. It was the worst peacetime naval disaster in Australia's history. The tragedy was followed by much controversy and two royal commissions. The Melbourne went on to sink a US warship, the destroyer Frank E. Evans, in South-East Asia in similar circumstances on June 3, 1969.

The annual Sydney to Hobart yacht race was hit in 1998 by a severe storm, which blew up very quickly. Warnings were not upgraded in time. Amplified by the shallows of Bass Strait, the fierce winds conjured up monster waves that sank five boats. Of 115 yachts that started, only 43 made it to Hobart. Six yachtsmen were killed, 55 were winched to safety and 20 boats were towed ashore. The coroner inquiring into the disaster found that management of the race had been grossly deficient.

TEMPEST Despite Australia being such a dry continent, rain and wind regularly wreak havoc. On December 24, 1974, people celebrating Christmas Eve in Darwin were expecting "a bit of a blow". The cyclone season is an annual event for local residents and they awaited Cyclone Tracy with unwarranted confidence.

Arriving at midnight, Cyclone Tracy made the church bells peal madly. The ferocity of the winds was off the scale: at 295 kmh, the measuring instruments failed. About 66 people died, although the precise number is not known because there could never be accurate accounting. Some 20,000 people were made homeless. The naval patrol boat HMAS Arrow was destroyed.

Above Two days after the cyclone the strain shows on the face of this woman, carrying her two children at Darwin airport. This photo won a Walkley award. (Photo: Vic Sumner)

Top right The reopening of the ice-works was a cause for celebration – and a long queue. (Photo: Rick Stevens)

Bottom right The clean-up begins. A tree, stripped bare, becomes a makeshift line to dry sodden clothes and bedding.

Top Anything not tied down was at the mercy of the winds. (Photo: Rick Stevens)

Above Shaken by the cyclone's power, Helen Greentree sits outside her tent, her dog Tiffany clutched to her chest and her shotgun – to frighten off looters – resting on her lap. (Photo: Vic Sumner)

BUSHFIRES Our love affair with the dense, tinder-dry bush that surrounds Sydney and many other Australian towns contributes to a nervy stand-off each summer between firefighters and the forces of nature.

On Black Thursday — February 6, 1851 — fires raged across Victoria, intensified by temperatures of 47 degrees Celsius. At least 10 people were killed and the fires caused wholesale damage to stock and other property.

On January 13, 1939, known as Black Friday, several bushfires joined together in Victoria. They formed a deadly wall of fire that swept everything before it. After three days the confirmed death toll was 71 and there were scores of people still listed as missing.

And then came Ash Wednesday, on February 16, 1983. Fires swept through Victoria and South Australia, driven by gale-force winds and accompanied by blistering 40-degree temperatures. The fires directly killed 76 people, incinerated more than 3700 buildings, destroyed forests and turned farmland to ash.

In NSW, over the summer of 1993–94, Sydney was ringed with smoke and flames, with 90 fires burning from the Queensland border to the south coast. Lives were lost at Bathurst, Como in Sydney's south and Lake Macquarie.

In the summer of 2002, bushfires were fought on a daily basis. The national capital had its turn during January 2003, when widespread fires roared through Canberra's suburbs, destroying 500 homes and killing four people.

Right The morning after the fright before. On Sunday, January 19, 2003, Canberra residents awoke to scenes of devastation. In Duffy, on the city's western fringe, rows of houses, such as these along Eucumbene Road, were wiped out. (Photo: Pat Scala)

Below right We won't stop till the stumps burn. Cricketers in Cessnock play despite the distractions. (Photo: Darren Pateman)

Below On the worst night of the 2003 Canberra bushfires it was almost as if the sky was alight. (Photo: Nick Moir)

EARTHQUAKE At 10.27 on the morning of December 29, 1989, the Newcastle earthquake, in an area of the nation that had been categorised as zero risk for earthquake, shook buildings up to 340 kilometres from its epicentre in inner Newcastle.

Measuring 5.6 on the Richter scale, the quake caused $1.5 billion damage, killed 13 people and injured 167 others. More than 30,000 buildings, including the Newcastle Workers Club, were damaged — 192 were so badly affected they had to be demolished. A further 178 had to be partially demolished.

Top Rescue crews work to find survivors trapped under rubble beneath the awning of the Kent Hotel in Hamilton, Newcastle, after the 1989 earthquake that shocked a complacent nation. (Photo: Darren Pateman)

Above Carol Coxhell was counting takings in the office of the Workers Club when the earthquake hit, just before 10.30am. A colleague heard her call "What's that?" before she was buried by the collapsing building. Here, her son Stephen attends her funeral. (Photo: Steven Siewert)

Right Caught off Vaucluse in 1935, this impressive-looking tiger shark was claimed as the largest ever caught by a rod and line. (Photo: Harry Freeman)

Below Marcia Hathaway, a 32-year-old actress, was wading in shallow water at Sugarloaf Bay in Sydney Harbour when a bronze whaler attacked. An ambulance called to nearby Mowbray Point was unable to make it up the steep slope with Hathaway on board. Eventually, she was carried up the slope by stretcher but died on the way to hospital. (Photo: Noel Stubbs)

SHARKS Sydney's beaches are safer than they once were. Rips will always be a problem but sharks, which terrorised bathers in the 1920s and 30s, conjure more fear than warranted by their actual threat. The regular attacks, which claimed arms and legs and many lives in the early years of surf swimming, provoked public and governmental consternation. Beaches were netted from the late 1930s, a program that has been successful, but at the cost of 150 and 200 sharks a year. Long-time netman Jim Lumb was clear about his priorities in 1996. "The proof is in the eating, mate. No one has been killed since '36. People want it out here."

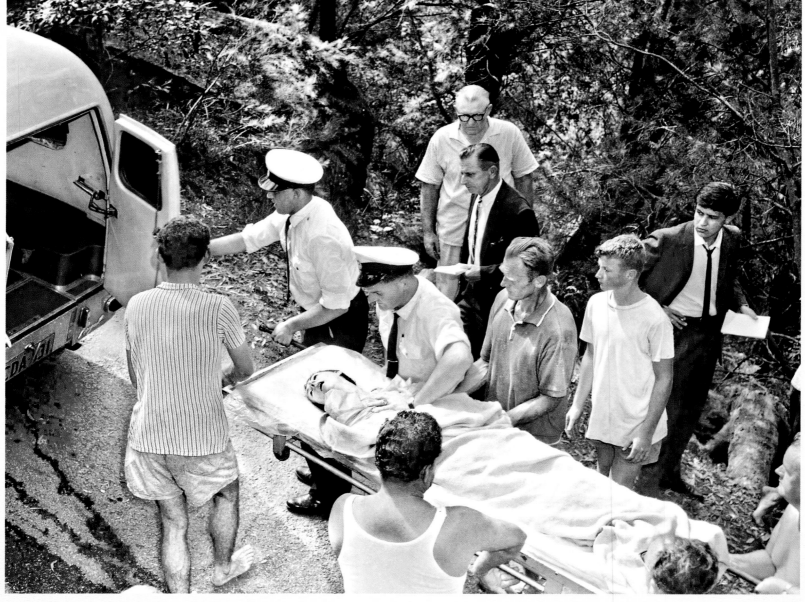

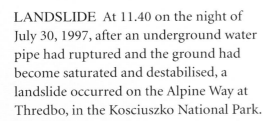

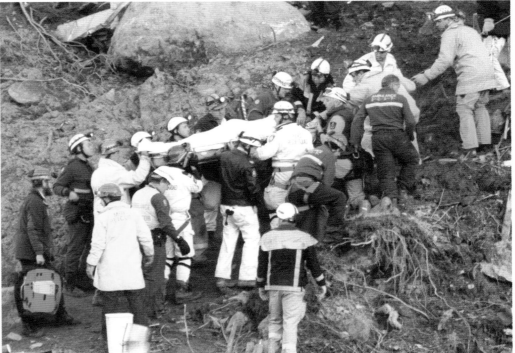

LANDSLIDE At 11.40 on the night of July 30, 1997, after an underground water pipe had ruptured and the ground had become saturated and destabilised, a landslide occurred on the Alpine Way at Thredbo, in the Kosciuszko National Park.

A mass of 1300 tonnes of earth and rock hit Carinya Lodge, killing the one occupant, and then hit Bimbadeen Lodge, killing 17 of the 18 people trapped inside. One survivor, Stuart Diver, was rescued after being buried for nearly 66 hours.

Top Rescue work at the landslide at Thredbo, 1997. (Photo: Mike Bowers)

Above Stuart Diver is pulled from the wreckage (left) and is borne to safety (right). (Photo: Dallas Kilponen)

Above After the deluge, food was dropped by parachute into Maitland's main street.

Right In the 1962 floods at Raymond Terrace, a rowboat was the most appropriate form of transport. (Photo: A. Kemp)

FLOODS Australia's waterways can never contain the huge volumes that the heavens occasionally offer up. The result has been a series of catastrophic floods.

An early insight into their power came on June 26, 1852, when a raging flood swept through Gundagai in southern NSW, killing 77 people and carrying off all but four houses. The substantial hotels in South Gundagai and the stores at North Gundagai were completely washed away.

Late summer in 1955 brought another massive deluge. Flooding was widespread across the state but reached catastrophic proportions in the Hunter Valley. In the disaster, 22 people died and thousands were left homeless.

Flooding is a feature of Australian rural life. When the floodwaters do not come as torrents, they just rise, often spreading across thousands of square kilometres and lasting weeks or months. Farms can be cut off for long periods, sheep and cattle are at

great risk — both of being swept away and of starving in the aftermath — and road and rail links are costly to repair.

In 1974 there was major flooding to eastern Australia and it was particularly severe in Brisbane, where heavy rain, associated with the decaying Cyclone Wanda, inundated the city. The waters rose for several days in Brisbane and in other centres, including Ipswich, peaking on January 29. When the flood receded, more than 6000 homes were missing, wrecked or full of slime. Fourteen people lost their lives.

Even when there is plenty of warning, rising floodwaters have an irresistible force and an inevitable impact.

In April 1990, the Bogan River in NSW's far west burst its banks, and the levee banks erected round the town of Nyngan did not hold. Almost all the town's 2500 residents were evacuated to Dubbo as floodwaters metres deep spread through the township.

Top Flooding at Maitland was so severe some survivors were forced to ride the houses to safety.

Above Water covers this road in Sydney's west in 1986. (Photo: T. Gunn)

Left Up to 141 millimetres of rain fell in an hour in Sydney in January 1999, turning Coogee into a lake. (Photo: Nick Moir)

CHAPTER FOUR

Gold!

. . . and the people rush

BY JOHN HUXLEY

The night too quickly passes
And we are growing old,
So let us fill our glasses
And toast the Days of Gold;
When finds of wondrous treasure
Set all the South ablaze
And you and I were faithful mates
All through the roaring days!

— Henry Lawson

Readers of *The Sydney Morning Herald* of May 16, 1851, might easily have been forgiven for missing a small news item dropped unobtrusively into its column of Daily Intelligence. This small item has since been described as the newspaper scoop of the century: "It is no longer any secret that gold has been found in the earth in several places in the western country," the story ran, sniffily adding, "It appears that this colony is to be cursed with a gold-digging mania."

Within a week, though, guarded "Granny" *Herald* — a nickname first used only a few years earlier — had in effect joined the rush, setting aside its considerable misgivings and sending its special correspondent, "a gentleman of great intelligence" called Gideon S. Lang, to the diggings. "I reached Bathurst on Saturday," Lang, an eminent explorer and pastoralist, reported breathlessly, "and found the gold mania still more violent than in Sydney, and much increased by the arrival of a man with a piece of gold, three and a half pounds weight, which he turned up, as he says, like a root of potatoes."

Although the level-headed Lang was sceptical of alarming claims that shepherds across the colony were deserting their flocks to join the rush for the "auriferous materials", he confirmed that many artisans, small tradesmen and domestics had left their jobs and were heading for the gold-washings. "About 100 people are now daily proceeding to the diggings, but every day the numbers are augmenting."

The would-be diggers were often ill-equipped for the enterprise. "The stupidity

of many is almost beyond belief," Lang noted. "Numbers I passed on the road [lacked] provision of any kind, either food, or bedding; one, an Irishman evidently, had nothing whatever but a pick without a handle, which he carried over his shoulder by the point, with the air of a second Cortez marching upon Mexico."

News of fresh diggings, discoveries and even gold deliveries were multiplying almost by the hour. Prices of basic foodstuffs, such as flour, sugar and biscuits, were doubling, trebling. The cost of a basic wooden cradle, used by the miners to wash for gold, had soared.

The front pages of the *Herald* were already filling with classified notices from those looking to exploit the rush by offering to buy and convey gold and, more frequently, to supply those who daily left the city in search of it. G. Hamilton's, of Hunter Street, Sydney, offered "kiln-dried biscuits, made on purpose for the diggings". Mr Henry Fisher,

Above Many of the political principles that guided Australia for nearly two centuries were cast in the heady atmosphere of the goldfields. Over nine months in 1860 and 1861 at Lambing Flat, NSW, bands of gold-hungry men turned on the Chinese miners. A Miners' Protective League sought the expulsion of Chinese, repeal of gold duties and parliamentary representation.

Left *We Find Gold in Our Claim*, a sketch from the *Herald's* weekly masthead *The Sydney Mail*.

Pages 138–139 Port Kembla steelworks grew from a single blast furnace with a capacity of 800 tons of steel a day in 1930 into one of the heavy industrial hubs of the nation. Its peak workforce approached 20,000 in the 1980s. Current production is 5 million tonnes a year. (Photo: Peter Morris)

Top Many mining operations, such as this windlass featured in 1908, relied for their success more on ingenuity than technology. (Photo: George Bell)

Above Success had many fathers but failure was a lonely experience.

142 THE BIG PICTURE

of George Street, opposite the burial ground, had strong colonial rum "made expressly to save 100 per cent on the carriage up to the mines". Suddenly, everything from English-built dog carts "for conveyance to Bathurst" to "Family Asperient Antibilious Pills" that protected miners from the harsh conditions was up for sale.

And the rush had scarcely begun. Ultimately, as Stuart Macintyre notes in *A Concise History of Australia*, it was to transform the colonies. It was to have the most profound economic, political and — especially in terms of immigration — social impact. The gold rush was, in the words of Catherine Spence, a young Scottish woman settler, a "convulsion [that] unfixed everything".

More than that, it generated the first of many waves of immigration that have continued into the 21st century, millions of boat and plane people following the First Fleet to turn Australia into a country of immigrants.

Not surprisingly however, back in that heady, momentous month of May 1851, the *Herald* struggled to comprehend the unprecedented movement of men and materials. "If we attempt to compare the first four months of the year, when Australian gold was a thing unheard-of, with the last two weeks of the current month of May, when Australian gold is the only thing thought of, we shall be at a loss for any metaphor that can adequately illustrate the stupendous change. If we were to say that

the colony has been panic-stricken, that the whole population has gone mad, we should use a bold figure of speech, but not much too bold to indicate the fact. It is as if the Genius of Australia had suddenly rushed from the skies, and proclaimed through a trumpet whose strains reverberate from mountain to mountain, from valley to valley, from town to town, from house to house, piercing every ear and thrilling every breast: 'THE DESTINIES OF THE LAND ARE CHANGED'. "

But for immense good, or unimaginable bad? For curse, or "lucky country" comfort? For the short term, or the long haul? The *Herald* remained unsure. Of course it lacked the benefit enjoyed by historians of hindsight but, more important perhaps, it was being rushed to resolve long-standing misgivings, ambivalences and fears within the colony that had attended outbreaks of gold fever almost since the first days of European settlement. For as the historian Marjorie Barnard explains, "From the very beginning gold and rumours of gold haunted the Australian story."

The first reported find, at least by a European, was, she recalls, a tragi-comic fiasco. The principal character was a convict called Daley who, as early as August 1788, produced a clod of earth speckled with particles of yellow metal which he claimed to be new-found gold. Far from being remembered as the founder of a mineral and mining industry now worth about $65 billion a year and employing a workforce of more than 90,000, Daley was exposed as a fraud. He had seeded the earth with glittering fragments collected earlier. He was flogged and forced to wear a canvas coat emblazoned with the letter "R" for rogue.

In 1815 convicts cutting a road to Bathurst reported seeing gold specks. Eight years later, James McBrien, a surveyor, discovered the first alluvial gold, in the sand near the Fish River, close to Bathurst. In 1830 a convict found gold in the same district and was flogged on suspicion that he had stolen

The good times roll

Many businesses in Sydney and Melbourne flourished with the gold discoveries of the 1850s, and the skylines changed rapidly. *The Sydney Morning Herald* began in a simple stone outbuilding in lower George Street (bottom right) and its quarters remained modest until the rush when it moved in 1856 to purpose-built premises (above) facing Hunter Street. The proprietor, John Fairfax (right), had left England in 1838, a bankrupt newspaper proprietor. The rivers of gold that flowed from the discoveries at Ophir and Clunes substantially increased advertising volumes and took him back to England in prosperity.

Returning in 1852 to Leamington in the English Midlands, Fairfax paid his old debts, incurred through libel actions. He then made plans for the future, buying a Cowper printing machine and a steam engine to drive it, thereby making the *Herald* the first Australian newspaper to switch from hand printing.

Before he left Leamington, he offered advice to intending immigrants to Australia: "To the young man of industrious and sober habits, and of moral character, whose anxiety is to pursue a course of honest perseverance unappalled by difficulty or danger, I say go. To the idle, the dissipated, the drunken, he who is reckless alike of his own peace and the sorrow he causes to others, I say stay."

Above A tempting way to find gold was to steal it – either from the miners themselves, as Mad Dan Morgan is sketched doing, or from the coaches used to bring the precious metal back to the city. Notorious for his savagery, Morgan had a price of £1000 on his head by the time he was shot and killed in Wangaratta in 1865.

Far right Sydney did not have its first power station until 1904 but, hidden away in the Southern Highlands of NSW, the mining town of Joadja Creek kept the home lights burning, producing kerosene, oil and candles. The only way into the town of 1200 – mainly Scottish miners – was the white knuckle railway line, which ran down a 45-degree slope, a trip that put visiting soccer teams at a significant disadvantage. The mine closed in 1906.

it. In 1839 the Polish-born explorer Paul Strzelecki found gold at the Vale of Clwydd, in the Lithgow district. The governor of NSW, George Gipps, determined to keep the find secret, in case the news provoked a convict outbreak. Such was the perceived power of gold to divide and disrupt the fledgling community.

When the Reverend William Branwhite Clarke, an Englishman with a Master's degree from Cambridge University and a long-standing interest in literature and geology, found gold, first near Hartley in 1841, then a few years later in the Pages River in the Liverpool Ranges, the response from Gipps was equally paranoid. Presented with the minister's specimens, he allegedly exclaimed, "Put them away, Mr Clarke, or we shall all have our throats cut!" Thus, according to the historian Ann Moyal, was the tireless, far-sighted Clarke, a contributor to the *Herald*, denied the recognition and reward that his role in the nation's gold beginnings deserved.

Most of the credit went instead to Edward Hammond Hargraves, who was perhaps not so much a successful miner as what Moyal describes as "Australia's

first successful, and hugely rewarded, public relations man". Born in England in 1816, Hargraves came to Australia as a sailor. He had been a fisherman in the Torres Strait, a small-time squatter in the Illawarra and an innkeeper near Gosford, before deciding in 1849 to join many of his adopted countrymen in the rush to the newly discovered goldfields of California. It was, wrote Charles Bateson in *Gold Fleet for California*, the greatest migration since the Crusades. In two years, more than a quarter of a million people from around the globe rushed to California. Hargraves was one of about 7000 Australians and New Zealanders who made the long haul to San Francisco.

So strong was this drift of workers from booming NSW, and so frantic the clamour from employers already deprived of convict labour, that the NSW government was compelled to rethink its policy of hushing up local discoveries. It is important to realise that at that time the wool industry accounted for half of Australia's export earnings.

The governor held grave concerns that by encouraging the search for gold in the colony, there would inevitably be economic, political and, thereby, social consequences for the pastoralists. Nevertheless, under the circumstances, the politicians acted promptly. In 1849 a government geologist was appointed. Suddenly the government was eager to find a new source of wealth and to develop mines, and prepared to reward those who made this possible. Enter, stage left, the portly Mr Hargraves.

Although moderately successful compared, at least, with most Australian "Forty-niners" who returned broke and dispirited, Hargraves became convinced that greater riches awaited him back home in NSW, where he recalled rock formations resembling those of the auriferous hills of California. He was roundly ridiculed: "There is no gold in the country [Australia] you're going to, and if there were that darned Queen wouldn't let you dig for it," one miner told him. Hargraves returned to Australia on the

ship Emma in January 1851, and set out, alone and on horseback, to prove his theory. Having passed through Bathurst, he arrived on the 11th day at Guyong, where he enlisted the assistance of John Lister, the 18-year-old son of a local licensee.

Exactly what happened next is shrouded in legend. But according to Hargraves's own colourful account, he and Lister were riding down the Lewis Ponds Creek, a tributary of the Macquarie River, when he felt surrounded by gold. He announced to his incredulous helper, "We are now in the goldfields." Whereupon Hargraves took up a pick, scratched the gravel off a dyke and with a trowel dug a panful of earth, which he washed in a waterhole. It produced a little gold. Hargraves washed five more pans of earth, obtaining gold traces from all but one. He was satisfied. "This," he exclaimed to his guide, "is a memorable day in the history of NSW. I shall be a baronet, you will be knighted and my old horse will be stuffed, put into a glass case, and sent to the British Museum!" It was February 12, 1851.

Remarkably, details of this and the subsequent discovery at Ophir on the Macquarie River, where four ounces of gold, worth about 30 shillings, were recovered, continued to be disputed for almost another 40 years, until a government select committee investigated the various claims and counter-claims. In 1890 it ruled that although Hargraves must be credited with having provided the expertise and the equipment, John Lister and two brothers, James and William Tom, who had been recruited to the prospecting party, "were undoubtedly the first discoverers of gold obtainable in Australia in payable quantities". Belatedly the three men were awarded £1000 to share.

It was a pittance compared with the rewards paid in 1851 to Hargraves after his find was presented to the government and checked by its geologist. Although his horse never made it to the museum, he was given £10,000 and a life pension, made a commissioner for lands and presented in

1854 to Queen Victoria. Marjorie Barnard writes that, whatever the truth of the matter, Hargraves's gold "had given the government a trump card that would end forever attempts to reintroduce transportation under one name or another; would re-establish prosperity; and stop the drift to California."

Today, Ophir — named by Hargraves after King Solomon's city of gold — is a sleepy backwater, with much to attract the curious visitor but little to suggest the frenzy that engulfed it a century and a half ago. Within a fortnight of the find being made known, 600 men were working Summer Hill Creek. At the height of the mania, Sydney was almost emptied of able-bodied men, while more than 2000 were squeezed into Ophir.

Life on the diggings was far from easy. The extent of human suffering increased as winter set in, losers overwhelmingly outnumbered winners, and easy alluvial gold was panned out. Nevertheless, within weeks the *Herald* had decided that the gold rush was a Good Thing, "one of the most remarkable phenomena in the history of the world, designed by Providence in order to populate the Australian wilderness".

As news came of further discoveries in NSW and Victoria, notably at Clunes, Sydney stores sold out of pick-axes, shovels and wheelbarrows, and the *Herald's* circulation soared. New readers scrambled to catch Lang's latest report, and the newspaper predicted "population and wealth will flow in upon us in copious, rapid and continuous streams". And so it did for some, including the *Herald* itself which, fattened by special weekly gold supplements, quadrupled both in circulation and in size, from four to 16 pages. Of the London papers, only *The Times* was bigger. With additional staff and presses to accommodate, the newspaper moved in 1856

Above To gold the glory, coal the grime: always the poor relation, coal was first found at Newcastle by escaped convicts in 1791. Initially sold to Bengal, India, in 1799, coal remains the nation's most important export commodity. A coal seam under Sydney Harbour was first reached in 1902 and the Balmain colliery, where these men worked, stayed open until 1931. Gas extraction from the bottom of the harbour continued until 1950.

to its new solid stone offices on a triangular site bounded by Pitt, Hunter and O'Connell Streets.

Immigrants needed little encouragement to seek their fortune in Australia. Stuart Macintyre quantifies the impact: "The millions of pounds of gold bullion that were shipped to London each year brought a flow of imports [in the early 1850s Australia bought 15 per cent of all British exports] and reinforced the local proclivity for consumption. The goldfields towns also provided a ready market for local produce and manufactures." The first railways were constructed, the first telegraphs began operating, the first steamships plied between Europe and Australia. And the population expanded at a rate unmatched by early

convict transportation, by the influx of labour to build the Snowy River scheme after World War II, or by the "£10 Poms" of the 1940s, 50s and 60s.

In just two years the number of new arrivals was greater than the number of convicts who had landed in the previous 70 years. In 10 years, the non-Aboriginal population trebled, from 430,000 in 1851 to 1,150,000 in 1861. In a decade, Victoria's numbers increased sevenfold to more than half a million, as towns such as Ballarat and Bendigo boomed, giving the new state numerical supremacy over NSW, and Melbourne a decidedly larrikin cultural ascendancy over Sydney, exemplified by the rip-roaring Melbourne Cup horse race.

Most of the newcomers were British, as

before, but there were also Americans and other "foreign" Europeans from France, Italy, Germany, Poland and Hungary, many of whom had just lived through a decade of revolution and republican uprising. And about 40,000 Chinese arrived, far and away the single largest foreign contingent and sufficiently "different" to be identified as a specific threat to social and economic order.

Gold had turned the tables on the pastoralists who, fearful that their place in society and their workforce on the land would decline, regarded the rushes with such alarm that some called upon the government to declare martial law and prohibit digging at Ophir. Gold had also given Australia a multicultural jolt, quickly turning the colonies into what later generations would call a "melting pot". Inevitably, such massive economic, political and social changes were not to prove trouble-free, especially in and around the goldfields.

In 1861 antipathy towards the frugal, hard-working Chinese exploded into violence when encampments at Lambing Flat, near present-day Young, were attacked and the "orientals" driven from the diggings. It was an incident in which Macintyre detected the origin of "a racial strain in popular radicalism" and, it might be added, in mainstream thinking into the 21st century.

So pervasive is this strain that it remains a recurring topic for social commentary. As the former prime minister Malcolm Fraser

once remarked, if Melburnians had been asked 50 years ago whether they favoured the prevailing rate of Greek migration they would almost certainly have replied in the negative. But few today would deny that they have made an enormously positive contribution to the community.

So, too, have most Sydneysiders come to recognise the worth of the Vietnamese, 200,000 of whom flowed through when Australia opened its doors at the end of the Vietnam War. Similarly, one day Australians may come to respect more the contribution of asylum seekers from the Middle East and elsewhere.

Looking back 150 years, more remarkable perhaps than the occasional outbreak of hostility was the relative ease and lack of violence with which the colonies accommodated such a huge and sudden influx of men and money. Only at Eureka, at Ballarat, Victoria, did unrest run out of control. There, in November 1854, a long-running dispute, primarily about the administration and enforcement of mining licences, came to a violent climax when government troops stormed a makeshift stockade erected by rebel miners, resulting in the death of more than 30 men. Almost unnoticed by historians, a similar confrontation had been narrowly averted at Turon, near Bathurst. Matthew Higgins, author of a paper on the "near rebellion" for the *Journal of the Royal Australian Historical*

Top BHP, now merged with Billiton, is the great success story of Australian mining with operations around the globe in coal, metals and petroleum. Iron ore remains a cornerstone of the company's business, dug from mines such as Mount Whaleback in Western Australia. (Photo: Glenn Campbell)

Above Diamonds had long been found in Western Australia but in the 1970s a geological detective project led to the discovery of the Argyle diamond mine, now the world's largest producer. (Photo: Erin Jonasson)

Society, relates how a Wesleyan minister, the Reverend William Piddington, intervened to prevent bloody confrontation. The near rebellion ended with a cricket match between a police team and miners' XI. On this occasion, at least, the miners won.

Gold fever continued to thrive for several decades. Further gold discoveries were made at Araluen, Adelong Creek, Hanging Rock, Kiandra, Grenfell, Lucknow, Hill End and elsewhere, until the last big strike at Wyalong

in 1893. As Marjorie Barnard concludes, gold probably expedited rather than radically changed the course of Australia's development. But it provided the basis for a multibillion-dollar mining industry, as other valuable metals were rapidly unearthed: copper at Cobar, NSW; tin at Inverell; lead, silver and zinc, famously at Broken Hill in 1883; and so on.

Arguably, though, not even the Poseidon nickel boom, sparked by a discovery at Mount

MR SMITH WITH KATHLEEN, 19 MTHS.

MRS SMITH WITH JAMES, 7 MTHS.

MICHAEL, 16

MAVOURNEEN, 14

NITA, 13

PAULINE, 12

EILEEN, 10

PATRICK, 8

KEVIN, 7

SUSAN, 5

THE SMITHS

Windarra in Western Australia in 1969, which boosted Poseidon share prices from 75 cents to $280 in just four months, matched the gold rush in terms of feverish activity and long-term impact. Gold ensured that, although the wool industry reinstated itself as the staple, the old pastoral days would not return. It taught men and women from many backgrounds to co-operate. It gave them political rights and a taste for high wages. It put Australia on the world map. After gold,

truly, "nothing would be the same again".

Though the gold rush was relatively short-lived, the people rush has continued in fits and starts to the present day. For more than two centuries immigrants have been the face and, more importantly, the future of Australia, regularly refreshing and rejuvenating what has been, until very recently at least, a young nation. Even today, their expectant eyes still peer from the pages of the *Herald*.

Below After World War II, when gold would no longer draw migrants in their thousands, the Australian government funded a massive drive to encourage British migration. Find or borrow £10 for each adult and Australia would pay the rest; children came free and – in cases such as the Smiths and Lennons in 1956 – in great numbers. Nearly 1 million £10 Poms made the journey in 30 years after the war.

ND MRS LENNON KEITH, 7 MTHS.

ANDREW, 20, AND WIFE SADIE

JIM, 19, AND WIFE ISOBEL

SADIE, 18

MARIE, 14

VERONICA, 12

THERESA, 9

JEAN, 7

AGNES, 6

ANGUS, 5

PATRICIA, 3

THE LENNONS

The people rush

In 1791 there were 87 free settlers in NSW and Norfolk Island. At the start of the 21st century, more than one in five of Australia's inhabitants were born elsewhere; a higher proportion, as Stuart Macintyre points out, than in Canada, the United States or any other settler society.

Between times, the human wave has ebbed and flowed strongly. Sometimes it was assisted, sometimes not. Usually it was welcomed, occasionally not. But always it was based on the nation's needs — be they sheer numbers, certain skills or a specific sex — and an individual's assessment of the competing economic opportunities, political obligations and civil liberties that provide the foundation for a better life.

Although Governor Bligh had proposed regulations aimed at attracting an industrious, respectable farming class as early as 1807, it was not until 25 years later that the land and emigration commission was created in Britain to assist migration. Over the next three decades about 340,000 Britons — 1088 shiploads — came to Australia. In the first four years on the scheme, more than 3000 single women arrived. At the same time, in 1837, the first Chinese labourers came to Australia. Local opposition deterred countless more. Though many of these migrants packed their bags with short-term, get-rich-quick ambitions, most of the half million from Britain, some 60,000 from Continental Europe and 42,000 from China who came to colonial Australia in the 1850s decided to settle.

Over following decades net migration rose and fell, almost in proportion to the level of employment and other economic activity: during the 1890s depression, numbers slumped before gradually reviving; in 1912, almost 90,000 immigrants entered Australia, the highest intake since the gold rush. Many barely had time to settle before going off to fight and die for the empire.

Falling birth rates in the 1930s and

Above Fijian-Indian students leave the Maloja in Pyrmont, Sydney, 1937. (Photo: K. Rainsford)

Left When the Johan de Witt left Europe in 1947 with 700 Jewish refugees aboard – many of them survivors of the Nazi death camps – it provoked a furore in Australia with the minister for immigration, Arthur Calwell, coming under attack. Even so, Calwell decided to enforce a quota allotting no more than 25 per cent of berths to refugees. An exception was made for the Johan de Witt as it had sailed under conditions to which no British migrant should be subjected. Clearly these men, women and children arriving in Sydney in March, 1947, had no complaints.

a painful demonstration of Australia's vulnerability in the war-torn 1940s prompted a new push to attract migrants. The former prime minister Billy Hughes said in 1937: "Australia must advance and populate, or perish." After the war, when the population had climbed to only 8 million in 160 years, Arthur Calwell targeted an annual growth rate of 2 per cent, half of it imported.

The "£10 Pom" scheme was introduced, as well as special arrangements for other, displaced Europeans. Many, as the historian John Moloney explained, were "'Balts', 'Dagoes', or 'Reffoes', nicknames which did not necessarily imply either suspicion or rejection, but merely an acceptance that the

'new Australians' were different to those of the old variety."

Nevertheless, between 1947 and 1973, immigrants from the United Kingdom constituted 41 per cent of the total intake of more than 2.5 million. Despite the cessation of assisted passage, abandonment of the White Australia policy and diversification of the overall intake, the Poms have kept on coming. More than 200 years since the first British settler arrived, more than 150 years since the first people rush, census figures show that 37 per cent of Australians have United Kingdom ancestry, more than the proportion who reported Australian ancestry.

Above The promised land wasn't meant to look like this: sparse cabins, bare floors and crook food. British migrants were unimpressed by conditions in the temporary camp at Bathurst in 1951, as authorities found themselves overwhelmed by the postwar influx. "My wife broke down and wept but that was only the first impression ... She is alright today," explained Kenneth Mann of Birmingham.

Left Two more young Italians about to disembark from the Viminale in 1937 to begin new lives. (Photo: Bertram Jones)

Right In 1976 there were 2400 Vietnamese-born people in Australia. Risking their lives on decrepit boats such as this one moored at Darwin in 1981, refugees came to Australia in their thousands.

Below Many Vietnamese, such as this group who reached Sydney in 1977, arrived in comfort through official channels, flown in from camps in South-East Asia. Twenty years later, the Vietnamese had become the nation's fifth-largest migrant group. (Photo: Ton Linsen)

Below right When pro-democracy protesters were massacred in Tiananmen Square in 1989 Australia offered resident visas to 42,000 Chinese students. Many took up the offer, transforming some Sydney suburbs, among them Ashfield, where the Go Go Supermarket is run by former students Jacqueline Wong and Frank Cai. (Photo: Stephen Baccon)

Above Sir Robert Menzies declared himself British to his bootstraps, but the nation no longer is. The scale of postwar immigration has made Australia one of the world's most diverse communities. NSW's smartest students of the millennium captured the changed face of a country where more than one-quarter of the population trace their history to countries other than Britain and Ireland. (Photo: Peter Rae)

Above How the river runs: the Snowy River, pictured here at dawn at the foot of Mt Kosciusko. (Photo: Nick Moir)

Far right top The first taste of Australian education for miners' children was Happy Jack School, which opened in Khancoban in 1955. The original building remains in use. (Photo: R. Stewart)

Far right bottom Some winter days the wet clothes were as likely to freeze as they were to dry. Mia Dolega Jasienska hangs out the washing.

The miracle from Snowy River

When construction began on the Snowy Mountains Hydro Electric Scheme in 1949, the prime minister, Ben Chifley, called it "the greatest single project in our history". As a feat of engineering, it probably still is. In 1967, the American Society of Civil Engineers rated the scheme as one of the seven civil engineering wonders of the modern world.

The Snowy became one of those big-picture, nation-building exercises. Some called it Australia's "coming-of-age", proving that it was a self-assured nation in its own right. The construction brought an exhilaration to rival the completion of the Harbour Bridge

that had gone before, and the Opera House which was to come. Afterwards, as much of the nation's infrastructure was allowed to run down and governments made budget deficits economically unfashionable, critics asked whether such a scheme would have been possible in the last quarter of the 20th century.

The Snowy Scheme diverted the waters of the Snowy and Tumut Rivers, via tunnels, through the Great Dividing Range to the Murray and Murrumbidgee Rivers to irrigate the inland plains. On their way, the waters would generate electricity for the NSW, ACT and Victorian systems.

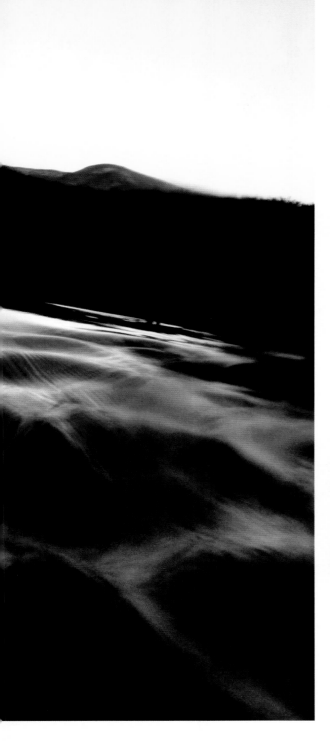

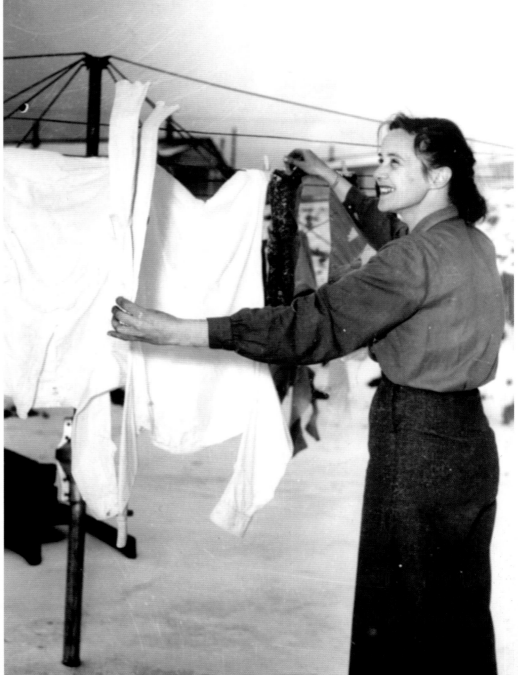

A total of 12 tunnels stretching 140 kilometres, 16 dams, seven power stations, a pumping station, 49 camps and townships and 1600 kilometres of roads and tracks were built. The townships of Adaminaby and Jindabyne were flooded and moved. It took 25 years, cost $820 million and was finished on time and within budget.

The scheme is a monument to multicultural Australia, having brought together a workforce of more than 100,000 men and women from 30 countries. The obvious downside was the drying up of the Snowy River, a process still being addressed.

Right Many voices needed to find one tongue: Josef Tezik and co-workers tackle the intricacies of English grammar at a class in Cooma in 1951.

Far right top Eileen Hudson, wife of Sir William Hudson, the first commissioner of the Snowy Mountains Hydro Electric Authority, cuts the ribbon to open the Guthega Tunnel in 1954.

Far right bottom This road crossing of the Snowy, pictured in 1951, offers barely a portent of the scale of the enterprise on which the nation had embarked, nor the volume of water to be contained and redirected.

Below Faces of the old world in a new land: some of the men who built the Snowy Mountains Scheme, heading off to work in 1950.

Above Jindabyne is one of 16 dams in the Snowy. Workers also drove 140 kilometres of tunnels through the mountains and built 80 kilometres of aqueducts and seven power stations.

Black and white photography

The first *Herald* photographer was George Bell. Already responsible for some of the finest images in *The Sydney Mail*, he switched papers after the *Herald* got past its reluctance to use photographs and showed the arrival of the US Great White Fleet in 1908.

A photograph of Bell astride a horse with a heavy full-plate camera stares down from the walls of what some still call "the darkroom". In reality, the *Herald's* last darkroom was at our old building at Broadway, from which we moved in 1995. Each generation has clung to the older cameras until forced to change: from the bulky full-platers used early in the century to the Ihagees of the 1930s, and the classic Speed Graphic, in use from the late 1940s to the early 60s, when the *Herald* took the quantum leap to 35mm.

We look at Bell and his bulky equipment today and wonder how he and

his colleagues managed. But no doubt he had marvelled at the previous generation, who had struggled with wet plates, and before that the daguerreotype and its impossibly slow exposures.

Hanging out of a helicopter or a light aircraft with modern digital SLR cameras is still a challenge. But in 1911 a New Zealander, Joseph Hammond, took Bell on a short flight in his fragile Bristol biplane to take what were possibly the first aerial shots of Sydney. They took off from Ascot racecourse, where Sydney Airport's domestic terminal now stands. After a short loop over Botany Bay, they flew over Marrickville and the Cooks River. Because the day was foggy, Bell's picture spread in *The Sydney Mail* of Wednesday, May 10, 1911, had to be sharpened by artists.

It was the start of something big. Today, using a global positioning system (GPS), we can position helicopters with complete

Top far left Pipe, billy, dog and towel: what more did the swagman of 1910 need? (Photo: George Bell)

Bottom far left The man behind the *Herald's* first camera, George Bell. (Photo: H. H. Fishwick)

Left Having turned back the Japanese, Lee Robinson and a native of New Britain watch the Australian governor-general, the Duke of Gloucester, pass by at Jacquinot Bay in June 1945. (Photo: Ray Olson)

Below With not a hair out of place: this image, from 1911, showed how a new generation of cameras could capture moving images.

Bottom A spot of bother: kids inspect the wreck of a beach patrol plane in Harbord, 1935. (Photo: Thomas Fisher)

accuracy, years apart, to take "then and now" pictures.

A headline in 1911, "Photographic Extraordinary: Highest speed snapshot taken in Australasia", trumpeted a breakthrough piece of equipment. A "between-the-lens" shutter allowed exposures to be taken at 1/2000th of a second, heralding a whole new world. The image accompanying the headline was of a man in mid-leap, captured in detail, and described as "incomparably fine". Before this the slower focal-plane shutters produced what the article described as "comet-like streakiness" when trying to render fast-moving objects.

For those digging through the millions of negatives in the *Herald's* archives, it is not the big events that have the most impact, even though there are many powerful images. It is the day-to-day work of *Herald* photographers that surprises and enthralls.

Above The Fairey IIID seaplane, built of wood and cloth: the first flight around Australia, an epic of 90 hours' flying time in April and May 1924, was made by a Fairey.

Above Sustained by their capacity to shock and awe, AC/DC wrote the book on bad boys made good. Bon Scott signs up a new fan in 1976. (Photo: Ton Linsen)

Right January 1971 was a big month for music festivals, first at Wallacia and then the rain-affected Fairlight Blues and Heavy Music Festival at Mittagong.

Left Living next door to Elvis: Lance and Irene Mortlock share their home town of Parkes with the annual invasion of Elvis impersonators. (Photo: Steven Siewert)

Below Established in 1951 to help overcome a manpower shortage, the Women's Royal Australian Army Corps was disbanded in 1985 after women were integrated into the army. (Photo: David Bartho)

CHAPTER FIVE

Literary Life

Writing up a storm

BY SUSAN WYNDHAM

On Saturday, December 28, 1946, under a headline that has aged badly, *The Sydney Morning Herald* announced the results of its first literary competition: "Woman Wins £2000 Novel Prize".

The page-one story is a nugget of Australian cultural history for reasons both hoped for and unplanned by the paper's editors. In launching Ruth Park's career as a novelist linked with Sydney, it also marked a new era of urban fiction that seemed inevitable as the country emerged weary from two world wars and an economic depression. Along the way, Park's book lit the flames of a controversy that would consume the *Herald* and its readers for weeks and hasten a new round of the slum clearances that wiped out tracts of old Sydney.

Perhaps the editors had an inkling that they were challenging readers with the choice of Park's story about a poor family in the inner-Sydney slums of Surry Hills. A review by Shawn O'Leary on the same day's book pages pleaded for a broad-minded reading: "Paradoxical as it seems, *The Harp in the South*, although it is strong meat for the weak-stomached, is a moral book … If the book is super-realistic, it is never deliberately bawdy."

Ruth Park had no idea of the trouble ahead when she wrote *The Harp in the South*. A young New Zealander who told the *Herald* she had crossed the Tasman in 1942 to marry the writer D'Arcy Niland and become part of the country's "growing literary tradition that gripped my imagination", she plunged straight into the poverty of freelance journalism and a wartime housing shortage.

While she and Niland worked frantically to establish writing careers and a family, they lived in makeshift accommodation, from a Kings Cross "flatlet" to rooms above a shop in Devonshire Street, Surry Hills.

In her 1993 autobiography, *Fishing in the Styx*, Park remembered the suburb of decaying Victorian terrace houses as "notorious for minor crime and farouche social behaviour … a queer, disreputable

Above Six-year-old Surry Hills resident Raymond returns home through the alleys from a movie. Children would forgo meals – and shoes – to save pennies so they could escape to the world of the picture palace.

Previous pages When there's not much in the way of home comforts, you've got to take fun where you can find it. These Surry Hills children mount some merry-go-round horses from a travelling carnival.

little village, half-hidden under the hem of a prosperous city".

So when Niland persuaded his wife to attempt her first novel for the *Herald's* literary competition, she re-created the Dickensian world where she had lived for two years without bath, gas or sufficient daylight, fighting rats and bedbugs, and amid extreme poverty, drunken brawls, wife-beatings and a murder on her doorstep.

Her novel centres on the Irish-Catholic Darcy family, residents of the fictional 12½ Plymouth Street. Challenging the mores of the day, it follows the adolescent daughter Roie through her sexual initiation with a Jewish boy, her frightened run from an abortionist, an attack by drunken Dutch sailors and the contentment she finds with a part-Aboriginal husband and their baby in a room of her parents' house.

The book might seem sentimental now but its head-on portrayal of sex, violence, misery and rough language still, as the *Herald's* reviewer wrote, "bludgeons the reader about the brain, the heart and the conscience".

This was a long step away from earlier Australian literature, which was dominated, at least in the popular imagination, by the rural romanticism of Banjo Paterson and Henry Lawson. Women such as Henry

Above Surry Hills rooftops in 1928. Residents were used to living close to their neighbours but the difficulty of finding money to pay the rent during the Depression forced young couples to stay at home with parents. The population of the suburb, with its narrow streets and houses, became even denser.

WOMAN WINS £2,000 NOVEL PRIZE

'Herald' Awards Announced

The prizes for the three best novels in the Literary Competitions conducted this year by "The Sydney Morning Herald" have been awarded as follows:—

FIRST PRIZE (£2,000): Miss Ruth Park (Mrs. D'Arcy Niland), of 20 Crystal Street, Petersham, New South Wales, for "The Harp in the South."

SECOND PRIZE (£1,000): Mr. Jon Cleary, who is visiting England, for "You Can't See Round Corners."

THIRD PRIZE (£500): Mrs. G. H. Job (who writes under the name of Esther Roland), of "Ruardean," Central Avenue, Indooroopilly, Brisbane, for "I Camp Here."

JUDGES COMMEND 10 OTHERS

In addition to the three prize-winning novels, the judges have especially commended 10 other novels, the names of which appear in the Book Pages of the "Herald" to-day.

Of 175 novels which were submitted, the judges found 48 were worthy of serious consideration as possible prize-winners.

"This display of talent," they say in their report, "exceeded the expectations of the judges, and distinctive evidence of literary quality marked the 15 stories which were then selected as finalists, from which to make the choice of awards."

The judges state that, apart from the prize-winners and the commended novels, the entries included a number of stories which did not have the literary merit required for such valuable awards, but which were competently written in their particular type of fiction.

The judges estimate that about two dozen novels, entered for the competition, are worthy of publication and would find an interested reading public.

£5,000 For Novelists

Under the terms of the competition, the three prize-winning novels, for which a total of £3,500 is awarded, are available for serial publication.

The conditions also provide that the "Herald" may acquire for serial publication other novels submitted on payment of £150 for each novel.

The "Herald" now announces that it is acquiring serial rights for 10 additional novels from among those commended by the judges and others submitted. This involves an additional payment of £1,500 to Australian novelists, making the total assistance arising from this year's competition £5,000.

All these Australian novels will be presented to "Herald" readers during the coming year.

STORY SET IN SURRY HILLS

Following is an outline of the | The author, Ruth Park, is a

Handel Richardson, Miles Franklin, Katharine Susannah Prichard, Christina Stead and Kylie Tennant had established themselves — but sometimes under male pseudonyms and with more overseas than local support.

Australian publishing was limited by the paper and labour shortages of World War II, combined with the eternal curses of geographical isolation and small population. There was one publisher, Angus and Robertson, a mighty but somewhat arrogant establishment.

Miles Franklin and Dymphna Cusack parodied the contemporary scene in a 1945 play, *Call Up Your Ghosts*. An American GI visits a city bookshop to buy books about Australia but he is fobbed off with American and British titles and the argument, "And there isn't any Australian literature yet. It doesn't pay."

The *Herald's* proprietors, the Fairfax family, set out to discover new talent when it established a grant of £30,000 to "encourage the development of Australian literature and art". As well as the novel prize in 1946, there were prizes for short stories, war stories and poems — the most generous awards ever offered in the country.

In its December 28 editorial headed "Growth in Our Literature", the *Herald* noted that Australia had produced a national literature — mostly bush ballads and short stories — before it became a nation. Using a marker of success still heavily relied on, the anonymous writer listed Australian books that had found international recognition, such as Henry Handel Richardson's *The Fortunes of Richard Mahony*, Joseph Furphy's *Such Is Life*, Xavier Herbert's *Capricornia* and Ethel Turner's *Seven Little Australians*. But he was pleased to report that the *Herald's* search had elicited a new generation of sophisticated, confident writing.

The high quality of the 175 entries impressed the judges, Dr A. G. Mitchell, of the University of Sydney; T. Inglis Moore, a lecturer in Pacific Studies at Canberra

University College; and Leon Gellert, the *Herald's* literary editor.

They awarded the £1000 second prize to an even tougher novel set in Paddington and the city. In Jon Cleary's *You Can't See Round Corners,* a young SP bookie slides from army deserter to murderer after his girlfriend refuses his sexual advances. Third prize of £500 went to a more traditional story set on a Queensland station, *Camp Here* by Esther Roland. All three winners were serialised in the newspaper over the next months, as were 10 more novels that the judges considered interesting to the public.

The public didn't even wait to read the first full-page instalment of *The Harp in the South* before giving their assessment. Park and her husband attended a Catholic Mass

Above Ruth Park working from home in 1951, with one of her five children under the table. She told the *Herald* in 1985 she had grabbed writing time between changing nappies and shelling peas, and clean-typed the pages over the double bed at night.

Top far left Oranges for the poor at St David's Church, on Arthur Street in Surry Hills, 1935. These days the building hides under a thick coat of vines and has been turned over to commercial offices.

Bottom left The *Herald* editor, Hugh McClure Smith, presents Ruth Park with her £2000 prize.

Above One house, three generations: for many families, it was put on a brave face and unite against those who would question the reputation of Surry Hills.

that weekend and were "stricken" when the celebrant devoted his sermon to the wickedness of the *Herald* and the books it promoted.

Park and her novel dominated the newspaper's letters page. The most heated correspondents condemned the unread book as vulgar, blasphemous and corrupting. "Book Lover, Sydney" congratulated the proprietors on their efforts to promote cultural development, then complained, "I was interested to read the summaries of the three winning novels, but somewhat disappointed to notice that they all sounded rather sordid. I know the modern idea is that to portray 'real life' one must make it stark. But why?"

Readers attacked Park as a communist, a capitalist and an exploiter. Some were offended on behalf of all Irish Catholics and Surry Hills residents. Others couldn't believe slums existed in beautiful, middle-class Sydney. There was great concern about the image of Australia that would be carried overseas.

On Saturday, January 11, 1947, the whole letters page was given over to the novel, and the *Herald*'s managing director, Warwick Fairfax, had his say in an accompanying article, "Why We Print the Story". Emphasising the imaginative quality of fiction, he argued — perhaps more forcefully than Park would have liked — that novels did not give an accurate description of life at a certain time or place, whether "Surry Hills today, London a hundred years ago, Timbuctoo in the Middle Ages or anything else". Nor were they a plea for remedying social evils or a means of recommendation to the world. "The question of what anyone thinks of Australia after reading *The Harp in the South* matters as little as what they think of medieval Denmark after reading *Hamlet*."

In fact, more than half the hundreds of letters to the editor backed Park. Comparing her with Charles Dickens and Emile Zola, they praised her vivid writing and her bravery in exposing urgent problems. The real blame lay with "the dull social conscience" of the people and their politicians.

At last the *Herald* sent a reporter out. On January 18, "Surry Hills Thinks Hard About Itself" quoted the residents of a small street who had read or, more often, heard about *The Harp in the South*. While a few proudly defended their home ("I'd rather be here than a lot of places in Redfern, or Ultimo, or Erskineville, or the 'Loo"), most confirmed Park's observations.

"The story is wonderful," said an elderly widow. "I'm keeping it to read all over again. A smack in the eye for some of those landlords, I say." An invalid pensioner described chopping wood three times a day for a fuel stove, bathing her children in the wash tub and taking herself to the bathhouse up the hill for one shilling and threepence. Others spoke of bedbugs, and landlords who lived "in their shells" on the other side of the harbour. A "large woman" said, "It's a lovely story but with a serial you read a part and then get muddled after you have a few drinks."

Park contacted the more well-meaning letter writers, suggesting they form an organisation to help the underprivileged. She also offered a guided tour of Surry Hills slums to anyone who wanted proof of their existence. The only response came from Pixie O'Harris, the children's book illustrator, who threw herself into harassing the city council

and the NSW housing department to step up their slum-clearance programs.

D'Arcy Niland, who would within a few years publish his beloved rural novel *The Shiralee*, wrote a defence: "Why the Hovel Novel". In private Park was supported by other writers such as Kylie Tennant, Jean Devanney, Christina Stead and Vance Palmer, and reviled by Miles Franklin who was a failed entrant in the *Herald* competition.

Over dinner with one of the judges, Tom Moore, the sharp-tongued Franklin commented on Park's book. "I liked the buggy parts much better than the sentimental," she said. In her diary for January 21, 1947, she let fly that *The Harp*

Above A couple kiss in a dimly lit Surry Hills alley in 1950. With mum, dad, grandma and the siblings a hindrance to young lovers' privacy at home, they stole it back in parks and lanes.

Above Ruth Park talks to Surry Hills locals about the new housing commission scheme for the suburb, in December 1951.

"entirely lacks architecture, that there is a withering lack of an independent or able intelligence behind it".

Part of Park's prize was guaranteed publication by Angus and Robertson. "It's not the kind of book A&R cares to publish but we have a gentlemen's agreement with the *Herald*," grouched the company's famed senior editor, Beatrice Davis.

A week later Park had a cable from the British publisher Michael Joseph Ltd, to whom she had sent galley proofs: "*Harp in the South* superb magnificent stop excepting *How Green Was My Valley* best novel Michael Joseph has had printing doubled." Houghton Mifflin published the book in the US and both countries produced laudatory reviews that appreciated its humour and humanity as well as its documentary precision.

When Angus and Robertson finally released the book in 1948, good reviews followed. Since then it has never been out of print. It has been translated into 38 languages, shortlisted for literary prizes, dramatised on television and, most ironically, became required reading for Higher School Certificate students.

Park reconsidered the controversy in her autobiography and found Jon Cleary, who went on to great success as a novelist, had received "the usual single ratbag letter" after the *Herald's* serialisation of *You Can't See Round Corners*. She concluded that she had offended by being a woman and a foreigner. However, she also stirred productive discussion about censorship, taxation of literary prizes (she ended up with only £800 of her prize money) and "modern literature".

Left Children's book author and illustrator Pixie O'Harris, griddle scones at the ready at her home in Vaucluse, led the charge for slum clearance.

Below The Devonshire Street housing project under construction in 1960. The section of Riley Street in the centre was grassed to become Ward Park. The row of terraces on Devonshire Street where Ruth Park lived when she arrived in Sydney had already gone – replaced by Devon Court, the three-storey red brick building in the centre.

In 1949 she published *Poor Man's Orange*, the successful sequel to *The Harp*, and she has been one of Australia's most prolific and popular writers for adults and children, print, radio, television and stage.

Now in her 80s, Park still describes the aftermath of the *Herald* prize as "devastatingly painful to me at the time", but acknowledges it "was certainly my launching pad as a novelist". Living in a pleasant seaside suburb, she has mixed feelings about her impact on Surry Hills.

Anyone who goes looking for the Devonshire Street house she lived in 60 years ago will find instead stern rows of Housing Commission flats. In the '50s they seemed a great improvement over tenement houses, but today they are a blot on the expensively restored streets of Surry Hills.

Battling through

Industrial unrest and unemployment had already begun to bristle beneath the roar of the 1920s, but the Depression came suddenly.

Australia was particularly vulnerable when Wall Street crashed in 1929, with imports exceeding exports, a dependency on agriculture and pastoral production, and a heavy overseas debt.

So the shock waves from New York hit Australians with swift and punitive force.

Ruth Park, who chronicled the effects of the Depression on working-class Australians in her novels, quoted a survivor in an article for the Fairfax weekly, *The National Times*, in January 1974.

"It came all at once, over four or five months. Creepy it was. Closing down sales first. Then you'd notice empty shops, and more and more door-to-door hawkers with home-made clothes, pegs, flower seeds, knitted baby bonnets.

"People were laid off, always the oldest and the youngest, but we thought it was just temporary. A recession, like. Then one morning I saw that the factory chimney down the road wasn't smoking. Can't tell you how that hit me, as though I'd been slammed in the chest with a hammer. I knew then though. We were for it."

In June 1930 prime minister James Scullin sought economic advice from the Bank of England. Otto Niemeyer, head of the advisory delegation, addressed the Australian premiers

at the suggestion of the British Government. His advice was stark: to retrench, economise, reduce tariffs and stop borrowing.

"Life in Australia is over-luxurious," Niemeyer later concluded from the safe distance of New Zealand and, despite strenuous arguments from dissenters that his measures would place further pressure on Australia for the benefit of British industry, the advice was implemented.

Unemployment in NSW was then 21 per cent, and it hit nearly 32 per cent in mid-1932.

The situation was almost as damaging to workers' dignity as it was devastating to their livelihoods: "What mockery was the ceremony at the Cenotaph to one who had escaped the shambles of Gallipoli to starve in his native land!" exclaimed a letter writer to the *Herald* in 1930.

It was manifest in the growing dole

Above Children whiz down the road near Sydney's Oxford Street in their billycarts. *The Bat* poster was for a silent horror movie released in 1926.

Above The great Australian escape: crowds on Manly Beach, Christmas Day 1930.

queues, the soup kitchens, the eviction riots, the swagmen and the formation of shanty towns in Brighton-le-Sands, Rockdale, Long Bay, Clontarf and La Perouse, in the Royal National Park, in caves overlooking the harbour — wherever there was some vacant public space or a sympathetic council.

They used corrugated iron, cardboard,

driftwood and hessian to build shelters in the dunes; in 1932 there were at least 332 people living in the La Perouse camp of Happy Valley alone.

Many of these people remained living there until 1939 when the golf club, to which the federal land was leased, evicted them. The club did not intend to use the land, it

was reported in the *Herald*, "but the shacks offended the eyes of the well-to-do people who played golf there".

By then the NSW government was claiming that the worst of the Depression had been shaken, a prediction that proved optimistic when the nation was engulfed by World War II.

That brought a cure for unemployment, but new pressures took its place: wartime controls on food, clothing, petrol and liquor, building restrictions and, at the close of the war, a housing shortage.

To hundreds of thousands the hope and prosperity created by the so-called wool boom of the 1950s seemed a long time coming.

Top The cheapest food source in town. Prawning in the mist of Sydney Harbour in the 1930s.

Above Shanty town at Happy Valley, La Perouse.

Above Young boys tuck into soup provided by the Sydney City Mission in 1949. The coal miners' strike that year lifted unemployment in Sydney's industrial suburbs and soup kitchens returned in many suburbs for the first time since the Depression, though many people were too proud to go.

Right Police evict 28 caravan families from vacant land in Kingsford in 1948. The landlady – with plans for a block of flats – was on hand to supervise.

Top right Ration queues were common – this one in 1946 was for cigarettes and tobacco at the Hyde Park kiosk.

Bottom right A power strike in 1945 forces Botany Municipal Council to meet by the light of hurricane lamps.

CHAPTER SIX

A Sense of Style

To see and be seen

BY VALERIE LAWSON

Below Star of the Ballets Russes, Irina Baronova, in her dressing room at the Theatre Royal in 1938. She was known as a "baby ballerina", along with the young dancers Tatiana Riabouchinska and Tamara Toumanova, because she was made a principal dancer at age 14.

Previous pages The foyer of the Hotel Australia, in Castlereagh Street. The old Art Deco building was Sydney's finest hotel and social focus. From 1891 when it opened, society gathered there for balls and the Thursday night dinner dances. It was pulled down and replaced by the Harry Seidler-designed MLC Centre in 1978.

192 THE BIG PICTURE

Assembled on a London railway platform the 64 members of the hastily formed troupe, the Monte Carlo Russian Ballet, faced a monumental journey to the other side of the world. Anxious and excited, already home-sick yet eager for the beaches of the Pacific, many believed they were going to a land where savages still roamed.

Australia! This was a cultural expedition like no other. With their luggage full of tights, pointe shoes and leotards, and their pockets and handbags stashed with cigarettes and chocolates, the dancers waved their tearful friends goodbye and clambered onto the boat train. Six weeks later they landed in Australia.

It was 1936. They found not savages but a welcome that depicted them as "fairytale people" — artists who inspired other artists. It wasn't just their look, their costumes, their sets, their fashions, their manner; it was their air of exoticism. Painted, sculpted, photographed and feted, they brought a new kind of glamour to Australia, post-Depression.

More than just dancers, they were the celebrities of their day, portrayed as exotic Russians, although many were English, Scandinavian or French. The Monte Carlo Russian Ballet was the first of three such groups touring Australia from 1936 to 1939, all billed as offshoots of the Ballets Russes de Monte Carlo.

In the first group, the stars were the sparkling Tamara Tchinarova, later to marry the actor Peter Finch, and the Danish Helene Kirsova, who posed for press photographs holding an immense blue velvet kangaroo. On the next tour, the starriest ballerina was Irina Baronova, a blonde, coquettish soubrette, who appeared in ads promoting face powder and nylon stockings. On the last of the Ballets Russes tours, the glamour girl was Tamara Toumanova, a dark-eyed and sensual siren who inspired artists, photographers, poets. And always in the wake of the stars was a corps of golden girls, each with admirers in train.

These were the right companies at the right time, bringing the outside world into a country that was hungry for beauty and artistic inspiration. In Sydney alone, over a nine-week season in 1936, the Monte Carlo Russian Ballet attracted an audience of more than 90,000 people. Women dressed for

their shows in long, clinging gowns, their hair waved and shaped to the head, their necklines sparkling with jewels.

The press covered the opening night as if it were a royal tour, noting that Mrs Charles Lloyd Jones was wearing "a lovely Schiaparelli gown of chalk-white suede crepe, beautifully tailored, with a short cape, square-shouldered, of quilted taffeta". In the audience, the *Herald* went on, the women's heads were "dressed with thick wreaths of frangipani and gardenias" and "the sharp gleam of diamonds caught the light". Luxurious furs covered "perfectly

Above A scene from *Le Carnaval*, performed by the Ballets Russes at the Theatre Royal in January 1937. Starring Helene Kirsova and Roland Guerard, it was performed in a program with *La Boutique Fantasque* and *Les Presages*.

Above Tamara Toumanova, principal dancer with the Ballets Russes on the last of the 1930s Australian tours, laden with gifts.

Right Peter Finch at Mascot Airport in 1956, before leaving for Alice Springs for the Australian premiere of *A Town Like Alice*, in which he played the leading male role. He was then married to the Ballets Russes dancer Tamara Tchinarova, but their marriage was nearly over. They would announce their separation a month later and Finch would marry twice more. Finch was born in England, grew up in Australia and acted on radio and the stage before he was spotted by Sir Laurence Olivier and moved to London to further his career in 1949.

tailored gowns scintillating with diamante embroideries and corsage posies of orchids", and one could see "sudden spots of colour as scarlet-lacquered fingernails gave reassuring pats to curled coiffures …"

As the married women were all known by their husbands' names and defined in print by their jewels and clothes, they seemed like possessions.

Yet in these social and artistic circles, as in so many spheres of Australian life, women held indirect power. It was women who set the social agenda, who encouraged, entertained and persuaded.

But their voice was limited. From the early 1920s — two decades after women gained the right to vote in 1902 — through to the 1960s, their power was exercised obliquely, through the arts, through social life, through community work.

Women dominated the most pictorially interesting pages of the local press, both in the editorial columns and in the display advertisements. Advertising artwork showed women joyfully displaying the newest stockings or in backless evening gowns smooching with their men as they sold the joys of stout or fruit cup.

There was, however, a sense of women
remaining in their place, expressed, for
example, in ads for vitality pills headlined
"Keep Your Husband", then, in smaller type,
"and yourself in top form". One spread in
the *Herald's* "women's supplement" showing
an array of men's fashions was headlined: "A
Page for Wives".

In advertising space and in editorial
photographs, men and women were to
be seen smiling, comfortable (except in
the many constipation ads), relaxed and
affluent. The women's pages, however,
represented only a slice of Australian life.

The Fairfax executive Rupert Henderson,
who drove the *Herald's* editorial for much
of the mid-20th century, thought that
women in the main loved to read about the
most privileged women of Sydney, and the
women's page editors loyally obliged. The
pages of the *Herald* and its rivals covered
the lives of the old moneyed families in
Sydney's east and north, in the Southern
Highlands and northern peninsula, and their
city and holiday playgrounds, among them
Romano's restaurant in Castlereagh Street,
Prince's restaurant in Martin Place, the Hotel
Australia, Royal Randwick and Palm Beach.

Right The Levy party at the opening of Romano's in 1939. "The Levy gang" owed their moniker to Patrick Levy, who started his own stockbroking firm, and were regulars at the trendy nightclubs and restaurants of the day.

Below Milling crowds at the opening night of the Olivier season at the Tivoli Theatre in June 1948. The then governor-general, William McKell, and actor Chips Rafferty were among the socialites, theatre identities, politicians and diplomats.

Far right A policeman caught below the canopy of streamers as SS Stratheden departs Sydney in February 1948, bound for England. About 3000 people watched the P&O liner sail from Pyrmont.

Through these reports and their accompanying photographs, social historians can assemble a mosaic of detail: who went where, what they ate, what they wore, who was on the sidelines looking in, and what was considered of weighty importance.

At Prince's and Romano's, we see men wearing wing collars with black tie, and men and women smoking, drinking spirits or hock. Tables, laden with a cluster of plates and cutlery, are set for five-course meals. Dinners and lunches were served, in the main, by Italian waiters recruited by the city's two leading restaurateurs, Azzalin ("the dazzlin'") Romano and Jim Bendroit. The guests danced the tango, the Lambeth Walk and the waltz, and they looked, on average, about 48 years of age.

In May 1939 the *Herald* reporter Jack Meander (a pseudonym for David D. McNicoll) wrote: "Romano's opened last night with a smile from Mr Romano, a bow from Luigi, a twinkle from Mr Davico and a chord from Bert Howell and his band. One or two people in Sydney were not there. The rest were a sea of orchids, rolled hair (blondes predominating), furs and white ties … Glimpsed coming in: Mr Frank Lubrano, leading Italian resident of Sydney, connoisseur of good living; Mr Smuts, manager of the Hotel Australia, connoisseur of good service; Mr Walter Pye, connoisseur of good clothes.

Above The then prime minister, Robert Menzies, and Mrs Stewart Jamieson at Prince's restaurant in July 1939, three months after Menzies assumed leadership of the United Australia Party from Joseph Lyons, who died in office.

Right Romano's, the elegant Castlereagh Street restaurant that was the social epicentre of Sydney through the 1940s and 50s. Restaurateur Azzalin Romano, some-time racehorse owner and sly grogger, and his wife offer party favours to guests.

"Jewels! Mrs Sam Hordern, a late arrival, with diamond and ruby earrings. With her were Mr and Mrs Geoffrey Ashton up from their property, Markdale, outside Goulburn. Mrs Jim Bancks, wearing her famous pendant, a huge ruby set in it … Saw Bill McMahon walking in with Mrs H. C. Osborne looking more soignee than ever."

On Thursdays, the big day for women's news in the *Herald*, readers could check who had been lunching with whom the previous day. Connie Robertson, the women's editor of the *Herald* from 1936 to 1962, would stand at the top of the stairs at Romano's looking down on the crowd, tapping her teeth with her pencil, and choosing the favoured ones for portraits. At Prince's, Robertson and her team of reporters would be greeted by Jean Cheriton, or "Cherry" as she was known, who claimed to know all the society women of Point Piper and Bellevue Hill. At work, Cherry served reporters with coffee and chicken sandwiches. She always wore a hat, black suit and white gloves and pinned a fresh camellia or bunch of violets on her lapel. Robertson and her colleagues on rival newspapers and magazines kept files on families, from matriarchs to the newest offspring. Their christenings, balls, weddings and parties were solemnly reported, along with extraordinarily detailed descriptions of their dress.

In Sydney, the leaders of the social pack were those who made their names and their money in sugar, coal, the law or the media. They included the Knoxes, Stephens, Allens, Wentworths and Fairfaxes.

A subset of this subculture could be seen most weeks at Darling Harbour, Walsh Bay and Circular Quay, from where the ocean liners would sail for the six-week journey "up over" to the northern hemisphere. Every Thursday representatives from the Orient Line, P&O or Matson Lines met reporters at the Man O' War steps at Bennelong Point. Ferries or launches took the reporters, early morning, to the liners moored off Watsons Bay. There the race was on to find interesting

faces and interesting stories for the papers next day. A typical headline in September 1937 was "Mariposa Brings Many Travellers Varied Experiences Abroad".

The idea that news came from "out there" rather than from home continued into the 1960s when reporters still met international flights to find out what returning Australians had done in New York, Paris, Rome or London. When the Australian economy was driven by the boom in wool in the 1950s, the emphasis in reporting swung to the world of the wool brokers and to retail dynasties, especially the Lloyd Joneses, led by the formidable hostess Lady Hannah Lloyd Jones. At the time, the annual Wool Ball

and the Sheep Show were classic, important Sydney events, as were golf club balls, the Black and White Ball, charity lunches and dinner dances at the Hotel Australia.

Charity work gave many of these women a sense of purpose at a time when marriage frequently meant the end of their careers. To see them at charity balls, twirling in white tulle ballgowns with bell-shaped skirts, one would think that women's lives had continued from the 1930s in an unbroken line of comfort.

But those women's expectations had been radically changed by World War II. When it began, 644,000 Australian women earned a wage or a salary. By 1944, that

Top The *Herald* women's editor Connie Robertson, in white coat and sunglasses, interviewing women army recruits in Townsville during World War II.

Above Connie Robertson, in Hollywood with Buster Keaton in 1939.

Right When *Herald* heavyweights decreed that overseas war reporting was unfit for women and denied Connie Robertson a tilt at the job, the numbers were on their side. This was the *Herald's* subeditors room, with the chief subeditor, Charles Theakstone, in the centre.

number had increased by about a third as they replaced men in the workforce, from butchers' shops to police stations to munitions factories. A handful of women journalists covered the war, although most, like Robertson, were not permitted to go abroad as war correspondents. In 1942, with the virtual disappearance of the *Herald's* women's pages, Robertson was permitted to play at being a war correspondent as she visited women's army and air force camps

in Australia. The tour was arranged by the department of information.

The war had also marked a change in direction in Australia's cultural life. From 1913 to 1939, theatre producers such as J. C. Williamson promoted the idea of Russian music and Russian dance. After the war the emphasis swung to Britain, with an influx of British cultural imports in tours arranged by the British Council and the Australian Elizabethan Theatre Trust. From

Left *Herald* staff reporter Annette Fielding-Jones posing as a model on Rowe Street, Sydney, a bohemian street of artists, theatres and high fashion.

Britain's point of view, it made sense to keep Australia as close as possible at a time when the US was becoming a stronger force economically and culturally in Australia. Britain sent cultural emissaries to Australia, among them the Ballet Rambert, Laurence Olivier, Vivien Leigh, Ralph Richardson, the honorary Englishman Robert Helpmann, Tyrone Guthrie and Anthony Quayle.

The lingering ties to Britain culminated in the royal tour of 1954, and with it a last surge of patriotism. Concluding her detailed and glowing report in the *Herald* on the Queen's arrival in Sydney, Robertson wrote: "Poised, youthful, feminine, perhaps slightly withdrawn into her own pools of silence from which she gains so much strength, the Queen might have been any young woman on a great occasion. Yet there is something of splendour; behind that fragile glimmer of gold there is the full panoply of the throne."

Above Hat fashion. A buxom statue, a butterfly and a horse in military garb decorate this 1953 hat.

Far right In the 1940s al fresco dining came into vogue and cafe tables such as these were set up on footpaths.

Even as Robertson wrote her purple prose, an era was ending. Still ahead was the influx of non-Anglo Saxon migrants, the impact of American television, jet travel and the women's movement of the 1960s. And, again, there were hints of the future in the press. Instead of artwork of women putting children to bed and dancing in the arms of men in tuxedos, ads promised ease of living through super-modern washing machines and "no more dry-cleaning" with wash-'n'-wear, drip-dry American fabrics such as Crilene. By 1957 Joern Utzon had won the competition to design the Sydney Opera House, the song of the year was Slim Dusty's *The Pub With No Beer*, Patrick White's *Voss* was published and Nino Culotta wrote of the migrant experience in *They're a Weird Mob*.

The days of looking outwards and upwards, of attempting to emulate some already forgotten way of life in Britain, were well and truly over.

Far left A stylist plants the final touches on a "coronation hairstyle" at Kings Cross Salon in June 1953. Sydneysiders spent the big night flitting between parties, watching the harbour fireworks or staging their own. An estimated 45,000 attended the official pageant at Sydney Showground. The 300 Australians present in the London Abbey "did Australia great credit both by their gowns and their headdresses", the *Herald's* women's section reported on June 4, although it appeared they slightly misjudged the style: "In most cases the frocks of Australians were more elaborate or heavily beaded; English women preferred a simpler cut and relied on jewelled tiaras or necklets to provide the touch of splendour."

Top left Artists touch up a giant poster of the Queen and Prince Philip that adorned a city building during the 1954 royal tour. The federal government spent more than £96,000 on decorations in towns and cities in the lead-up to the tour in a frantic effort to ensure the country showed its best face.

Centre left Mothers gather with their children to watch the Queen pass through Sydney in 1954. The long wait for a glimpse had begun the night before. Some people pitched camp at Farm Cove and others brought blankets and food. When her ship came into the harbour, the Queen was met by boats and surfers who paddled out to greet her.

Left A fashion shot in 1953, the year of coronation mania. Australia caught the fever from Britain, and evening wear "fit for a queen" led the season. Designers were inspired by the tiaras and coronets already in the news, and colours such as "crimson, sceptre gold, garter blue and imperial violet", the women's section of the *Herald* explained on May 18, under the headline "Coronation Goes to the Head".

PORECASTS (for 24 hours from 6 a.m.): CITY: Sunny. Mild. NW winds. Ex. max. temps. City 65, Liverpool 65 degrees. N.S.W.: Fine NE half and coast. Elsewhere showers develop. (See p. 12)

SUN: Today rises 6.55, sets 4.53. MOON: Rises 1.17 a.m., sets 1.11 p.m. TIDES (Fort Denison): High, 3.42 a.m. (4ft 6in), 4.37 p.m. (4ft 8in), Low, 10.7 a.m. (1ft 4in), 10.49 p.m. (1ft 10in).

The Sydney Morning Herald

No. 41,022   Telephone 2 0944   One Hundred and Thirty-ninth Year of Publication   18 PAGES & TV Guide   PRICE 5c

Nixon sees step to peace in talks today

HONOLULU, Sunday. — President Nixon flies from Honolulu to Midway Island today for talks which he believes will be a "very important step" towards peace in Vietnam.

There is widespread speculation that he and South Vietnam's President Thieu will agree at the talks to announce a start on the withdrawal of about 50,000 U.S. troops.

Mr Nixon added fuel to the speculation when he declared in an off-the-cuff statement on arrival in Honolulu yesterday:

"You know how tremendously important it is that we find a way to bring an end to the war in which we are now engaged in Vietnam and bring an end to that war in a way that it will promote the cause of real peace in the Pacific and not plant the seeds for another war.

"We believe that this meeting in Midway will be one step in that direction — a very important step, as will be indicated by the results of that meeting and other events that will follow."

Ways of boosting South Vietnamese involvement and including the National Liberation Front in South Vietnam's political life after a cease-fire, without bowing to demands for a coalition Government before free elections, are to be discussed by the two Presidents on the mid-Pacific atoll.

EVERY STEP

Mr Nixon is due at Midway at 10 a.m. (7 a.m. Monday, Sydney time).

American officials said last night that there were no major areas of disagreement between Washington and Saigon.

They said the Midway talks had been arranged to help the Allies decide on co-ordination positions in the peace negotiations at a time when the Communists seemed seriously interested in ending the war.

Before he left Honolulu, Mr Nixon had talks with the chief advisers who are accompanying him to Midway, but no statement was issued.

Before he left Saigon last night for the Midway talks, President Thieu said that South Vietnam was taking every possible step to find a just peace.

(A.A.P.-Reuter.)

PAGE 3: 600 Reds killed in two days; PAGE 5: Village of the dead; the Australian wounded.

THREE AUST. MEN DIE IN FIERCE CLASH

Three Australian soldiers have been killed in three separate clashes with enemy troops in Phuoc Tuy Province, South Vietnam.

Seventeen other Australians have been wounded, in many grenade, rocket and mortar attacks at or near Nui Dat.

Australian troops have killed about 100 Vietcong and North Vietnamese in Phuoc Tuy Province in the past week, in the biggest action since May, 1968.

VILLAGE BATTLE

NUI DAT, Sunday.—The worst battle has been at the little rubber village of Binh Ba, five miles north-east of here, where Australians have killed 54.

Most were killed on Friday in a day-long effort to push North Vietnamese and Vietcong out of the village.

The others were killed yesterday when a North Vietnamese Army company was hit in the rubber plantations outside Binh Ba as it was trying to break through to the village.

Another force of about 100 North Vietnamese, in camouflage suits, were pushed out of nearby Duc Troung where the civilian population of Binh Ba were sheltering. At least six were killed there.

In the last week the 6th Battalion, operating in rubber plantations and jungle areas from just north of Binh Ba to the Long Khanh Province border, 15 miles from here, have killed 40 Vietcong and North Vietnamese in mostly scattered contacts.

Mortar attack

CANBERRA, Sunday.— The Australians killed were: Private Barry James, 21, single, from Toowoomba, Queensland, of the 6th Battalion, Royal Australian Regiment; Private Wayne Teeling, 21, married, National Serviceman from Clovelly, N.S.W., of the 5th Battalion, R.A.R.; and Corporal David Brennan, 22, single, from Bathurst, N.S.W., of the 9th Battalion, R.A.R.

Private Teeling was shot on Friday during a fierce 7½-hour battle in which 27 enemy soldiers were killed according to Army authorities in Canberra.

Private James was shot during a contact with the enemy north of the Australian Task Force base at Nui Dat last Thursday.

Corporal Brennan was killed during a mortar attack on Friday.

● Seventeen Australian soldiers injured in Vietnam. See Page 5.

● Seventeen Australian soldiers injured in Vietnam. See Page 5.

LATE NEWS

Fine day, change later

Sydney's fine weather should continue today, but a cold southerly change is expected late tonight.

Yesterday was the first day for six days that Sydney did not have rain. There was dry weather over most of the State.

Thredbo had the lowest minimum temperature at 19 degrees and also the lowest maximum, 34 degrees.

The Bureau of Meteorology last night predicted a maximum temperature of 65 degrees for the city and Liverpool today.

Yugoslav consulate damaged by blast: bomb fear

An explosion, believed to have been caused by a bomb, rocked the Yugoslav Consulate in Knox Street, Double Bay, early this morning.

Shattered glass was scattered along the footpath and smoke gushed from the windows.

Police cars and the fire brigade rushed to the consulate.

The fire brigade said the explosion was caused by a bomb.

Mrs G. Cooper of Ocean Avenue, Double Bay, heard the explosion.

"My God," she said, "It's either a bomb or a safe, I've never heard such an explosion in my life, before.

"It vibrated right up Ocean Avenue and that is quite a long way from here."

Mrs M. Forster, of New South Head Road, Double Bay, who lives a quarter of a mile from the Consulate, said: "We were all in bed when the explosion woke everybody.

"All the doors and windows of the Embassy were blown out and all the windows in the shops on both sides of Knox Street. As far as we could see nobody was hurt."

A crowd of nearly 400 people stood outside the consulate this morning as police investigated the bombing.

Police said a bomb had been placed in the doorway of the consulate.

Police said that 10 shops in the shopping centre near the consulate were damaged by the explosion.

Windows were blown out and police had to secure the premises for the owners.

Shops damaged included the New World Supermarket and the Customs Shop.

Success on killer illness

After a nine-year effort, research workers in Sydney and Melbourne have found a treatment for pulmonary embolism, a blood-circulation condition which is often fatal.

Pulmonary embolism may strike patients who have been in bed for a long time after surgery or women after childbirth.

But preventive action and new forms of treatment have greatly reduced its toll.

The condition is due to the breaking-away of blood clots which tend to form in the leg veins after prolonged periods in bed.

The clot, which may be the diameter of a pencil, passes back to the heart, then out into the pulmonary artery of the lung, finally lodging in one of the smaller branches of the lung.

● Cont. page 7

Aid planes to Biafra

GENEVA, Sunday.—The International Red Cross today gave the go-ahead for its planes based in Cotonou, Dahomey, to resume night mercy flights into Biafra.

But planes on the other Red Cross base on the island of Fernando Poo will remain grounded for safety reasons.

---

400 GIRLS COLLAPSE IN POP SCENE FRENZY

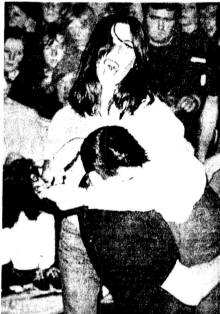

One of the scores of girls who were carried screaming from the pop concert at the Sydney Showground yesterday. About 400 girls collapsed.

Another member of the audience is carried out by an attendant.

Hysteria at the Showground

By MIKE HENDERSON

About 400 hysterical teenage girls collapsed yesterday during a pop music spectacular in the Horden Pavilion at the Sydney Showground. Three were taken to hospital.

Forty police were rushed to the pavilion to reinforce the four police and 20 bouncers on duty when it looked as if the crowd of 7,000 screaming fans was getting out of control.

Two Central District Ambulance men and two police revived the girls overcome with excitement or crushed in the crowd.

Most of the girls were 14 or 15 years old.

Two of those taken to St. Vincent's Hospital were treated for bruises and abrasions. The third had been overcome by fumes from a smoke machine used in one of the acts.

Ray-O-Vac batteries last night for the spectacular as part of a transistor-battery sales campaign. Admission was by showing one of the company's batteries.

Six Australian pop groups — Tarman Shud, Heart 'n' Soul, Velvet Underground, Flying Circus, Masters' Apprentices, The

Dave Miller Set — and two current pop idols, Ronnie Burns and Russell Morris, entertained the crowd through 1,200-watt amplifiers.

The music reached the pitch of a jet warming up, and communication in the pavilion had to be made by hand signals or writing.

Most of the 20 "bouncers" were labourers recruited from the City Markets at $10 for the afternoon.

They dragged bodily the young girls who collapsed near the front of the crowd.

Police and bouncers locked arms to push back the teenagers to prevent those in front being crushed against an iron scaffolding framework set up to protect the stage.

TACKLES

One bouncer used tackles to push back the front row of young girls.

Some of the girls who were semi-conscious when carried to the first-aid section. Others were still screaming and shaking all over.

They were deposited on a blanket-covered layer of cardboard near the front, where the ambulancemen and police gave them water, or made them sit with their heads between their knees.

Some girls simply lay there, sobbing, their hair matted with sweat, their faces flushed and tear-streaked, their lips trembling.

After a few minutes they would go out and join the

Elections 'a shot in arm' for A.L.P.

By IAN FITCHETT, Political Correspondent

The Labor Party sees the retention of Bendigo and a drift of almost 9 per cent to Labor in Gwydir in Saturday's by-elections as a "shot in the arm" for the party.

Mr A. D. Kennedy, a 29-year-old High school teacher, is regarded as certain to win Bendigo on preferences by a narrow majority.

The Country Party will hold Gwydir, but with a reduced majority.

The party leaders read vastly different meanings into the results.

The Prime Minister, Mr Gorton, said he believed the Liberal Party and its candidate in Bendigo, Councillor R. W. Cambridge, had done very well.

This was considering the A.L.P. had an absolute majority of primary votes at the last three House of Representatives elections for Bendigo and that by-elections traditionally went against the Government.

The "shot in the arm for Labor" was the reaction of the A.L.P. Leader, Mr E. G. Whitlam.

The Country Party Leader and Minister for Trade and Industry, Mr J. McEwen, said: "I had no doubt we would win Gwydir although a new candidate could not be expected to have the same majority as Mr Allan, who was in the Parliament for 16 years."

D.L.P. claim

The leader of the D.L.P., Senator V. C. Gair, claimed that his party was the only one which could take comfort from the Bendigo poll.

He said the A.L.P. dropped six per cent and the Government two per cent on 1966 while the D.L.P. vote remained as solid as ever and in fact showed a slight increase.

It is believed that Mr Kennedy's winning majority in Bendigo could be less than 200 votes.

Figures at the close of counting today were:
A. D. Kennedy (A.L.P.), 19,394; W. Cambridge (Lib.), 14,536; P. Brennan (D.L.P.), 5,343; L. Hutchinson (Ind.), 2,673; C. Candler (Ind.), 570; informal, 575. Total, 43,091; electors on roll 47,881.

Results at 1966 general election were: Beaton (A.L.P.), 23,191; Dunphy (Lib.), 16,062; Dreschler (D.L.P.), 5,640; informal, 697; total, 45,590.

The closeness of the Bendigo poll was not a surprise as Mr Kennedy was a new Labor candidate who was regarded as a marginal man although the A.L.P. has held it since 1949.

BEST CHOICE

Observers believe that Councillor Cambridge was a far better local candidate for Bendigo than Labor's Mr Wal Lee, who was first given endorsement, and that this fact adds to the importance of Mr Kennedy's performance.

Mr Kennedy was relatively unknown in the electorate until he won endorsement.

When Mr Lee was stood down, the Liberal Party decided he would get the Ben-

digo endorsement if Councillor Cambridge were defeated in the by-election.

This decision is likely to lead to a damaging split in the party in the electorate by the end of the year as Councillor Cambridge has stated he will not stand aside without strong protest.

GWYDIR

No vote cast by 11 p.c.

CANBERRA, Sunday. —Final figures for tonight in the Gwydir by-election after today's count, which included an additional 500 postal votes and about 500 postal votes, are:

R. J. D. Hunt (C.P.), 19,700; R. B. Nott (A.L.P.), 17,718; Informal, 370; Total counted, 37,588.

This gives Mr Hunt a majority of 2,182 with only about 2,000 postal votes to be counted.

There were 54,196 people on the roll and about 5,000 have not voted.

In the 1966 Federal election for the seat, only 2,351 of those enrolled failed to vote.

The Leader of the N.S.W. Opposition, Mr P. D. Hills, said in Sydney the results in Gwydir indicated that, if the trend was followed in a State election, a Labor Government would be returned in N.S.W.

● Country Party facing stiff test — Page 5.

Man six hours on 150ft tower

A young escapee from an Orange psychiatric hospital spent six hours up a 150ft radio transmitter tower near Parkes before police helped him down early yesterday.

Several months ago, the man was taken to the hospital after climbing the same tower and threatening to hang himself with a length of rope.

He made yesterday's climb about 7 p.m. The tower, which is operated by

and spoke to the man through loud-hailers.

After several hours at the top of the tower in bitter cold, he began to climb down, but after descending only about 30 feet, he halted his descent.

Four police skindivers from Sydney, with training in rescue work and were on duty in Parkes, were called in.

Two of them, Sergeant M. J. Bennett and Senior-Constable R. Young, climbed the tower and managed to bring the man down about 1 a.m.

INSIDE

Qantas Boeings sold to U.S.

Qantas has sold four of its remaining six early-model Boeing 707 aircraft to a major American airline, Braniff International.

The general manager of Qantas, Captain R. J. Ritchie, and Braniff officials signed the contract of sale in Sydney on Sat-

urday, by several international airlines, in the remaining two aircraft, and he expected them to be sold within a few weeks.

Captain Ritchie said that the four Boeings had been sold at a substantial profit, but he declined to reveal the price paid by Braniff for commercial reasons.

The four Boeings have

They are the 707-138B type aircraft, a smaller version of the large 338C intercontinental type, 21 of which now make up the Qantas fleet.

Qantas originally had 13 of the smaller type.

The four aircraft will be painted in Braniff colours before being flown to the American airline's home base at Dallas, Texas, later

policy through the years—to buy technically and commercially sound aircraft for which there was a continuing, world-wide, commercial airline demand.

He recalled that all the aircraft types that Qantas had bought since World War II — Constellations, Super Constellations, Boe-

Big carbide plant fire

HOBART, Sunday.—A fire in the transformer building of the Commonwealth Carbide Company plant at Electrona, near Hobart, last night caused $150,000 damage.

The second crippling fire at the carbide works in less than a half year, it de-

In 1789 Governor Phillip and an entourage of about 60 sat through a convict performance of an English stage favourite, *The Recruiting Officer*. The show, put on to mark the birthday of King George III, was described by Watkin Tench with the kind of charity normally reserved for an over-enthusiastic school play: "Some of the actors acquitted themselves with great spirit and received the praises of the audience." Tench records that it was all done in the light of "a dozen farthing candles stuck around the mud walls of a convict hut". History recalls it as the first theatrical performance in the colony, but for Tench and the rest of the audience it was an "opportunity of escape from the dreariness and dejection of our situation".

Officialdom had mixed views on the desirability of organised public performances in the early stages of settlement, probably guessing that for convicts the temptation to pick a pocket or a fight or generally misbehave would be too much. But as the immigrant population grew, prospects brightened and Levy's Theatre Royal opened in late 1832 with a melodrama called *Black-Eyed Susan*, followed by a farce called *Monsieur Tonson*, all to the accompaniment

of the band of the 17th Regiment. *The Sydney Morning Herald*, then less than two years old, said in a review: "On Wednesday evening the Comic Muse made her debut in the colony with a good grace ..." It then went on to make a few suggestions on smartening up the scenery and shifting and improving the house lighting.

The real take-off point for live performance — particularly by overseas

Above Advertisement in the *Herald* for the first professional theatre performances in Australia, 1832. The new Theatre Royal was still under construction, so the proprietor, Barnett Levy, fitted the hotel with a temporary stage.

Top left Surrounded by onlookers, Anna Pavlova clutches bouquets. The Russian ballet dancer delighted Australians during her 1926 and 1929 tours, but her enduring legacy is the meringue dish named after her.

Bottom left Sarah Bernhardt, who visited Australia in 1891, was the biggest star in French theatre, and perhaps the world, in her time. She continued to act even after she lost one of her legs in a stage accident.

Above Roy Rene, aka Mo McCackie, was the top name in Australian comedy before the advent of television, and sometimes shocked with his early explicit language on stage – including his "how come every time I write F you see K" skit.

Right The face of a comic genius: singer, dancer and larrikin comedian George Wallace. He was born in 1895 and started his acting career in vaudeville, before trying radio and film.

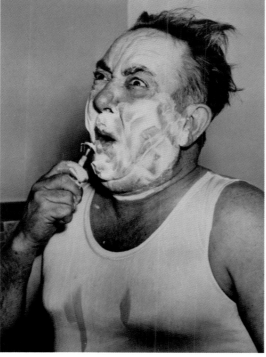

artists — came with greater prosperity in the cities and towns after the discovery of gold; and sometimes — with the lavish spending of suddenly rich miners a big lure — on hastily assembled stages on the goldfields. Lola Montez entranced and shocked with her spider dance; Sarah Bernhardt served up the classics, often in French; and sundry touring companies danced, juggled and declaimed.

The entrepreneurs behind these shows rose and fell, but great survivors such as J. C. Williamson and the Tait brothers made it into the century of federation just as the flickering curiosity of silent film shaped itself into a real threat. Stage drama was worst hit, but vaudeville — with stars such as Roy "Mo" Rene and George Wallace — still drew the crowds, at least until the double hit of radio and the depression in the 1920s.

The Taits tried movies and their production, *The Story of the Kelly Gang*, the world's first feature film, was screened in 1906. By the 1930s movies had found their voice and commandeered grand old live theatres or paid for the rise of new ones. Rene and Wallace stood in front of the camera too but their live magic was lost. Radio produced the first cross-pollination — later matched by television — as families around the nation leaned towards the "wireless", wishing they could see, not just hear, the characters in favourites like *Dad and Dave* and *Blue Hills*.

As drama prospered in the new media, keeping it alive on stage fell to work-by-day, play-by-night actors and theatre hands, and diehards such as Doris Fitton, whose vision sustained The Independent in Sydney from 1930 to 1977.

In 1981 the *Herald's* highly influential drama critic, H. G. Kippax, paid tribute to true believers like Fitton and Allan Wilkie in the face of the great cinema eclipse, but reminded readers of the long failure of the wider theatre community and its audiences to embrace local productions. He pointed to a *Herald* editorial of 1889 which observed: "That same tacit prejudice that seems to exist against anything local is the worst obstacle to be overcome …" Kippax jumped ahead to another *Herald* editorial, a 1964 lament that despite the rise of funded arts bodies, talented local dramatists could not get even short seasons of their work produced by professionals. And he noted that from the opening of the Theatre Royal in 1832 to 1981 only four performers had created anything approaching a furore: Bernhardt, Dame

Above Tivoli circuit star Jim Gerald and the Gay Girls Chorus, circa 1925.

Above left Shooting the 1934 film *Strike Me Lucky*, starring Roy Rene and Nat Phillips, who formed the comic team "Stiffy and Mo".

Right The prime minister, Robert Menzies, and his wife, Patti, sit serenely front and centre of the dress circle at the Sydney Tivoli in 1963. They saw *The Sound of Music*.

Top far right The playwright, the actress and the seventeenth doll, 1956: Ray Lawler, author of *The Summer of the Seventeenth Doll*, with the female lead, Fenella Maguire. The critics declared the play proof that Australian theatre had come of age.

Bottom far right The American crooner Johnny Ray and fans at Luna Park in 1956. Australian support for his weepies is credited with rekindling his career.

Below Frank Sinatra got the fans going on his 1961 Australian tour, gathering outside the Sydney Stadium in coats, heels and floral skirts. Built as a boxing and wrestling venue and just down the hill from Kings Cross, Sydney Stadium saw many rock 'n' roll greats before it came down in 1973.

Nellie Melba, Pavlova and the Oliviers with the Old Vic Company.

Kippax had already done much to encourage genuine talent. His praise for David Williamson's play *Don's Party* was seen widely as final proof of the arrival of a new wave of Australian theatre, the first since Ray Lawler's *The Summer of the Seventeenth Doll*, and even more promising.

Such was the power of praise or criticism from a journalist known for his balanced and constructive writing. Kippax was critical of the handling of federal arts funding in the early 1970s and this broadened in April 1975 to an editorial criticising the Whitlam government. On Kippax's death in 1999, Graham Freudenberg, the ALP's senior speechwriter, was quoted in his obituary as saying it was this editorial that "first set the line which would doom the Labor

government that, on moral grounds, it should be destroyed by any legal means".

It was a similarly rocky road for ballet and opera as the multimedia age gathered pace, but with keepers of the flame like dance maestro Edouard Borovansky, and the Williamson companies with an opera tradition going back to Nellie Melba, they soldiered on until growing audiences and outside funding ensured their survival — and a home of their own.

The rise of grants and awards also helped authors, and weathering the Depression, a war in which we fought off an enemy at our doorstep, and the pursuit of postwar prosperity unleashed powerful themes. But the backlash Ruth Park faced for daring to expose the reality of slum life in Sydney was no isolated experience, and it was a slow plod to wider sales of Australian writing.

Above The Beatles lifted the bar on frenzy with their Stadium shows in 1964. With the screaming and fainting not many got to hear the music.

Right Ringo Starr, who missed the early part of the tour because he was having his tonsils out, completed the line-up on the Beatles' hotel room balcony.

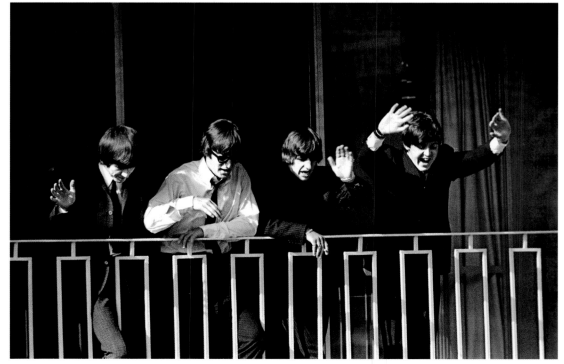

Above Policemen hold back the tide of fans screaming for the Beatles outside the Sheraton Hotel, where they stayed in Sydney during their 1964 Australian tour. Some fans tried to climb into their rooms but were removed by police.

Left George Harrison, Paul McCartney and John Lennon ambush the chef at the Sheraton Hotel.

Top left Robyn Nevin was the youngest actor to graduate in NIDA's inaugural year but emerged disillusioned and worked at the ABC for several years before returning to the craft. She is the CEO and artistic director of the Sydney Theatre Company.

Top far left Doris Fitton with the theatre cat. Fitton established the Independent Theatre Company in 1930 and moved it into a tram depot-cum-vaudeville house in Miller Street in 1939. Ruth Cracknell, Leonard Teale, Helen Morse and Jeannie Little were among the actors to perform there, and one of the directors, Robert Quentin, went on to co-found NIDA. The theatre closed in 1977.

Bottom far left David Gulpilil was a shy 17-year-old when the British film director Nicolas Roeg plucked him out of Arnhem Land to star in *Walkabout*. Roles in *Storm Boy*, *Crocodile Dundee* and *The Tracker* followed, topped off by an Order of Australia.

Centre left The young mechanical engineering student David Williamson discovered the joys of theatre at Melbourne University. He wrote his first full-length play, *The Coming of Stork*, in 1970, but made his name with his second, *The Removalists*, a year later. A prodigious body of work followed, concluding in 2005 with *Influence*, which he said would be his last.

Left John Bell nurtured Australian drama through the Nimrod Theatre Company, which he co-founded with Ken Horler in 1970, the Old Tote Theatre and the Bell Shakespeare Company, which he founded in 1990. The self-confessed Anglophile also acted in England in the early 1960s, where he married his acting school sweetheart, Anna Volska.

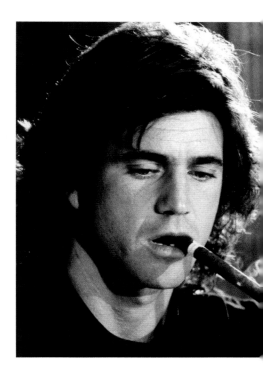

Above The sixth of 11 children, Mel Gibson came to Australia from the US aged 12 and learnt his acting at NIDA. He became one of its most generous benefactors after becoming a superstar.

Top left The doyens of contemporary Australian film: director Baz Luhrmann – another NIDA graduate – and actress Nicole Kidman arrive at the premiere of *Moulin Rouge*.

Top far left Cate Blanchett shot out of NIDA in 1992 and caught the attention of local theatre and television producers almost immediately. She made her feature film debut in 1997 with Bruce Beresford's *Paradise Road* and won an Oscar in 2005 with *The Aviator*.

Bottom left The Australian actor Judy Davis in Hyde Park in 1977, the year she graduated from NIDA. The following year her career was kickstarted with the film adaptation of *My Brilliant Career*.

Bottom far left Hugo Weaving being made up for his role in *Priscilla, Queen of the Desert*.

Top The pianist Roger Woodward was composing his own tunes by the age of two and playing Chopin's *Etudes* before breakfast by age 13. He began playing for international audiences in the 1960s when he was in his 20s.

Above David Helfgott, the pianist whose life and battle with mental illness were documented in the Oscar-winning film *Shine*, is congratulated by maestro Tommy Tycho.

Right Graeme Murphy, head of the Sydney Dance Company, started ballet at age 14 and went on to become one of Australia's most brilliant choreographers.

Left Walmajarri dancers in Canberra perform on "the big Ngurrara painting" that maps the Great Sandy Desert. It was the largest Aboriginal artwork ever to be painted on canvas and was used as evidence for a native title claim in 1997.

Bottom left One of the leading lights of the avant-garde artistic movement in Australia, Brett Whiteley lived, loved and painted at the extreme edges of possibility.

Below The sitters: the retired NSW governor Sir Roden Cutler, composer Peter Sculthorpe, artist Margaret Olley, author Thomas Keneally and entertainer Barry Humphries pose at the Art Gallery of NSW with their Archibald portraits in 1992.

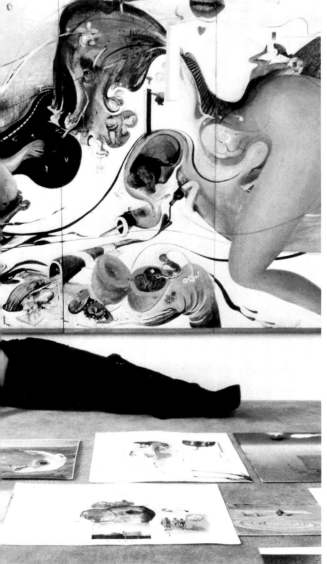

and her progress in international air races was closely followed. There was a sense that women had broken through.

In 1925 *The Sydney Morning Herald* boldly stated its views in an editorial: "The duty of the man is as much to the home as is the woman's; and the duty of the woman to the state is just as much as the man's. We grant these things almost as axioms now; but we have taken a long time to admit them, and the admission has been very hardly forced from us. It is difficult to understand now, and it will probably become absolutely incomprehensible with the passage of a few years, why we ever

considered it wrong for women to vote or enter parliament."

But if the *Herald* fancied equality was all but achieved, it was premature.

When World War I broke out in 1914, women were not allowed to enlist and their offers to serve in auxiliary roles were usually rejected, although many served as nurses. Women's participation in the workforce did not increase significantly. Instead they were confined to farm work, caring for the children, knitting socks, sending comfort packages, raising money and supporting returned officers.

There were advancements towards equal opportunity made during this time, Patsy Adam-Smith argues in *Australian Women at War*, but almost all of them were quashed by the Depression. By 1939 however, women were no longer prepared to accept this relatively benign role and demanded to contribute more actively to the World War II effort, in the armed forces and the workforce. That there was an urgent need to employ all possible labour caused some discomfiture to the government, where there was concern women would take men's jobs after the war because they were cheaper to employ. The

Above Women machinists work in the Commonwealth Clothing Factory in 1939.

Top far left Aviator Nancy Bird, then 19, and her plane in 1934.

Bottom far left A woman making "sun glare goggles" for allied air forces in 1944.

Above The life of Sydney University women undergraduates was viewed with pity, observed the *Herald* in a report accompanying this image in 1934. In fact, insisted the paper's women's supplement, "Their cup of life is filled to the brim."

Labor government eventually decided in 1941 to approve the interim employment of women until men became available again.

There was slow recognition for the women who were in the line of fire. Nancy Wake, whose courageous work for the French Resistance movement earned her the highest British, French and US government honours, was not honoured in Australia until 2004. Many Australians may have first learnt of her "hair-raising" activities in a chatty article on the women's page of the *Herald* in January 1949, alongside European winter fashion.

The next strides in the women's movement were not made until the 1960s with the rise of feminism and the galvanising

power of Germaine Greer's book *The Female Eunuch* in 1970.

Although the number of women in the workforce had increased dramatically since the war, the women's movement held an uneasy relationship with the unions, which were slightly dismissive of women but also saw them as the future of their membership.

In a country which propelled industrial legislation for women so vigorously in the 1890s — with the Children's Protection, Factories and Shops, Married Women's Property and Early Closing acts — one of the most basic tenets of equality was not firmed up until 1969. That was the first test case establishing the principle of equal pay for equal work.

In 1972 a second test case expanded this principle to equal pay for equal work of equal value. The Women's Electoral Lobby, also formed in 1972, forced the major parties to elevate women's issues, and played a role in the election of the Whitlam government. In following years legislation was broadened: the 1983 Sex Discrimination Act was passed, making it illegal to discriminate on the basis of gender, marital status or pregnancy. Unpaid maternity leave was achieved in 1979 and parental leave in 1992. These victories helped the campaigns of others seeking tighter legislative or workplace protection, with significant compliance rules to ensure non-discrimination on the grounds of handicap, race and religion.

Above This woman, one of 2000 marchers in the 1969 annual May Day parade, wore part-skirt, part-trousers to drive her message home.

Above left Women unionists outside Parliament House in 1958. They planned to have a rally demanding equal pay, but instead held a rally to congratulate premier Joe Cahill, who had the same day promised to introduce it before the next election.

CHAPTER SEVEN

Market Forces

Living in the seventies

BY ROSS GITTINS

A young person will hate them for doing so, but every early baby boomer can recall the days when kids leaving school or uni could walk straight into a job without fuss. Just before I finished at the University of Newcastle in late 1968, I took the train to Sydney and, after a day of walking in off the street to the big firms of chartered accountants, retired to my sister's house to consider the job offers I'd collected from each of them. I picked the one with the highest pay, a sum that greatly impressed my girlfriend: $4000 a year — almost $80 a week!

When, in 1973, I chucked in that job to take a year off and do a course in journalism just for the fun of it, I had no fear about regaining employment. When the time came I'd simply wait for the next Saturday, buy a copy of the *Herald*, look up all the job ads in the "Men and Boys" columns for accountants and pick the one that looked the most interesting. I'd ring them up on Monday morning, saying, "I've got good news for you — I'm willing to take your job."

As it turned out, I took a job as a 26-year-old cadet journalist on the *Herald*. But, at the time, that assessment of the little trouble I'd have getting back into accounting was quite realistic. A year or so later, it wouldn't have been.

What a different economy we live in today. I've seen my own kids struggle to find a decent job after completing uni. And today the starting salary for graduates is about 10 times what I got in 1969.

The funny thing is that economists can date precisely the point when our economy — and all the developed economies — changed from benign to malign, from stable to dysfunctional. The event that triggered it was the oil shock of Christmas 1973, when the cartel formed by the Organisation of Petroleum Exporting Countries (OPEC) quadrupled the world price of oil from $US3 a barrel to about $US12 a barrel. And if you are converting currencies here, this was another time, another place, and the Australian dollar was worth $US1.49 in 1973.

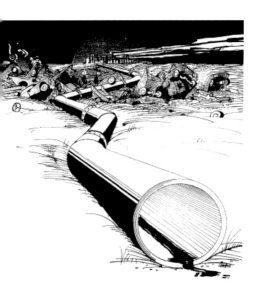

Above The world economy and the suburban bowser remain inextricably linked to the amount of oil flowing. (Illustration: Jenny Coopes)

Previous pages Flights of fancy: the revolution in air travel threw open the doors to cattle class in the 1970s. Lobsters always travelled first class.

That first oil shock — there was another in 1979, which lifted the oil price to $US36 a barrel — had two conflicting effects on the developed economies. It greatly raised the prices of petrol, home heating, plastics and all other goods derived from oil, and all goods and services requiring transportation. But as well as being inflationary, it was also deflationary — the oil price leap involved a huge transfer of income from the developed countries to the oil-exporting countries — mostly in the Middle East. It made us poorer, with less to spend on anything else.

Before the following year was over, most countries' inflation rates were heading for 20 per cent or more, the world had plunged

Above The snake of inflation squeezes the public and politicians. (Cartoon: Larry Pickering)

Left The Australian car industry peaked in the 1970s. Then came the cutbacks, closures and retrenchments. Here, the last Commodore rolls off the line at Holden's Pagewood factory in 1980.

Below First tapped in 1964, Bass Strait still holds Australia's largest oil reserves. Since 1978, Australian supplies have been sold at the prevailing international market prices.

into severe recession and unemployment was shooting up. A new and ugly word was coined to describe this unprecedented and ugly situation: stagflation — the paradoxical combination of a stagnant economy and high unemployment with high inflation.

It's taken our economy the best part of 30 years to recover its equilibrium, to stop the violent rocking of our economic rowing boat and get both inflation and unemployment back down to something like where they were before 1974.

Looking back, economists identify 1974 as the seminal year in the history of the world economy since the end of World War II. It signified the end of the Golden

Above All out, brothers: here Sydney City Council workers vote to continue their strike in August 1970.

Top right In a foretaste of a decade of virulent industrial campaigns, building workers across Sydney went on strike in 1970, seeking a $6 a week pay rise. They were branded terrorists by the commissioner of police, Norm Allan, who mobilised all available detectives and uniformed officers. (Photo: Bob Rice)

Bottom right In 1981 a Cremorne sales manager, Leanne Hayward, led a conservative backlash against the union movement, organising an anti-strike march through the city streets. Not all marchers and watchers found common cause.

Age of the immediate postwar period, when economies grew strongly year after year without needing much attention, inflation stayed low and full employment — an unemployment rate of less than 2 per cent — was a persisting reality.

Those who grew up in the 1950s and 60s assumed that the way the economy performed then was normal — the way it had always performed. Their parents, having endured the Great Depression of the 1930s, knew better. But as the 1970s and 80s rolled on, economists came to realise that a misbehaving economy wasn't abnormal so much as reasonably typical of the way it had performed throughout most of the 20th century.

So it was the first 30 years or so after the war that were abnormal. They were, indeed, a golden age — the developed world's best period of economic performance either before or since. In a speech he gave in 1997, appropriately titled "The Economics of Nostalgia", the Reserve Bank governor, Ian Macfarlane, offered several explanations for that relatively brief period of cloudless sky.

There was a gap to be made up after the Depression and the destruction of the war. The 1950s and 60s were a period of postwar reconstruction with massive investment and "catch-up", particularly in the countries most devastated by the war, such as Germany, Italy and Japan. Much of that investment was made possible by America's Marshall aid plan, itself proof that we can learn from our mistakes. Rather than the retribution that followed World War I — and contributed to

the rise of Hitler — the aftermath of World War II was characterised by magnanimity and an effort to ensure order and co-operation in the world economy through the establishment of institutions such as the International Monetary Fund (IMF), the Organisation for Economic Co-operation and Development (OECD), and what is now the World Trade Organisation (WTO). Of course, a major motivation for the Marshall plan would have been to save Europe from the blandishments of Soviet-sponsored communism.

The inter-war Depression prompted the erection of high protective barriers around the developed economies, which made things

Right In 1974 the unemployment rate doubled, although it was still only 4 per cent. It kept on climbing throughout the term of the Fraser government, eventually peaking at 10.4 per cent in September 1983. Here, a morning queue at the Commonwealth Employment Service office in Crows Nest, 1974. (Photo: Rick Stevens)

Top far right Honest unemployed or dole-bludging bum? The Unemployed Peoples' Union challenged the stereotype. (Photo: Rick Stevens)

Bottom far right Gough Whitlam and his "welfare" bus. (Cartoon: Larry Pickering)

worse. After the war, international trade was liberated by various rounds of multilateral reductions in tariffs under the auspices of the General Agreement on Tariffs and Trade (GATT). Exports and imports grew rapidly, adding to the pace of economic growth. Barriers to the flow of capital between countries were reduced. So here we find the reinvigoration of one of the phenomena that has driven human progress since the time of Marco Polo. Globalisation advanced dramatically in the 19th century, only to be suppressed in the nationalistic and defensive economic errors of the inter-war period.

Although peoples and governments were eager for economic growth, there was widespread restraint in behaviour.

Parents who'd lived through the Depression were wary and saved much of their steadily growing incomes. Wage demands were moderate and consistent with the improvement in productivity, keeping inflation low. And people expected it to stay low; because they acted accordingly in their setting of wages and prices, it did.

Keeping true to the role delegated to them in the economic theories of John Maynard Keynes, governments generally managed their economies skilfully, balancing stimulus and restriction as they minimised the swings in the business cycle and, for the first time ever, made full employment a reality.

But then, in 1974, it all fell apart. The Golden Age ended, to be replaced by

something called the Great Inflation — the only period of sustained peacetime inflation ever. Before then, major periods of inflation had occurred only during wars. Until the period following World War II, the general level of prices had advanced little over the centuries. A rise in the price of bread or milk or any other household staple was a news story — and at street level it could replace the weather as a talking point. It was true that prices tended to rise during economic booms, but equally true that they tended to fall during slumps.

With the Great Inflation came steadily worsening unemployment rates, the term stagflation and the end of full employment. With the advent of stagflation came a major

change in the preoccupations of politicians. The state of the economy and its needs became — and remains to this day — the dominant political issue. And with this came a change in the news and in newspapers: news about the economy — about inflation, unemployment, interest rates, housing booms, taxes, budget deficits and trade deficits — moved from the back pages to the front page.

I joined the *Herald* in February 1974, a chartered accountant wanting to write about politics, but soon guided by wiser heads into the new growth area of economic journalism. Quite by chance, I was in the right place at the right time. I got in on the ground floor.

But could this rupture in the history of the world economy have been caused simply by a quadrupling in the price of oil? No, it couldn't. The oil shock was merely the most salient event of the period. Various adverse developments preceded it and, indeed, helped to cause it.

Though governments' use of Keynesian policy to manage demand was sober and sensible for the postwar period, towards the end it became ill-disciplined. Governments were mesmerised by the goal of full employment and neglectful of inflation. In Australia, as elsewhere, they tried to keep their economies running perpetually at full capacity, using budget deficits and low interest rates to maintain customer buying power whenever demand slackened. To retain full employment they were quite prepared to pay the price of a bit of inflation.

In their preoccupation with managing demand, economists took little interest in what was happening to the supply, or production, side of the economy. What was happening was an unending stream of usually well-intended government interventions in the economy, ranging from the nationalisation of industries, to laws protecting workers' rights, to controls over the prices of eggs and bread. Many of these interventions were aimed at

Above Popular protest took on increasingly creative forms in the 1970s: police speak to a university student. (Photo: Robert Pearce)

bringing stability to particular industries, but in the process the old price governor of competition was reduced.

By the late 1960s and early 1970s, several years of lax economic management in various economies — including a succession of large budget deficits in the United States, as Lyndon Johnson spent big on both the Vietnam War and his Great Society welfare programs — had caused inflation to break out of its usual 2 to 3 per cent range and start heading up.

As actual inflation rose, people's expectations about price hikes also rose. Unions began demanding higher wages to help ensure that the workers stayed in front and firms became more ready to raise their

Above Union muscle and emerging concern for the environment made a powerful combination. In Sydney, the Builders Labourers Federation secretary, Jack Mundey, led the fight to save The Rocks in 1973.

Left Squaring off: in 1974 at Macquarie University scores of students were arrested after 30 police cars arrived to break up a demonstration. (Photo: W. Black)

prices in response to actual or expected cost increases, leading to a self-perpetuating spiral of rising prices.

The world economic boom of the early 1970s also caused increased demand for many foodstuffs and raw materials, leading to big rises in the prices of rural and mineral commodities (including those exported by Australia). As Macfarlane likes to remind us, Australia's annual inflation rate reached 10.4 per cent in the September quarter of 1973 — before the first oil shock.

So here we were in 1974 with the prices of virtually all commodities well up, with one exception: oil. Long-term contracts had held the price of oil below $US2 a barrel for many years. And now the US dollar was

falling, making matters even worse for the oil-exporting countries. So eventually they rebelled, formed a cartel and pushed the price up to compensate. In other words, the first oil shock was less a cause of the problem than an effect of it.

Even so, the mutually contradictory nature of the oil shock and the advent of stagflation left the developed countries confused about how to respond. Should they tighten policy: raise taxes, cut government spending and increase interest rates to fight inflation, or loosen policy to fight unemployment? They alternated between the two and found themselves deeper in the mire. Inflation worsened and so did unemployment. And their citizens were experiencing unthought-of impositions, such as peacetime petrol queues and pep talks about trading in the gas-guzzler for a more compact car and caring for the environment by cutting down on pollution.

What came next was a crisis within the economics profession. The simple Keynesian analysis that had dominated both academic economics and government economic policymaking since the war was seen to have failed. The Keynesians' famous Phillips curve — named for the New Zealand economist Bill Phillips — promised them a

A Special Pre-election Appeal
To Prime Minister Malcolm Fraser

Top Record numbers of whales passing Sydney in 2005 are living testament to the successful anti-whaling campaign. Here, an advertisement published in the *Herald* in 1977.

Above Terania Creek, near Nimbin, was a focal point of conflict between loggers and environmentalists.

Right What goes up must come down: the rise of the car was matched by worsening air pollution. Friends of the Earth members spray a car with a sweet smell in 1972. (Photo: Keith Byron)

straightforward trade-off between inflation and unemployment, but management of demand offered no means to deal with both high inflation and high unemployment at the same time.

Enter Milton Friedman and others with the revival of an old idea in economics, renamed "monetarism". They believed that inflation was "always and everywhere a monetary phenomenon". Prices rose for no reason other than the excessive growth in the quantity of money in circulation. So central banks needed merely to limit the quantity of money they supplied and prices would stop rising. Once businesses, unions and the public realised such a policy was being followed, inflation would quickly abate with little disruption to the economy.

Australia took up the experiment and began setting money-supply targets after the Fraser government was elected in late 1975. It didn't abandon the practice until early 1985, when the Hawke government realised that its deregulation of the banks had sent the various measures of the money supply haywire. What re-emerged was an old forgotten truth: if you raised interest rates high enough you'd put the economy into recession and the recession would bring the inflation rate down — but if that was all you did, once the economy was back on its feet the inflation rate would start rising again.

Ultimately there emerged a conventional wisdom that draws from both Keynesian and monetarist schools. The Keynesians have prevailed to the extent that it remains accepted that governments can and should intervene — to counter the business cycle and stabilise the growth in demand by stimulating or restricting it as appropriate. But the monetarists have prevailed to the extent that the manipulation of interest rates (monetary policy) has replaced the manipulation of government spending and taxation (fiscal policy) as the main tool to influence how we spend our hard-earned dollar. Central banks — in Australia the Reserve Bank — have been given independence of the elected government and most have established targets for the rate of inflation as their guiding principle. As the events of the 1990s have demonstrated, an insistence on keeping inflation moderate does not involve tolerating perpetual high unemployment. Quite the reverse. The old, much-maligned (and much-ignored) slogan of the Fraser years, Fight Inflation First, turned out to be right.

This was the developed world as reshaped by the oil shock and stagflation. The specific story for Australia has its own differences. Apart from the growing lack of discipline in wage- and price-setting in the late 1960s and early 1970s, Australia's

Above The rugby tour by the Springbok team in 1971 brought the question of South Africa's apartheid policies into Australian lounge rooms and sporting arenas. Sporting boycotts meant the Springboks did not return until 1993.

Left Land rights became a rallying point for both black and white.

move to double-figure inflation rates was explained less by the first oil shock than by the earlier boom in the world prices for our rural and mineral commodities. And also by the McMahon government's failure in 1971 — because of considerable resistance from the Country Party — to limit the inflationary consequences from the sudden leap in export earnings by adequately revaluing the Australian dollar. Because Australia was largely self-sufficient in oil production and it wasn't until the late

1970s that the Fraser government brought the price of local oil closer to global levels with "import-parity pricing", it took some time for Australian motorists to join Europe and the US in experiencing the full effect of the OPEC price hikes. A year after the first shock of late 1973, retail petrol prices had risen by only 18 per cent. But after three years the increase was 50 per cent, after six years it was almost 150 per cent and after a decade it was more than 300 per cent. By the time the Whitlam government was elected in

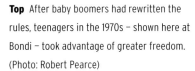

Top After baby boomers had rewritten the rules, teenagers in the 1970s – shown here at Bondi – took advantage of greater freedom. (Photo: Robert Pearce)

Right Men also broke down many doors in the 1970s, including those to the labour ward. Larry McPherson with his wife, Suzanne, meets his Father's Day present, Amie Letitia. (Photo: John O'Gready)

Centre When women charged into the workforce, child care became a crucial concern. By 2005 nearly half of all children under five attended child care before they went to school. (Photo: Martin Brannan)

December 1972, the seeds of inflation were already well sown. And many of the factors adversely affecting our economy during its term came from abroad and were beyond its control. The new government didn't know what hit it. Its ministers had lived through more than two decades in which the economy performed well with little need for detailed attention. They assumed the economy would continue generating wealth on automatic pilot while its leaders focused on redistributing the wealth and clearing what they perceived to be a 23-year backlog of needed social reform.

All the world's governments were muddled in their response to the first oil shock, so it would be unreasonable to expect our government to have quickly perceived how radically the game had changed. After

all, it took economists up to a decade to fully digest what had happened and why.

That said, very many of the economic policies the Whitlam government pursued served to make matters worse. And most were misjudgements a continuing Coalition government would not have made. In particular, Whitlam's succession of treasurers — but particularly Dr Jim Cairns — permitted government spending to more than double over the course of its three budgets, with the growth in tax revenue falling far behind. Clyde Cameron's policy of using the federal public service as a "pacesetter" in the improvement of workers' pay and conditions — including the granting of maternity leave, extended holiday leave and the 17.5 per cent holiday leave loading — added greatly to

employers' wage costs. Combine that with the defects of the arbitration system — which took pay rises won by strike action in one industry and quickly flowed them on to all other industries — and you see why average weekly earnings leapt by 70 per cent in three years, far in excess of the growth in prices and productivity. It took more than a decade for this "real wage overhang" to be overcome. The annual inflation rate reached 17 per cent in June 1975.

In the 30 years since then our economy has experienced two ever-more severe recessions — in the early 1980s and early 1990s — but has finally returned to something approaching its former stability. The inflation rate averaged about 10 per cent in the 1970s and 8 per cent in

the 1980s, but since the early 1990s has averaged 2.5 per cent — equal to our best performance in the Golden Age and right in the centre of the Reserve Bank's target range. Most of the developed countries had inflation under control by the 1980s; we took longer. But how did we do it? The severity of the early 1990s recession helped, but inflation would have rebounded long ago had that been the only factor.

In the postwar years, economists thought in terms of just one form of inflation, later dubbed "demand-pull". When demand for goods exceeded their supply, this would force up their price. But as they studied the puzzle that is stagflation — prices rising while demand was weak — economists realised it must have been caused by a different form

Above For every great invention there's a lemon squashed under the wheels of progress: in 1949 a Harris Park barber saw great potential in this electric shave bar.

Top right More than just wheels of convenience: in the 1950s, there was one car for every 10 adults; now two in every three adults have a car of their own. When trains and buses ground to a halt, as they did during this strike in 1951, so did the traffic in North Sydney.

Consumer society

Frugality died in Australia with the end of the Great Depression and wartime austerity. In its place came the seemingly endless rise of the consumer society, built on the back of rapid growth in both disposable income and credit.

Great leaps in technology and productivity bore a rich harvest and every new toy — from transistor radios to today's video-capable mobile phones — was picked over and inspected. Anything that worked — for us — was bought quickly and in great quantity. Theoretically, cars and refrigerators

and non-fuel stoves could last a lifetime, but that reckoned without the driving force of what the Joneses were doing and the lure of the "latest model".

Radio was the first of the modern luxury entertainment devices to enter the front door of our homes in the 1920s. First it was a bulky pseudo-furniture item in walnut veneer sitting on the floor and called a wireless, often replacing its old-hat predecessor, the upright piano. After World War II, bakelite and direct power let the radio jump on to the mantelpiece,

Above With the war won, it was time to hit the shops. Christmas Eve, 1946.

Left The 1935 Electrical and Radio Exhibition at the Sydney Town Hall offered a foretaste of the 1950s, showcasing all manner of labour-saving devices in the "completely electrified home". (Photo: Harry Freeman)

Top Television, the drug of a nation: Bill Golding's family switches on in April 1957. (Photo: Harry Martin)

Above McDonald's first Australian managing director, Donn Wilson, in 1971. The company now has 730 outlets. (Photo: Brian Cameron)

Top centre The rise of the do-it-yourself market – shoppers at a Sydney hardware store in 1957. (Photo: Harry Martin)

just in time to make space for the product explosion of the 1950s.

Television arrived in 1956 as the great suburban roll-out began, and played a major role in selling all manner of consumer dreams. It took nearly 20 years for colour to arrive but, since then, home viewing has morphed into wide-screen, stereo, plasma and digital formats. VCRs came and went and most homes now have more than one screen. A quarter of homes have a pay-TV service, and waiting to take control of home entertainment are millions of home computers, with high-speed internet connections poised to multiply viewing options.

More than half of all television viewers watch programs from the comfort of an air-conditioned home, often in a room that was once the rumpus or games room and is now the entertainment centre.

A similar number of Australians have two or more cars parked in the double or triple garage. In 2001 more than 6 million people travelled to work by car, about 10 times the number who went by public transport.

Some revolutions now seem passe: the vertical griller didn't stick around for long, and even the once-ubiquitous electric frypan seems so very 1960s among the gleaming array of seldom-used, one-purpose, one-touch gadgets in our custom-designed kitchens.

Food is no longer something Mum makes, a transformation typified by the growth of McDonald's, which opened its first Australian store at Yagoona in 1971 and now dominates the fast-food industry from 730 outlets across the country. Even breakfast is increasingly an eating-out experience and the hunt for the perfect cup of coffee has become an obsession.

Few leave home without a mobile phone and texting users are a safety hazard on the road and on footpaths. More than 2 billion text messages were sent in Australia in 2004 on 15 million mobile phones.

Top Supermarket aisles were the place to be in Sydney in 1963.

Above The consumer revolution remade the home. (Illustration: Harry Afentoglou)

Colour photography

Right More than window dressing: the glass-cleaning business in the city centre calls for a fearless constitution and the skills of a mountaineer. (Photo: Nick Moir)

Below Your turn to mow the lawn: the deposed occupant of the Lodge, Paul Keating, shows the garden to its new tenant, John Howard, in March 1996. (Photo: Mike Bowers)

Colour photography was slow to elbow its way into the *Herald*. Despite the arrival of instamatics and mini labs, newspapers were held back by printing — and time.

Early colour required planning and preparation and was used only in "wraparounds" for special events, such as the official opening of the Opera House in October 1973. Photographers continued to load their cameras with black and white film for two more decades.

Colour news photographs began appearing in the *Herald* during Sydney's bushfire crisis in January 1994, with Will Burgess, a Reuters photographer, taking the first honours. Staff photographers soon

began shifting to colour and, by the end of that year, all assignments were shot on colour negative film — although almost all were printed in black and white.

When the *Herald* moved to Darling Harbour in 1995 the darkroom — the nerve centre of a photographer's world for nearly a century — was not needed; negatives were scanned directly into a computer. The real liberation of colour, though, came when the presses rolled in 1996 at Fairfax's new offset printing plant at Chullora.

Colour printing shaped the way photographers saw the world. Although the same rules applied, the elements that make a picture work were very different. This was

a huge challenge, but *Herald* photographers took it on with gusto. Awards soon followed.

Fast on the heels of colour was the digital revolution: true mobility had arrived. All *Herald* photographers had traded in their film cameras by the time the Sydney Olympic Games began in 2000. As long as you could power the cameras, computers and phone, you could capture and send images back to Sydney from anywhere in the world.

The results have been remarkable. *Herald* photography, which moved away from the time-honoured tricks and posed photographs to a more documentary style, has been recognised through numerous World Press awards over the past decade.

Above Princess bride: Mary Donaldson met her prince in a pub in Sydney, married him in 2004 in Copenhagen and went to live in a palace. With her new husband, Prince Frederik, Princess Mary dances the wedding waltz. (Photo: Rick Stevens)

Top Cabramatta's streets are alive with vivid cultural contrasts. (Photo: Palani Mohan)

Above Ansett Australia crashed and burned, but this flight to Tokyo just came to a shuddering halt. (Photo: Dean Sewell)

Above Games people play: ballroom dancing took a competitive twist at Sydney's Gay Games in 2002. (Photo: Steven Siewert)

Top left Police and Aborigines face off outside Redfern station in February 2004 after the death of 17-year-old T. J. Hickey. The night of confrontation highlighted yet again tensions between Aborigines and police. (Photo: Edwina Pickles)

Left Sucking up ash from burnt-out scrub, a willy-willy crosses the desert near Tennant Creek in the Northern Territory. (Photo: Ben Rushton)

Above and right Pigs might fly – and how! Miss Piggy leapt to a new world record of 3.31 metres at the 2005 Darwin Show. (Photos: Glenn Campbell)

Top far right In the African grasslands meerkats delight in rising from their burrows in the morning to catch some sun. At Taronga Zoo, they settle for a heat lamp. (Photo: Rick Stevens)

Bottom far right Out of the barrel: a bodyboarder rides his luck in the Shark Island Challenge off Cronulla in 2002. (Photo: Craig Golding)

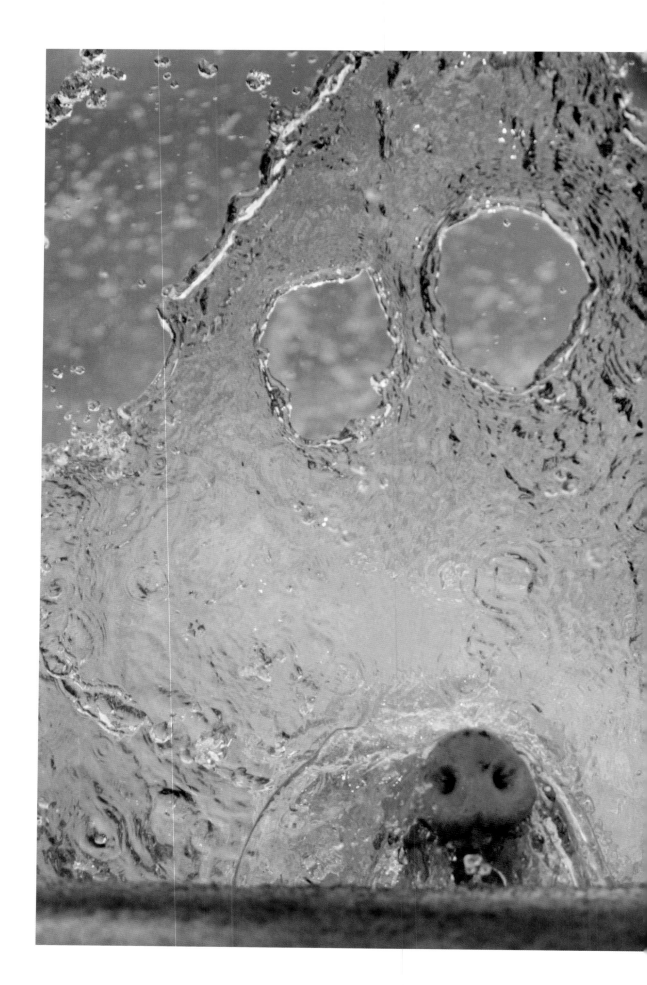

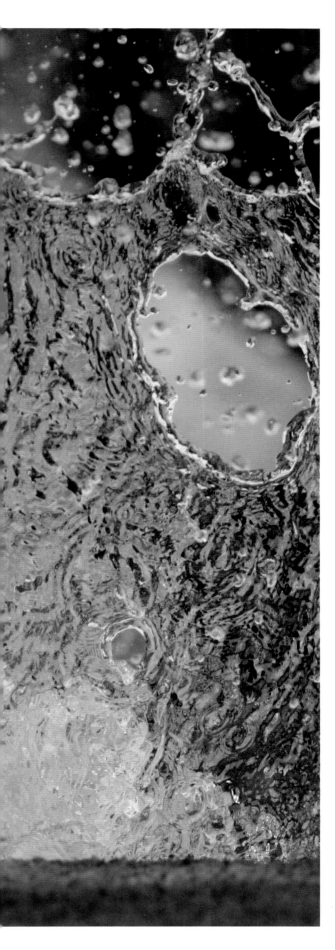

Above Terrorism is entrenched in the modern
vocabulary – and in the games children play.
A child with a toy gun on the cliff behind
Dreamland beach, Bali, plays make-believe
terrorist. (Photo: Tamara Dean)

Below On the eve of invasion in 2003, a young girl and her little sister emerge from the haze of heat and smoke from a petrochemical plant that glowers over their family tomato patch just north of the Iraq-Kuwait border. (Photo: Jason South)

Bottom Hold still – it won't hurt a bit: Sivash, a six-year-old Eastwood school student, begs to differ as he gets his measles jab as part of a national vaccination program. (Photo: Steven Siewert)

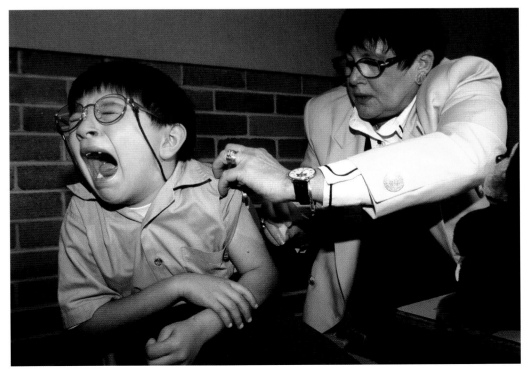

Right Villagers from Enarotali island, West Papua, who in 2000 were still living with no power or television, saw no harm in browsing and checking out *Grease*. (Photo: Jason South)

Below Let's dance: Nicola Cayless, with arms above her head, warms up for her weekly ballet class. (Photo: Penny Bradfield)

Below centre Not even death ends the desire for a water view: more than 250,000 people have been buried in Waverley Cemetery, first used in 1875. (Photo: Jon Reid)

Top Catch of the day: a seagull shows off lunch at the Sydney Fish Market. (Photo: Mike Bowers)

Above Fashion pit stop: Lulu Wagstaffe gets a quick makeover between shows at Australian Fashion Week in 2004. (Photo: Steven Siewert)

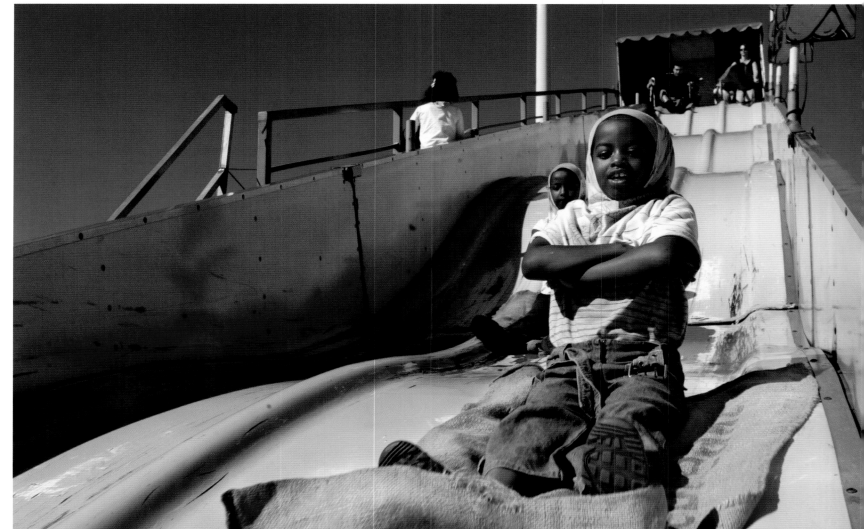

Top far left Just sniffing the breeze: a bearded dragon sits on the Cobb Highway, between Hay and Ivanhoe, as a storm front approaches. (Photo: Nick Moir)

Left Every year hundreds of the Northern Territory's finest Aboriginal footballers gather at Yuendumu, 300 kilometres north-west of Alice Springs, for a contemporary sporting corroboree. (Photo: Steven Siewert)

Below left Samiro Toore rides her own magic carpet at the Arabic Carnivale in 2004. (Photo: Steven Siewert)

Below Beware of low-flying kites and their handlers. Damien Beebe flourishes his stunt kite at Bondi's Festival of the Winds.

CHAPTER EIGHT

Diversions

Who took the comics?

by Peter FitzSimons

Sure, some other *Herald* aficionados tell the story of the welcome morning thump of the *Herald* landing on their doorstep as a pleasurable punctuation point of their childhood, but for us Fitzes of Peats Ridge it wasn't like that at all.

Dad would come up from our citrus orchard for his morning tea break and take the battered old ute by the name of "Morrie" down to the mailbox and be back just three jiffies later with mail and the paper to divvy up. The bills were for him, the cheques for Mum, and the paper was split between us. My older brothers were generally into the sport pages or the classifieds, where they searched for cheap second-hand cars; my sisters and Mum seemed particularly into Column 8 and something called the "Women's Pages"; Dad would, through the course of the day, read the whole thing from front to back. As the youngest of six kids, all that was left to me was Uncle Dick of *The Potts* fame, and for some reason I associate a particular *Potts* strip with the moment of shaking off mere kid-dom and becoming close to a man, dammit, even if chronologically I was only 10 years old.

The subject was "averages" and the tag of the cartoon was good ol' Uncle Dick saying: "Averages? I don't believe in averages! If you believe in them it says that if you've got your head in the deep freeze and your feet in the oven, you still feel pretty good on the average!"

Laugh? I should jolly well say I laughed, by golly I did, and I showed it to Mum and Dad and my brothers for good measure, demonstrating that I, too, could draw to their attention things from the *Herald* that demanded a wider audience. Sometimes we would also use the *Herald* to wrap whatever fish we might have caught on trips to Pittwater, tear it into bits to make a nest for pet mice, and make a sickly kind of papier-mache out of it. And Mum had a way of folding it that made an odd-looking hat which we would wear for reasons that escape me now.

But the *Herald* was like that. It was every bit as much a part of the family fabric of our lives as Holden cars, pumpkin scones, Sunday school and a rock-solid belief in the inestimable virtues of the Liberal Party. It was always just kind of there — solid, dependable and as unlikely to surprise as it was to disappoint. I had perhaps vaguely heard that there were other newspapers out there but (sniff!) they never really entered my orbit and, if I thought about it at all, I suspect I must have surmised that those papers were read by the same people who — if you can believe it — voted Labor.

It was only much later, when I was first published in the *Herald* — I couldn't say when, exactly, but I think it was around May 25, 1986 — that I began to understand the *Herald* the way I do now: as a living organism that really does change. I have always loved the line, "This is my grandfather's axe — my father replaced the handle, and I replaced the head", and the *Herald* is the same. It's still the *Herald*, and over decades it can appear fundamentally unchanging, but the changes are there all right.

Take the moment when a crossword first appeared, in 1933. There it was, a curious hotchpotch of black and white squares, the latter with some numbers in them, tucked well away into the back pages of the

Above Beatrice Bush sold newspapers on the corner on Victoria Road in White Bay for 25 years until her death in 1996, aged 71. The much-loved local character woke at 3.15am every day to sell the newspapers from 4am to midday.

Centre The comic book form became widely popular. Even political cartoonist Alan Moir used it in his long-running *Little Caesar*, which set current politics in Roman times.

Previous pages A ferry, the lap of the waves and a newspaper – downtime for Sydney commuters on an April day, 1935.

MORE AT: www.moir.com.au

women's supplement, which itself started in 1905.

9 ACROSS: the jury was still out.
7 DOWN: but before long, and for the first time, male readers could be seen buried in the pages reserved for their missus, pencil in hand.

As if proof were needed of their universal appeal, the story is told in *Herald* corridors of the time that one of the male compilers apparently proposed to his girlfriend in a series of daily clues. (Come to think of it, dear reader, if your father was once a *Herald* crossword compiler, it is quite possible you owe your very existence to the fact that your mum knew the English equivalent of the German word "jawohl"!)

It was, too, an auspicious day for the *Herald* when cartoons first started to appear, although the story of how they began is curious. In October of 1944 a printers' strike disrupted all four of Sydney's papers and, to tide over the readers, Fairfax provided a kind of composite paper, looking like the *Herald*, but which nevertheless included cartoons from the *Telegraph*, *Mirror* and *Sun*. They proved so popular that within two months of the strike ending the *Herald* was forced to climb down from the rarefied exile of its own pedestal and find some comic strips to call its own.

The one that became far and away the most popular, *The Potts*, had started life in the famous *Smith's Weekly* in 1920, penned by Stan Cross, and taken over by Jim Russell in 1940. In 1950 when *Smith's* died, the Potts family had to find somewhere to live and the *Herald* was its natural home — it proved an immediate hit with readers.

It continued until 2001 when Russell died, establishing a record for the world's longest-running cartoon strip. (And for the record, if you wonder what Jim Russell was like, Chips Rafferty once said to him: "Gor blimey, Jim, you're beginning to look more like Uncle Dick every day." Russell once acknowledged, rather ruefully, when accepting an award from the NSW minister for the arts: "I've grown more like Uncle Dick, and Uncle Dick has grown more like me. My wife says he is me.")

The *Herald* weather maps first appeared in 1877 and have continued since — with one notable gap. Shortly after the Japanese bombed Pearl Harbor on December 7,

Top Jim Russell achieved a record for the longest-running comic strip with *The Potts*, which he drew for 61 years. His career began at age 14, as a copy boy for *Smith's Weekly*. He joined the *Herald* team in 1951.

Above *The Potts* sometimes caused a stir with women readers.

Following pages, centre The first of about 40,000 "LB" crosswords appeared in *The Sydney Morning Herald* in 1935. Lindsey Browne (top) started compiling them to top up his wage as a cadet journalist. Browne proposed to his wife through these two crosswords, using the first letter of every across answer. Number 305 read I LOVE NANCY MOORE and number 316 asked WILL SHE MARRY ME. A few weeks later he let readers know the response with the last letter of every across answer: THE ANSWER IS YES.

COLUMN 8

*V*ALUES. Don Bradman, Test cricketer, can't remember the number of autographs he's signed—"must run into many thousands."

Marcus Oliphant, atom expert, can. He's never been asked for one.

* * *

*C*ANBERRA is guessing who will be next Governor of the Commonwealth Bank.

If the Prime Minister gets his way with Cabinet it is pretty sure to be Leslie Melville, whose room at the Bank bears the simple label "Economist".

* * *

*U*NFAIR TO MEN: One of Sydney's more classy hotels refused lunch yesterday to a man without a coat.

Opposite him a woman sat in comfort with her shoes off.

* * *

A.B.C. is supporting the move for sponsored sessions. The plan is for a third network to carry advertising, leaving FC and BL to share light and serious entertainment and Parliamentary broadcasts.

Revenue from licences doesn't allow them to compete with commercial stations for local radio stars, whose fees have trebled.

* * *

A FEVERED citizen invaded the office yesterday, whispering that a gang of Nazi spies was hidden under the timber in the barque Pamir.

The mission was to seize Professor Oliphant and torture him into telling the secret of the atom bomb.

To pacify him a reporter said he would pop down to the ship and see. The citizen pressed a Boy-Scout knife into his hand and hissed, "Take this. You'll need it".

* * *

*S*YDNEY'S Four Hundred are twittering about the form of invitation to Thursday's Royal Garden Party.

The honour of their company was sought by the Ministers of State, and not, as is usual, by the Governor.

Nobody will say why.

* * *

*D*AME ENID LYONS wants closer censorship of imported films.

All major American films which reach here have first been approved by the American Catholic League of Decency, whose members are pledged not to attend pictures which have been refused the League's certificate.

The same conditions do not apply in England, and American producers are complaining that English films are permitted a frankness they dare not attempt.

* * *

*S*HAKING out the moths from some things yesterday I came across a nice little notebook bound in pigskin—worth about 7/6 today.

The point is that it was one of those things whisky firms used to give away in the days when the customer was always right.

* * *

*T*HERE are some buxom lassies who will sweep you off your feet down at Wynyard.

After they've scattered the tea-leaves they get behind their brooms and charge into the crowds. It's great sport making the populace hop like sheep at a crossing—much better than can be got from such modern devices as vacuum cleaners.

* * *

*T*HE room we're in once harboured leader-writers. Among the books left behind is "The Psychology of a Primitive People."

Now you know who they write for.

Granny

Solution to Crossword Puzzle No. 305

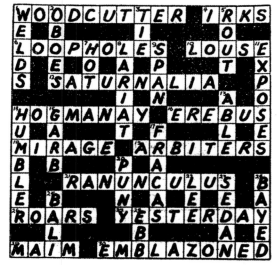

Solution to Crossword Puzzle No. 316

1941 — "a day that will live in infamy" — the *Herald* stopped publishing a detailed weather map and didn't publish one for the next three years, as "a security measure". (Visions come of the generals in Tokyo earnestly consulting the *Herald*'s weather page and saying, "The wind is blowing from the east, temperatures are moderate, and the tide is high: it's perfect invasion weather!")

And, finally, there is your favourite, and mine — Column 8. It began life with the signature of Granny on January 11, 1947, under the editorship of the legendary Syd Deamer, and an opening paragraph that set the tone for ever more: "VALUES. Don Bradman, Test cricketer, can't remember the number of autographs he's signed — 'must run into many thousands.' Marcus Oliphant, atom expert, can. He's never been asked for one."

Sure, over the years there have been a few changes. For instance, when it began it had on top a dear little old lady with

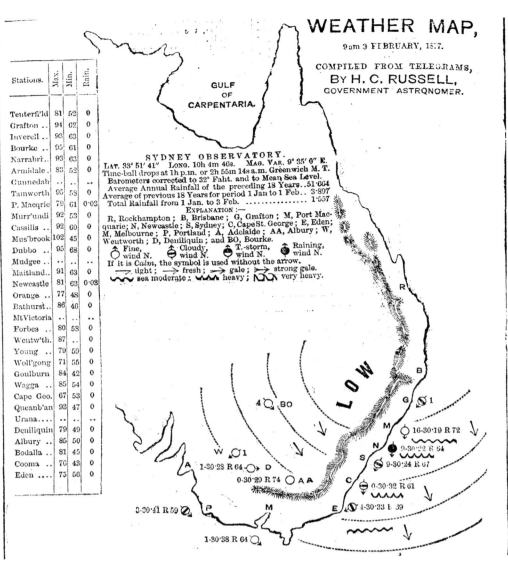

Stations.	Max.	Min.	Rain.
Tenterfi'ld	81	52	0
Grafton ..	94	62	0
Inverell ..	93	63	0
Bourke ..	95	61	0
Narrabri..	93	63	0
Armidale .	83	52	0
Gunnedah	..	..	..
Tamworth	95	58	0
P. Macqrie	79	61	0·03
Murr'undi	92	53	0
Cassilis ..	92	60	0
Mus'brook	102	45	0
Dubbo ..	95	68	0
Mudgee ..	..	..	..
Maitland..	91	63	0
Newcastle	81	63	0·03
Orange ..	77	48	0
Bathurst..	86	46	0
MtVictoria	..	..	..
Forbes ..	80	58	0
Wentw'th.	87	..	0
Young ..	79	59	0
Woll'gong	71	55	0
Goulburn	84	42	0
Wagga ..	85	54	0
Cape Geo.	67	53	0
Queanb'an	93	47	0
Urana....	..	..	..
Deniliquin	79	49	0
Albury ..	85	50	0
Bodalla ..	81	45	0
Cooma ..	76	43	0
Eden	75	58	0

knitting needles and a bonnet. Long story there but the short one is the other papers, much younger by far you know, used to make fun of the *Herald's* age.

So Granny, as some venerable readers still refer to the paper itself, just served it right back. The column's position hasn't always been the same, either (it's now on the back page of the front bit, if you know what I mean), but the values are the same, as witness my favourite item, which ran in 2001, penned by Column 8's other legendary editor, George Richards: "If Sydney's Olympic marathon blue line ever disappears, Annelise Pearce fears she will never see her parents again. 'Being country folk from Warialda, NSW, they find Sydney traffic bamboozles them easily, so they are quite happy to drive the very long route through and around many Sydney suburbs until they stumble across the blue line. They then follow it meticulously into the city to my Pyrmont home. They assure me it's a very scenic journey!'" True to the column's roots, it was pithy, connected the paper to the readership, was very Sydney/Australian and sort of made you feel all warm and fuzzy inside.

And so it goes on. These days it is my kids who wait their turn for the comics while my wife takes apart the real estate in Domain and I vainly try to do something that has appeared called sudoku, a mathematical puzzle that is driving me nuts. Some of the sections are entirely new, but the spirit of the paper — Sydney talking to itself in a still mostly sane way — goes on.

Top The first newspaper weather map for the *Herald* and Australia, 1877.

Above left The cricketer Don Bradman.

Above right The nuclear scientist Sir Marcus Oliphant.

The Herald: a taste of the first 10 years

BUSHRANGERS.

To the Editors of the Sydney Herald.

GENTLEMEN.—On the 25th of October last, at about 3 o'clock A. M., I was awakened by the smell of burning linen or cotton, and on examining the different rooms and finding nothing wrong, returned to bed, but soon discovered the smell was encreasing, upon getting up again I found the house full of smoke, and, entering the parlour, I saw a door that leads out of it to the street, standing half open, which I had previously shut and bolted, and, on searching about in the dark, came in contact with a man quite naked; being unarmed, and also undressed, I was unwilling to grapple with him till I returned to the bed-room for a gun. Whilst there, he got out, and I pursued him so close that he left his shoes behind him. It was then day-break, I stationed watchmen at every place, thus left him no alternative but to lay for the whole of that day in a wheat field. I then proceeded to examine the house, and found many things misplaced but nothing missing except one knife. That evening I housed the pigs and shut up the milking cows and calves. I went to the stock-yard again after night and found the cows turned out and the gate open, I then went into the calve's-house and there found the burglar, with a rope in his hand; and, with the assistance of my men, made him a prisoner. We took him into the house, and on searching him found the knife I had missed concealed in a long leather breast pocket which he had for that purpose; during that day I carefully examined the house and discovered a breach made in the chimney by the removal of some stones and mortar, and a descent made from thence into the parlour fire-place. Doubtless his chief object was to get possession of a double-barrel gun which is generally kept over the mantel-piece in wet weather. I gave him some food, tied him to one of my men and marched him to Kiama, six miles, by torch-light, and gave him up to the police. His name is Robert Robertson, a Convict servant belonging to Mr. Smith of this place; he broke out from the Liverpool Hospital, and I believe is now awaiting his trial in Sydney Jail for a previous robbery.

— January 28, 1833

Timothy Brown, with a hook nose, and a very agreeable capacity of mouth, was charged with the following gastromatic pilfering:—Mr. T. Shadforth, his master, had a very pleasant field of peas. Timothy, as any other honest fellow might, had a taste for peas; but to relish them with a proper gout, he, as well as most people, knew that ducks, when properly stuffed with sage and onions, were quite the thing, accordingly he turned out of his nest in the morning, an hour before his fellow servants, and proceeding to the stables, roused up the poultry. Having chased the ducks into a corner, their eternal quack, quack, quack, aroused the servants, who turning out, observed Master Timothy wringing the head from a fine fat, young and tender drake. He then caught up another, felt it, but it would not do. Another and another succeeded, until at last the finger and thumb of Timothy's right hand decided that the breast of a young duck was just the thing. Off went the head, and away went Timothy and the ducklings. Six months to an iron gang.

— January 28, 1833

Eliza Doyle was charged with being found at large in George-street, gaping with open jaws at the various shops that fell in her way, instead of residing like a good subject at the Wollombi, and scrubbing the pots and pans in a peaceable sort of way. The Bench sent her to her own district to await the judgment of the Court there.

— March 14, 1833

CHOP & COFFEE HOUSE,

OPPOSITE THE ROYAL HOTEL,

GEORGE-STREET, SYDNEY.

———ooo———

T. MALONE,

BEGS to inform his Friends and the Public of Sydney and its vicinity, that he has fitted up the house lately in the occupation of Mr. M'Namara, opposite the Sydney Theatre, in the above line of business; where he purposes having constantly on hand,—

Mock Turtle, Vermicilli, and all other descriptions of Soups. Cold Meats, Hams, Tongues, Sausages, Cold Fowls, &c.

Steaks and Chops at ten minutes notice.

Coffee and Tea night and morning.

Pickles, sauces, &c., on the most reasonable terms.

All descriptions of made dishes got up on the shortest possible notice.

T. M. also begs to inform heads of families that he goes out Cooking for Dinners, Balls, and Parties as usual, when no pains will be spared on his part to give satisfaction.

☞ Potted Fish and Stewed Oysters every night

———o———

Dinners provided.

— March 14, 1833

CHALLENGE ACCEPTED.

———ooo———

WHISKER?

THE UNDERSIGNED accepts Mr. CHARLES SMITH's Challenge, and will run his thorough-bred English imported Race Horse, WHISKER, against Mr. C. SMITH's Horse EMANCIPATION, on the terms proposed by him, in his advertisement, dated *Beef Steak Corner, April* 22, for the sum of £200. The Challenge to be accepted within ten days from this date, and the Match to come off the last week in May, 1833.

H. BAYLY.

— May 2, 1833

TUESDAY.—William Flannigan, assigned to the Editors of the *Sydney Herald*, was placed at the bar, charged with absenting himself during the whole of the previous day.

Captain Rossi—This is not the first, second, or third time you have been before me. You know I don't care for the Press, or any paragraph you may write about me. You printers' devils give me more trouble than any other assigned servants. Most of the street robberies are committed by convict printers. I tell you publicly *I don't care for the Press.* I sentence you to receive 25 lashes.

— May 16, 1833

CAUTION.

THIS is to certify, that I, JOHN UNCLES, arrived in this Colony in the year 1827, per *Albion* (1) and obtained my CERTIFICATE OF FREEDOM, on the 10th April, 1833. All Constables and others are hereby cautioned not to molest me after this Notice, as I will hold any person so doing strictly responsible. My Certificate having been accidentally lost, I take this public method of noticing it.

General remarks—5 feet 6 inches, dark brown hair, hazle eyes, dark complexion, the fore finger off the right hand.

JOHN UNCLES.

Bong Bong 5th July, 1834.

— September 15, 1834

We have been particularly requested to draw the attention of the Police, to the indecent practice of persons bathing at all hours of the day, near the Soldiers' Point, Darling Harbour. There are a number of respectable families, whose windows overlook this part of the Harbour, to whom such practices are extremely disgusting. No person with common decency would insult females by exhibiting such scenes, and it is hoped, that the police will do their duty in removing the nuisance.

— March 2, 1835

We have just learned, upon good authority, that His Honor Francis Forbes, Chief Justice of New South Wales, takes his departure from this Colony, by the first ship for England. The respectable emigrant Colonists will congratulate themselves, and *we* here congratulate them, on this most auspicious event; satisfied as we are that not one—no, *not one*—of that body of Colonists will ever desire to see His Honor's face here again.

— February 22, 1836

FLYING KITES.—Not Commercial "kites," but those which little ragged urchins fly about the town both night and day are an abominable nuisance. Those in the day frighten the horses passing through the streets; and at night, kites with lanthorns at their tails are certainly dangerous in such a combustible town as this. These practices are contrary to the Police Act, and ought to be put down by the Constables.

— February 22, 1836

THE ABORIGINES.

A Contemporary of Friday week, by order of the Government House *coterie*, revives the subject of the alleged killing of some aboriginal natives by the party under the direction of Major Mitchell, on his late expedition of discovery. In reply to our statement that the allegation of any natives having been shot in the progress of that expedition, was unsupported by any *proof*, our contemporary quotes from the *Colonist* a statement on the subject, with which, we confess, we were previously unacquainted. The writer says, from, as he alleges, "indubitable authority."—

"It appears that two days after Major Mitchell had left Mr. Stapylton with the depôt party, he fell in with the same tribe of natives of which the chief had been shot by his party during the former expedition; this, coupled with the fact of the tribe being at least two hundred miles from the country where he expected to find them, naturally led him to look upon their movements with suspicion, which was greatly strengthened by their subsequent behaviour,* *showing evidently that an attack was meditated on the party; so hostile were their actions, that a native attached to the expedition, who in every instance showed the most pacific disposition, acquainted Major Mitchell that his "jin" had heard them concerting a plan to seize upon him and massacre his party. Notwithstanding* his strong representation it was not until he had been *followed three days*, during which time every means were resorted to, to disperse or avoid them, that finding the number daily increasing by the accession of wandering natives, and his men *becoming intimidated by their savage yells and actions*, and worn out by the necessity of constantly watching, he was induced to fire upon them *at the moment they were advancing with bundles of spears for the purpose of attack.*"

— January 12, 1837

PARTIES desirous of becoming Subscribers to the *Sydney Herald*, who reside in the Interior, and others who are not known, must give a respectable reference, or their orders will not be attended to.

— July 3, 1837

DOMESTIC INTELLIGENCE.

GIVE US BREAD!

The population of the Colony received an increase of upwards of twelve hundred souls last week, exclusive of the military. Three hundred and nineteen emigrants arrived from Ireland in the ship *Adam Lodge*, and three hundred and seventy-nine from Scotland in the ship *John Barry*, making the number of emigrants six hundred and ninety-eight; which with five hundred and twenty-five convicts that arrived by the ships *Mangles* and *Heber*, make a total of twelve hundred and twenty-three souls. Flour and meat in consequence must advance greatly in price.

— July 17, 1837

SHIP NEWS.

It is said the Chilian brig *Colocolo* left the harbour the other night without giving any information to the authorities that she was about sailing. The circumstance of this vessel being able to slip out in the night without any one being aware of it, reminds us of the very insecure state of the harbour. In the present disturbed state of Europe, nothing is more likely to take place than a war between some of the powers, and of course if there is a war England must be in it. The Russians, French, Americans, and Dutch have all visited this port and are well acquainted with the harbour, and in the event of a war we should certainly be favored with a visit by privateers, or perhaps a frigate, which would lay us under contribution to a pretty large amount. For the last five or six years we have been constantly hearing about building forts for the protection of our harbour, but at present nothing whatever has been done.

— July 20, 1837

A CONSEQUENCE.—"Now do you mean to say that you are an honest man?" asked a prisoner of a witness in the Supreme Court on Saturday. "If I was an honest man should I be in this Colony," was the rather puzzling reply of the witness.

— August 7, 1837

SLY GROG SHOPS.—The more we reflect on this subject the more we are convinced that it is the imperative duty of the legislature to take some more decided steps to put an end to the grog selling, but more particularly to the practice of carrying rum round in a cart, and actually seducing servants from their work. A few days ago, a man was brought before Messrs. Antill, Macarthur, and Thompson, sitting in Petty Sessions at Cawdor, charged with this offence. It appeared that the defendant was proceeding up the country with three drays; that he stopped on the farm of a gentleman in the neighbourhood on a Monday night, and sold some rum, and the consequence was that the next morning seven of the men were in a beastly state of intoxication, and four of them, fearing they would be punished, while under the effects of drink, took to the bush. The case being clearly proved the bench convicted the grog seller, and sentenced him to pay a fine of £30 for selling without a license, and £5 for selling to convicts. Now this is a case to which we particularly call the attention of the Chief Justice. His Honor lately said that masters must take decisive steps to put an end to the scenes of disorder that occur in the interior. Here is a farm with every thing going on quietly; the master sees that all his men are orderly and respectful when they leave off work, he retires to his cottage and upon getting up the next morning finds that the farm is one scene of dissipation, that seven of his men are in a beastly state of intoxication, and that four of them have taken to the bush; and as men cannot subsist in the bush without plunder, the next time we shall hear of them will most probably be when they are arraigned before the Supreme Court for some serious offence. We would respectfully ask His Honor what steps could have been taken by the master to prevent this scene from occurring.

— February 26, 1838

SEWERS.—We beg particularly to call the attention of the Governor to the necessity of making arrangements for laying down proper drains and sewers throughout the town. At present whenever the town is visited by such a shower as fell on Tuesday afternoon, the damage to property for want of drains and sewers is immense; besides which it is necessary for the health of the town that the streets should be properly drained.

— March 1, 1838

COUNTRY TOWNS.—The inhabitants of the towns of Parramatta, Windsor, Maitland, Bathurst, and Melbourne are reminded that after the 10th of August they will be liable to a penalty if the eaves of their houses are not provided with gutters, or otherwise so constructed as to prevent rain from dropping from the eaves thereof upon any part of the footways of any street or public place. The fine for this offence is fixed by the Country Towns' Police Act at five shillings for every day they may so remain unprovided

— July 29, 1838

The fact is, that the present system of taxation must be pulled down. Let us have Indian labourers upon every estate—do away with the Convict system—and the government of the Colony will be at the feet of the settlers. European labourers will make up the population. Indian labour will produce wealth; and every small emigrant settler, if industrious, can, in two years, pay for the introduction of three or four Coolies, to cultivate his farm. Let, then, the settlers—great and small—combine to achieve purposes so universally beneficial; and in a very few years, they may defy the Downing-street plunderers.

— October 15, 1839

The weed has other good qualities besides curing dogs of the mange: it cures men of diseases much more disagreeable—such as the propensity to grumble. The habit of smoking has greatly reduced the number of persons like yourself, querulous bipeds, who are miserable when they see others contented; and who would be perfectly happy were every one reduced to the same state as themselves. And now, having analysed all your arguments, and found them equally worthless, I bid you farewell with a piece of advice, which I hope you will follow for the future:—never again write on a subject of which you know nothing.—I remain, Sir, your obedient servant,

A SMOKER.

— January 26, 1841

Mightier than the sword

A *Herald* editorial of September 2, 1865, began: "People are often astonished out of measure if their letters to the *Herald* do not appear in hot haste, much more if they do not appear at all. Whenever any subject arises exciting public attention, we are inundated with correspondence."

Letters were scattered throughout the paper under the headline "Original correspondence". They canvassed questions such as the treatment of Aborigines, horse stealing, the notion that the bishop was looking after the colony's souls while the health of colonial bodies was being overlooked, and how bushranging decreased after armed escorts joined the mails. By 1930 they had earned their own column. Some topics are seasonal — daylight saving, the first cicadas of summer. Some prolific writers have earned obituaries. John Minchin, who researched letters debates at the State Library before adding to them, was described in a eulogy in 1993 as "a pillar of the church and a column of the *Herald*".

The growth of the fax, from the late 1980s, and then email, has made the letters page more topical. The letters editor receives about 500 emails a day — 95 per cent of the daily mail — about 20 faxes, and a similar number of stamped letters.

LETTERS TO EDITOR

AFFECTING ACCOUNT OF A FACTORY WOMAN.

To the Editor of the Sydney Herald.

Sir,—Considering your paper the best to lay our grievances before the public, I implore you to allow me a corner as an appeal to your sympathy, and urge you to advocate our cause. I trust in you as the moral reformer of the Colonial press, and I hope you will be able to suggest a remedy, while I trace the evil. As your paper is open to advocate the "rights of the people" you will not surely close it to the wrongs of the Factory women.

It is four years ago since I came here—the long voyage—leaving my friends which had brought me to reflection; I thought on the misery and disgrace I had brought on my friends with remorse, and wished, as I had left them heartbroken, to send them the comfortable news of my reformation. Never shall I forget my entering the Factory, or my joy at leaving it. I was assigned to Mr. ——, of Pitt-street; my spirit was broken, and I went, with subdued feelings, to my place—I had been idle at home, I was willing to work—I had neglected religion, and I now wished to attend to it—I wished for a guide, and expected one in my mistress: for, in my simplicity, I believed we were only to be placed with those who felt an interest in our reformation. Alas! how different I have found it. My mistress was a low woman, used bad language, quarrelled with her husband, and, the third night I was there, I had to assist a government man in carrying her to bed. In the morning she was for treating me, and said, "D——n it, Bet, take a glass; we all take a drop sometimes." I had promised, on my knees, before I left home, never to touch wine or spirits. My mother, my poor heart-broken mother, said, "Only promise me this, and I may see some comfort yet." Could I refuse this request? No! Could I break it? No! My vow was made on the deck of the *Melrose;* and my mother said, "Every day I will ask and implore God to bless and strengthen you, that you may keep this promise holy." Afterwards, when I have been tempted, the thought that my mother was perhaps then praying for me, kept me resolute and determined. Well, in this place I lived ten months, and here I daily witnessed little else than scenes of debauchery and drunkenness. My mistress had in her service two orphan emigrants—the poor girls may curse the day they ever saw her. One of them used to cry very much; but in time she sunk to a level with her leader. At last some respectable neighbours interfered (but how slow were they to do this); the character of the house was brought to the notice of the magistrates, and I was returned to the Factory. One of these poor girls died of disease about eighteen monts after, and the other now keeps a den of iniquity in —— Street.

Next for my second place:—I had scarcely entered the house ere I felt my mistress was respectable. The quiet order which prevailed, the sight of well dressed children, made me rejoice, and for a few days I enjoyed perfect peace. My mistress spoke to me kindly, cautioned me, and at night gave me a book and begged me to attend to my prayers. How soon I loved this woman;—how gladly I executed her orders; when she was sick I nursed her, and when she reposed confidence in me, oh! how much I wished my mother could see me respected and trusted But I was too happy here; a trial was in store for me. My master was blessed with an angelic wife, and yet he tried * * * How much I endured at last to avoid the pit I saw dug for me! But I was resolute: I could not tell my mistress; I did not dare to plant for ever a thorn in her bosom, so I became insolent, refused to obey orders, a constable was sent for, and then came the trial: my mistress said, "Only say you are sorry, and I will forgive you:" I said "I am glad I have done it; I wish to go to the factory." I felt I was leaving a mother, and yet I did not shed a tear until I had been three days in the Factory. My sentence being over, I was again sent to Sydney. My master had been at work here. My new mistress told me she had just lost her daughter (a falsehood) and was very kind to me; bought me new gowns, took me out with her shopping, made me take tea with her on Sundays, and pressed me to take one glass; my promise to my mother saved me. I had never been so kindly treated; the old lady put rings in my ears, said I was very pretty, but was sorry she must leave me, and bade me sit up for her: she then locked the door and left me; I threw myself on the couch and slept; I dreamt my mother begged me to go to the Factory; my old mistress tried to save me; yet I felt I should fall, and with horror I awoke. Scarcely a second after this, out of my mistress' room came my old master; I rushed to the door; I found I was alone with one who came for the worst of purposes: this was a fearful trial; but the grace of God enabled me to see my danger, and I saw I must dissemble to save myself: yet in that night I thought more of my mistress than of the sin. Ere day dawned he left me, and as I had an hour alone, the result was that I went out, gave myself up to the constable, and was returned to the Factory as a bolter.

Your obedient servant,

A FACTORY WOMAN.

[We are promised the continuation of this which is most respectably vouched for.—Ed.]

— February 19, 1841

The relationship between settlers and Aboriginal people sparked heated debate. A *Herald* editorial in 1842 called for the responsible squatters to "meet with the punishment due to the perpetrators of so diabolical an act". It drew the following response on December 7, 1842:

ORIGINAL CORRESPONDENCE.

"SOMETHING THAT MUST BE ENQUIRED INTO."

To the Editors of the Sydney Morning Herald.

Gentlemen,—Assured of your candour and courtesy, I beg leave to make a few observations upon your article of the 5th instant, bearing the title I have quoted above.

I perfectly agree with you that a statement of the destruction of fifty or sixty aborigines by poison should receive the attention of Government, and lead to an inquiry. Such acts are against the laws; they destroy the security of society. The man who murders a score of aborigines to day, is prepared by the dreadful deed to slay his countrymen to-morrow. Moreover, such deeds of blood bring guilt and retribution upon the colony. History illustrates the testimony of God, that he will punish the nations when he makes an inquisition for blood. Murder by poison is also so dastardly—murder at a feast by poisoning the emblems of hospitality and friendship is so treacherous—that the English spirit abhors and execrates it. The hand of murder under such circumstances is not red but black, and putrid with human gore.

I agree with you, that however awful the result, inquiry should be made. But when the station has been ascertained, when the culprits are pointed out with all the force of moral demonstration, where is your legal proof? The evidence of the surviving blacks cannot be taken; and, unless you obtain the evidence of an approver, or some marvellous exactitude of circumstantial evidence through the medium of European testimony, you fail.

You are aware that by the refusal of the Home Government to sanction the Bill for giving validity to the testimony of the aborigines, they are in a great degree placed beyond the pale of the law. And henceforth colonial heroes are less likely to be legally disquieted for having "quieted the blacks."

I, therefore, beg in conclusion to deprecate your calls upon the innocent squatters to absolve themselves by a denial, and upon Mr. Schmidt to substantiate the statement against the guilty party.

Australia adopted compulsory military training in 1911. Boys aged 12 and 13 had to train as cadets before graduating at 18 into the adult forces and those who failed to register were fined or jailed. A conscript's mother wrote on September 4, 1911:

TO THE EDITOR OF THE HERALD.

Sir,—I beg you will allow me space in your valuable paper to thank "Medicus" for his or her splendid letter in your issue of Saturday, August 19. It just expresses everything I and many other mothers would like to say. I am not at all clever at expressing my opinion or at writing letters, but "Medicus" has put it just right.

It is high time mothers had something to say on this subject of their boys being drilled and rushed about in back streets. My boy got a severe cold at the beginning of the training, drilling in a drizzling fog in a dirty back lane, but that of course is nothing. He is only a common boy. I never dreamed my boy would pass the doctor, as he has been suffering from a nervous disease for nearly two years, and has to take medicine three times a day, and I have to take him to the doctor every now and again, to see how he is going on. He is a tall lad, weedy and overgrown, with no stamina whatever. I have watched over him and tended him, and many a time I have despaired of his life; and now, by sheer care and watchfulness, he has reached 15 years of age, and he has to turn out to this. To learn to fight for what? We have nothing to fight for in the country. What working man has? We get our daily bread, if we have the ability to work for it. If something happens to lay us up, we go to the wall. We have to let the boy go to drill, or be fined, and we have no money to pay fines. I think it is high time something was done, as there are hundreds of boys like mine. Another thing, what about evening classes? My boy has had to give his up. Are these to go because the boys are to be taught to kill their fellow-men?

My boy's service book has a sentence in it at the end—"Australia gives us freedom." I don't think compulsory drill comes under the heading of freedom. I am, etc,

CONSCRIPT'S MOTHER.

The Dunbar, sailing from Plymouth, sank off South Head in 1857. A rescuer's son wrote on August 8, 1924:

WRECK OF THE "DUNBAR."

TO THE EDITOR OF THE HERALD.

Sir,—My father, Captain George Alfred Hyde, actually discovered the wreck when he went down Jacob's Ladder at 7 a.m. on August 21, 1857. He then saw the smashed up remains of the "Dunbar," also the more or less mangled remains of her 119 victims: he himself filled seven coffins with arms and legs and other fragments of poor humanity. He removed these in his boat to his boatshed on Gibson's Beach, in Watson's Bay, where they remained until the funeral. The sole survivor of the wreck, Johnson, was cast up by the sea on a ledge of rock, from which he was rescued in the following manner:—The top mast was taken from the Signal Station, a rope passed through the block on it; my father climbed out on the mast to lower down Antonio Woolier, a young lightweight man, who descended on a bow-line, and being swung in on the ledge, made Johnson fast to the rope. He was then hauled up, my father taking great care to prevent him striking against the rocks. Meanwhile the excited crowd on top, anxiously peering down, nearly pushed my father and other rescuers over. They were only kept back by vigorous truncheon work of the police present. Subsequently, my father was presented with a gold watch in recognition of his services, and Woolier received a handsome cash collection. Afterwards, the latter became the licensee of the "Dunbar Hotel," Rennie-street, Paddington.

I am, etc.,

A. MACARTNEY HYDE.

25 York-street, Aug. 7.

Australians rushed in 1954 to spruce up the nation for the royal tour, the first by a reigning monarch. On January 15, 1954, one concerned citizen wrote:

Queen's Journey To Newcastle

Sir,—I work in the city and have to travel each day over the route which the train, taking our Queen to Newcastle, will travel.

I am appalled at the thought of her Majesty seeing the untidy backyards, station yards, and refuse dumps, not to mention the drab railway stations, almost all the way to Epping. It is easy to imagine that those in charge of plans for the tour do not travel much along that line.

Although I would certainly like to be one of the crowd waving as the Queen goes by, I am ashamed to think of her Majesty being subjected to such a repulsive sight, when there is the beautiful Pacific Highway as an alternative route. There can be seen the fronts of dwellings and shops, and there, too, thousands of people could catch a better glimpse of the Queen.

(Miss) D. WEDDERSPOON.
Epping.

Right Australia's first minister for immigration, Arthur Calwell, set off after World War II to speed up the flow of "desirable" migrants – but he suspected claims of a shortage of ships was a ploy by Britain to stop the outflow of its citizens. A comment from Harry Eyre Jr.

Opposite page, top and centre right
Emile Mercier liked to take the layperson's view of events. These three cartoons, featured in the afternoon *Sun* in the early 1960s, look at new measures for beer and spirits, the boom in poker machines and the debate over a design for the Opera House.

Opposite page, centre left and bottom
George Molnar was a fine draftsman with a sharp eye. Here he looks at the alienation of Sydney's Opera House designer, Joern Utzon, the just-can't-win world of the newspaper editor, and the one-upmanship of modern living.

Below Alan Moir has been the *Herald's* editorial page cartoonist since 1984. Here he looks at the views of the Prime Minister, John Howard, on Aboriginal policy.

News Item: Mr. Calwell, the Minister for Immigration, has gone to London to seek ships in which to bring immigrants to Australia.

Calwell: "Is this the face to launch a thousand ships?"

RECONCILIATION..

Daily newspaper cartoonists are a select band: generally there are only one or two to a masthead, and when pens become swords their swipe is the most feared.

At times of national outcry over controversial political measures — from conscription to detention — one drawing from a cartoonist can be more devastating than a street march by thousands. On the other hand, when the nation is in shock or grieving, as with the Port Arthur massacre or the Bali bombing, they can offer solace with a single, affecting image.

There is no quicker way to learn about the mood of other times than by flicking through the cartoons on the editorial pages of old bound volumes. The *Herald* was a late adopter when it came to in-house cartoons, but in October 1944 Harry Giles Eyre, who signed himself Eyre Jr, started the ball rolling, and kept it going until his death 28 years later. Today there is some blurring of roles with other forms of illustration. But it is only the editorial page cartoonists who have freedom to roam across the issues of the day and to interpret them as they choose. Editors may reject their work but rarely do because they value the special bond cartoonists have with the readers.

In this unique role there are times when their insight can sway public opinion. Perhaps their biggest gift, though, is their ability to transform an errant or arrogant politician from rooster to feather duster with a few dozen deft strokes.

For a cartoonist there can be a special last laugh: more often than most people would guess, the ego of their victims overrides any hurt and they ask for the original work to hang on their living room walls.

"I asked for a short port snort, but this snort is too short a short port snort, sport!"

"This one'll sound a note of patriotism in your policy – when you hit the jackpot it plays 'Advance Australia Fair'!"

MOLNAR
80. 10. 73

*As I was going up the stair
I met a man who wasn't there.*

*"What we should worry about is not so much the futuristic design as the fear
of it being outmoded by the time they get it built!"*

*"Two gentlemen to see you. One because you didn't give a fair criticism of the
Government and the other because you did."*

"No, darling. Only common people eat in the kitchen. People like us cook in the dining-room."

"I need some more Valium...
I've just discovered my
son's on pot."

"I need some more pot...
I've just discovered my
mum's on Valium."

Top row Valium versus marijuana: Larry Pickering's double-take on society under pressure.

Right Emeric saw the pressure to boycott the 1980 Moscow Olympic Games in protest against the Russian invasion of Afghanistan as politics turning the Olympic rings into shackles. Australia sent a depleted team.

Bottom row Dogs and cockroaches talk in the wonderful world of Cathy Wilcox. These are all "pocket" cartoons, usually appearing as Wilcox's take on a news story of the day.

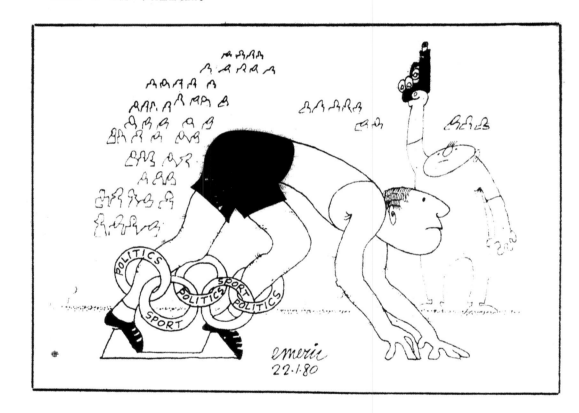

"...and you, the jury, must decide in your own minds if these publications stimulate feelings of an erotic nature."

Above Moves to ban raunchy publications brought out irreverence in Pickering. Here he depicts the wicked effect such works could have on common folk.

Left Rugby league became a television drawcard in the 1960s: *The Sun's* Steve wasn't far off the mark in predicting the rise of players hamming it up for the camera.

"It's been on ever since there was talk of televising Rugby League!"

Above Caught between warring factions: Wilcox on children coming home after a contact visit.

Above right The Woomera factor and the new Australian welcome from Wilcox.

Right and below right Alan Moir takes aim at Australia's detention policy, and presents an Aboriginal view on the arrival of the Tall Ships for the bicentenary.

HAPPY ANNIVERSARY

AUSTRALIA FAIR

Moir

REPUBLIC...

SYDNEY TRANSPORT PLAN

Moir

YES NO MAYBE WHY LATER DUNNO TRY AGAIN NOT EVER PRAPS NOT NEVER

Moir

Top left, centre and above More commentary from Moir: highlighting the Howard Government's treatment of asylum seekers; the morass of the republic debate; and a jibe at the former NSW premier, Bob Carr, and Sydney's transport troubles.

Bottom left Michael Leunig visits the edge of reality.

THE DAILY HORN
MAJOR CRACKS APPEARING IN EVERYTHING

Leunig

CHAPTER NINE

War and Peacekeeping

The world changes

BY PAUL MCGEOUGH

The 1990–91 Gulf crisis was the war in which governments and military thought they had the media figured. Reporters, they believed, had enjoyed a free rein in Vietnam and had lost that war for the United States and Australia. But the Washington spin — much of which has since been revealed as lies and manipulation — had actually allowed the US to persevere with its Indo-China adventure for 10 long and costly years before reporting from the war zone had chipped away sufficiently at public support to force a US withdrawal. To avoid a repeat during the Gulf crisis, the Americans turned to the British experience in the 1982 Falklands War. They had experimented in the invasions of Grenada (1983) and Panama (1989), but, according to commentator Phillip Knightley, their finessed execution of the grand design in the Gulf would go down in the history of journalism as the classic example of how to manage the media in wartime.

The bleak and isolated setting of the Falklands meant that London had absolute control over media access, so its Ministry of Defence was able to decree that only 17 carefully vetted British reporters would see action. The crippling ground rules included this gem: "Help in leading and steadying public opinion in times of national stress or crisis." The rest of the world's media, including the *Herald's* Peter Smark, were obliged to make what they could of MoD briefings in London, at which official spokesmen regularly came to the lectern to tell lies — of omission and commission.

In the Gulf crisis, the Americans and their allies ran the same "drip-feed" briefings in their respective capital cities and in Riyadh. The information released had been so expertly massaged that it could not be sensibly evaluated. They adopted a language that came from a new PR agenda designed to make war more palatable, a buzz-word video game of surgical strikes told in a dehumanising and high-tech script: people were "soft targets", civilian death and damage was "collateral damage" and mass

Above Soldiers from the 4th Battalion, Royal Australian Regiment (RAR) – posted for duty in Iraq – train during a brown out "at an undisclosed location in the Middle East", according to this photograph supplied by the Department of Defence in early 2003.

Previous pages Australian clearance diver Gavin "Rocket" Stevens on protection duty at the port of Umm Qsar, Iraq, in 2003. Divers had to clear mines from Umm Qsar and Az Zubayr and Al Faw peninsula. (Photo: Kate Geraghty)

bombing was merely "laying down a carpet". The only breach came when a senior US officer described the Americans' senseless mass bombing of the retreating Iraqi army at Mutla Ridge as a "turkey shoot". More importantly, there were none of the enemy "body counts" that became a daily scorecard by which some reporters had measured progress in earlier conflicts.

Journalists whose critique clashed with the view from Washington were warned that their Saudi visas could be cancelled; and although the Americans took pooled media teams into combat, they made it almost impossible for them to file ahead of their capital city colleagues, whose accounts of scripted official briefings shaped so much of the coverage. The Americans also set out to thwart the few "unilateral" reporters who chose to wander away from the Riyadh briefings to see what they might find in the

Left Sailors from HMAS Darwin at Sydney's Garden Island before their second tour of duty enforcing UN sanctions in the Persian Gulf in 1991. (Photo: Steven Siewert)

Below Australian Special Air Service (SAS) forces, a key part of Australia's commitment to the war on terrorism in Afghanistan, on patrol near Bagram in September 2002. (Photo: Simon O'Dwyer)

desert. In the race between "unilaterals" and "pool" reporters to reach Kuwait City on liberation day, the "unilaterals" — including the *Herald* — won. I was hitchhiking with an Egyptian general, who had volunteered to take me to the front line to see the fighting. Learning from the BBC World Service as the jeep headed north into Iraq that Saddam had surrendered, the excitable general wrenched the wheel to head east across the desert, blurting out: "Lunch in Kuwait city?"

But the media management policy worked. Just weeks after the end of combat, the Pentagon's chief public affairs spokesman, Barry Zorthian, poked reporters and editors in the eye with a summation to the National Press Club in Washington: "The Gulf War is over and the press lost."

We expect lies from the world's Hitlers and Saddams. But in his book *The First Casualty*, Knightley lists some of the great

Above Australian soldiers from the 2nd Battalion, RAR, land on Red Beach near Honiara, the capital of the Solomon Islands, as Operation Helpim Frens gets under way on July 24, 2003. (Photo: Kate Geraghty)

Right On June 8, 1965, members of the 1st Battalion, RAR, go ashore at Vung Tau, spearheading the Australian ground troop commitment to the Vietnam conflict. (Photo: Stuart MacGladrie)

Far right Australian armed forces take the salute in front of Sydney Town Hall during a welcome home march on June 18, 2003, at the end of their tour of duty in Iraq. (Photo: Peter Morris)

wartime lies by democratic governments: the number of ships sunk at Pearl Harbour; Britain's constant inflation of the number of German planes downed in the Battle of Britain and the truth of its attacks on non-military targets in Germany; Washington's suppression for six months of the Japanese kamikaze attacks in World War II and its claim that the huge bang in the New Mexico desert on July 16, 1945, was an "ammunition dump explosion" rather than the first atomic bomb test.

Fast forward to the Gulf crisis. The propaganda counterpoint to America's promotion of its clinically precise strikes on Iraqi military targets was the "Kuwaiti babies" story in which "savage" Iraqi soldiers had ripped premature babies from their incubators so that the machines could be looted. A sobbing 15-year-old Kuwaiti girl was brought before the human rights caucus of the US Congress to tell the story for the world's TV cameras. The war was over in 100 hours and another two years would elapse before it was revealed that her story was a fabrication — the girl was the daughter of the Kuwaiti ambassador to the US and had been coached by Hill and Knowlton, the global spin machine hired by the Kuwaiti government. By then it didn't matter; the story had served its purpose. Then president George H. Bush used it six times in his pre-war speeches, and in the US Senate, which voted to go to war by a majority of only

five, this "atrocity" was referred to by seven senators.

There were other untruths. The US constantly emphasised its use of "smart" bombs, but later it was revealed that they accounted for just 7 per cent of the munitions used, and of the 88,500 tonnes of bombs dropped, more than 70 per cent had missed their target. We were told of a 98 per cent "launch success rate" for 200-plus Tomahawk missiles — but this was revealed to mean only that they had actually left their launchers and had nothing to do with target accuracy. The US commander general Norman Schwarzkopf claimed 100 per cent success for the gee-whiz Patriot interceptor

for incoming Iraqi Scud missiles. But an Israeli study showed that the Patriot had intercepted just one of 42 Scuds launched by Iraq — and there was some doubt about that single success.

History may well record the lies and manipulation that preceded the US-led invasion of Iraq in 2003 as the greatest propaganda success ever. In a world still dazed by the senseless September 11 strikes on New York and Washington in 2001, the second Bush Administration argued that Iraq must be invaded because it had weapons of mass destruction — it didn't — and because of Saddam Hussein's links to the terrorist behind September 11, Osama bin

Laden — he had none. Without a casus belli, Washington then fell back on the genuinely appalling denial of Iraqi human rights, on which it had refused to act for decades. But as the reshaping of Iraq as a democratic beachhead in the Middle East entered its third year, the country remained a mess. A badly managed invasion had left it in the grip of an entrenched and vicious insurgency at the same time as religious and ethnic leaders squabbled among themselves without being able to form a government.

Washington was so desperate to see off Saddam Hussein that it had no regard for the legitimacy of its case for war, and it gave no thought to the aftermath. But in

Above Men of the 30th Battalion ready to leave Hay, south-western NSW, for World War I. Hay was one of Australia's most patriotic towns. About 4000 people lived in the district and about 600 men were eligible to fight. At least 642 enlisted, and 134 died.

the lead-up, before the scales were knocked from some media eyes, its manipulation of the media was masterful. Late in 2004 the "you just don't get it" put-down for those who dared to criticise the Iraq War and the so-called "war on terror" was evident in this chilling account by a writer for *The New York Times Magazine,* who had interviewed a senior White House adviser: "The aide said that guys like me [i.e. reporters and commentators] were 'in what we call the reality-based community', which he defined as people who 'believe that solutions emerge

from your judicious study of discernible reality'. I nodded and murmured something about enlightenment principles and empiricism. He cut me off. 'That's not the way the world really works any more,' he continued. 'We're an empire now, and when we act, we create our own reality. And while you're studying that reality — judiciously, as you will — we'll act again, creating other new realities, which you can study too, and that's how things will sort out. We're history's actors … and you, all of you, will be left to just study what we do.'"

We will never be perfect in reporting crises and conflict. But all this is a powerful case for the *Herald's* somewhat diminished network of on-staff foreign correspondents — it still shares bureaus with *The Age* in Washington, New York, London, Tokyo, Beijing, Jakarta, Bangkok and Jerusalem; and for its traditional preparedness to spend big to have reporters and photographers on the ground in times of war and disaster. The starting points for newspaper credibility have to be that all governments are economical and flexible with the truth, and that wire

service reports by the press in big-power countries cannot be relied on to see things with Australian eyes — particularly given the preparedness of successive Australian governments to give troops and legitimacy to the likes of the 2003 invasion of Iraq. The closer reporters are to the action and the more sceptical they are about the policies, speeches and actions of national and world leaders, the better their chance of uncovering at least a version of the truth for readers.

W. J. Lambie was the *Herald's* first war correspondent. He was blooded in a silly military outing in the mid-1880s amid grief in the colony of NSW over the death of Britain's General Charles Gordon at Khartoum, in Egyptian-controlled Sudan. The expedition, sparked by a letter published in the *Herald* calling on New South Welshmen to defend the empire in Sudan, comprised more than 700 men and 200 horses. They set off from Circular Quay in great excitement, but they were not really needed and saw little fighting. A handful were wounded, including the hapless Lambie, who was ambushed by rebels as he and Melvin, a colleague, rode to a telegraph station to file to Sydney. Breathlessly, he reported: "Turning in my saddle to see how things were going, I saw an Arab on a yellow camel, pushing forward to intercept Mr Melvin. This fellow had to be stopped if possible, for although our time might be pretty close, it had not come to the pinch when a man drops his mate and fights for his own life. I felt a sharp, piercing blow on my right leg below the knee. A red hole and a stinging pain showed what was the matter." Lambie recovered, but 14 years later his luck ran out during an ambush by Boer fighters as he reported on the Boer War for *The Age* — he was shot through the head and in the heart.

If Lambie wrote in the vein of the *Boy's Own Annual*, the next *Herald* war correspondent, A. B. (Banjo) Paterson, began a tradition upheld by nearly all who have followed him to history's battlefields.

Top This picture ran in November 4, 1899, with the simple caption: "Saying goodbye". It was among two pages of pictures commemorating the departure to the Boer War of NSW troops the previous Saturday.

Above A. B. (Banjo) Paterson covered the Boer War for *The Sydney Morning Herald*. He filed news stories and the occasional poem, drew battle scenes and took photographs.

Above Water carriers take a break from carting water to the front lines at Gallipoli during the heat of the summer months. (Photo: Phillip Schuler)

His despatches from the Boer War proved the enduring need to have independent witnesses to wars in which politicians are happier to send armies of young men and women than they are to have all aspects of the conflict dissected at home. Courageously, the newspaper promised readers that the poet's letters would be the stuff of history. And Paterson proved a more thoughtful correspondent than Lambie; filing, as the Fairfax historian Gavin Souter describes in *Company of Heralds*, "an uneasy

blend of delight in the sport of warfare, a certain amount of reluctant understanding of the Boer's cause, and dismay at the suffering inflicted upon the civilian population".

Every war has its intensely human element among the troops and civilian populations that get caught up in it. Their stories become a more meaningful account of what actually happens out there than are the official briefers' euphemistic "collateral damage" reports. Like this from Paterson, they need to be told: "We burnt a house belonging to the Boer commandant as a means of inducing him to come in and lay down his arms. The women were given 15 minutes to get their effects out of the house; they lost their heads, cried pitifully, and brought out all sorts of useless things — vases and photographs and so on — instead of bedding and eatables. Then the house was burnt and the army moved on.

Far left "Freighted with high hopes and stern resolves" was the headline on this picture showing the ferry Kulgoa loaded to the gunwales with NSW members of the Australian Expeditionary Force (AEF) on August 18, 1914. They were en route from Fort Macquarie (where the Sydney Opera House now stands) to troopships at Cockatoo Island. These formed part of the first Australian convoy heading for training camps in Egypt before the launch of the Gallipoli campaign.

Left Australian troops in trenches in the shadow of the Pyramids at Mena near Cairo during desert training in early 1915, ahead of the Gallipoli landings. (Photo: Phillip Schuler)

No doubt it is an advisable step — in fact, I remember writing from Bloemfontein and light-heartedly urging that it ought to be done — but when you see it done it is a different matter. When you really see women and children turned, homeless and crying, out on the open veldt — well, you want to be home and done with the war."

Some things have changed in war reporting — some have not. Lambie and Paterson went to war on horseback, in the same way as I had to for a time when covering the conflict in Afghanistan in the wake of September 11. However, there was to be none of this bareback freelancing in World War I. As a prequel to today's slavish systems of "accreditation" and "embedding", the Australian government declared that a single correspondent would represent all Australian papers. The membership of the Australian Journalists' Association selected C. E. W. Bean of *The Sydney Morning*

Herald. In uniform and with the rank of captain, he sailed for Turkey with the Australian Imperial Forces. At Gallipoli, he witnessed at close quarters the making of the Anzac legend; and, subsequently, as Australia's official war historian, he was seen as keeper of the Anzac flame. Les Carlyon, journalist and author of the best-selling *Gallipoli*, presents Bean as a man of humility and decency who approached his task with a quaint sense of duty, settling into a foxhole "with his clackety Corona typewriter, his brass telescope, his box of paints and his piles of blank diaries" to report a war as no other correspondent has done before or since.

Unfortunately for Bean, he was scooped in his own paper on the first reports from Gallipoli. As a *Herald* correspondent in the streets of Manhattan on September 11, I was able to dictate copy to Sydney on a mobile phone line kept open all night >292

Censorship

Top How the proprietors announced the 1944 censorship story to the public.

Above A Commonwealth policeman reads a banned copy of *The Sydney Morning Herald* while preventing other copies from reaching the streets at the height of the Sydney newspaper censorship crisis of April 1944.

The *Herald* locked horns with the government over censorship in World War I when news was vetted twice — once before it left Britain and again when it reached Australia. In World War II the issue became a bare-fisted brawl. Conflict began over the rationing of newsprint and then spread. Although proprietors accepted the "security" element of the censorship equation, they baulked at the duty being foisted on them to maintain "morale". They took to the ramparts against a directive by the Curtin Labor government that reports on industrial disputes must be vetted by the censor. In the face of the media outcry, the directive was withdrawn. Warwick Fairfax put a publishers' argument that is still good today. "Public morale in a democratic country like Australia derives its very strength from the belief that, broadly speaking, the public is being given full opportunity to acquaint itself with the truth and to judge accordingly. The public does not expect to know exactly how many battleships

or divisions or aircraft are here or there. But they are particularly resentful of complacency or over-optimism; and they do expect to be told when, in the view of observers, the position here or there is grave, just as they are told when it looks bright."

In 1944, when the censors blocked reports on the censorship row itself, Fairfax's R. A. G. (Rags) Henderson issued a statement setting out the more absurd censors' cuts, which *The Daily Telegraph* reported, leaving blank spaces for what the censor had excised. All hell broke loose — Commonwealth police raided the *Telegraph*, later ordering that the presses be halted, and impounded copies of the April 16, 1944, edition of *The Sunday Telegraph*. A publishers' council of war decided to fight. To test the law, the next editions of the *Herald* and *Telegraph* both ran material they had been ordered to cut. At the height of the drama, policemen were photographed sitting on bundles of the *Herald* that had been loaded on to trucks,

checking that there had been no breach of the law; over at the *Telegraph*, a policeman pulled a pistol on a truck driver as he ordered him not to leave the loading dock.

The publishers' final victory came not in a formal decision by the High Court but from a conference suggested by Chief Justice Sir John Latham. The outcome was a new code which, in part, read: "Censorship shall not be imposed merely for the maintenance of morale or the prevention of despondency or alarm. Censorship shall not prevent the reporting of industrial disputes or stoppages. Criticism and complaints, however strongly expressed, shall not be a ground for censorship. Defence security shall be the governing principle for every application of censorship."

About 2am on November 7, 1980, two hastily dressed court officials arrived at the *Herald* offices saying they had a High Court injunction ordering the *Herald* not to publish details from classified government documents on Australian foreign policy. Peter Bowers, the *Herald's* ranking executive on duty, demanded identification. The officials patted themselves down and could produce only a Grace Brothers charge card. Bowers, a man of plain words, was flabbergasted, saying they would have to do better than that to halt the presses.

A *Herald* lawyer arrived soon after and personally identified the officers. The presses were stopped, the offending story removed and, for the first time since 1944, a Sydney newspaper ran with blank space. The book that the documents were drawn from went on sale within days, but the case against the *Herald* proceeded. The federal government cited various transgressions, from threatening national security — embarrassing leading Indonesian political figures was nominated as a major concern — to infringement of copyright. Although the case was eventually settled out of court more than six months later, an order upholding copyright effectively blocked further publication of material. This was despite Mr Justice Mason's High Court judgement that he was "not persuaded that the degree of embarrassment to Australia's foreign relations which will flow from disclosure is enough to justify interim protection of confidential information", and a ruling that there had been no breach of the Crimes Act.

(Sydney time), updating minute-by-minute through seven editions as the Twin Towers collapsed and New York and the world went into shock. But in 1915 Bean's first Gallipoli despatch did not pass the censorship and telegraph maze until May 15, a week after the *Herald* had published a colourful account by the British reporter Ashmead Bartlett. In the absence of the internet and 24-hour television, however, Bean's account still had a fresh resonance for readers hungry for news from the front.

"The bullets struck fireworks out of the stone along the beach," he wrote. "The men did not wait to be sent, but wherever they landed they simply rushed straight up the steep slopes. Other small boats were digging

for the beach with oars. These occupied the attention of the Turks in the trenches, and almost before the Turks had time to collect their senses, the first boatload was well up towards the trenches. A few Turks awaited the bayonet. It is said that one huge Queenslander swung his rifle by the muzzle, and, after braining one Turk, caught another and flung him over his shoulder. I do not know if this story is true, but when we landed some hours later there was a Turk on the beach with his head smashed in."

In World War II the *Herald* had 23 war correspondents whose frustrations and travails are a lively thread in Souter's *Company of Heralds*. But it was not until 1942 that the paper started to bring some

of them to life for readers by tentatively abandoning the anonymous "by our own correspondent" and identifying some of these incredible risk-takers by name.

This team included Jack Percival who, with his family, was imprisoned in Japanese-controlled Manila for the duration of the war. On his release in February 1945, Percival had dropped a third of his body weight, but his first cable to Sydney was taken up with journalistic essentials: acknowledgement first; money second. His first cable demanded that his reports henceforth should carry his name because of what he had been through and it concluded: "HOW ABOUT SOME EXPENSES REGARDS ALL — JACK PERCIVAL". Fairfax's then

Below The *Herald* correspondent Jack Percival, and his wife and two-year-old son, were interned by the Japanese for three years in the Philippines during World War II. He survived torture and beri-beri, dropping 40 per cent of his bodyweight. Harry Summers, who covered the liberation of Manila for the *Herald*, reported back to Sydney that the Percivals' son had survived the ordeal well, adding "they must have gone without a lot themselves to give [him] something like the necessities in food."

Bottom The *Herald* war correspondent Roderick Macdonald covered the fighting in Italy for eight months before being killed by a mine in Cassino on May 8, 1944.

general manager, the enduring Rupert (Rags) Henderson, responded with equal brevity that "SELF AND EVERYONE IN OFFICE OVERJOYED", prompting Percival to pen one of Australian journalism's more wonderful expositions of the love-hate relationship between correspondents and editors: "Let me say this — the warmth of your cables gave me the most horrible sentimental reactions I've ever had. Guess it was like a dog that has been whipped and kicked about receiving a pat."

In Thailand the dapper Harry Standish eluded Japanese search parties that had been ordered to capture him for "spreading malicious anti-Japanese propaganda". In 1942 the editors ordered the Chungking-based Roderick Macdonald to get himself from China to West Africa for a landing that was expected to take place in Senegal. After

journeying by foot, mule, truck and a dozen aircraft, Macdonald landed in Gambia, next to Senegal. There, debilitated by malaria, he received a cable ordering him to North Africa; the landing, in fact, would take place in Algeria. Later he was aboard one of the flimsy gliders that spearheaded the first successful Allied move back into Europe, in July 1943: the invasion of Sicily from Tunisia.

Replacing Macdonald in Chungking, Selwyn (Dan) Speight found that the power supply in his primitive digs was so erratic that he had to buy candles "at great expense" only to have "rats gnaw through the walls to steal them, and I saw one of them run off with my lighted candle, still burning, in his mouth". No waiting in a capital city for the release of the next sanitised nose-cam video clips of missile strikes for him. Writing with a "somewhere in China" dateline, Speight

Below Members of a demolition squad stand in what remains of the kitchen and laundry of a Bellevue Hill house that received a direct hit when Sydney was shelled from the sea early on the morning of June 8, 1942.

reported from the perspex bubble of one of a fleet of US B-25 bombers as they attacked an ammunition dump in Japanese-controlled Burma: "We swooped on Mangshih out of a thunderstorm. The churn in my stomach stopped. I saw the bomb doors open and saw the bombs go down (before the other aircraft) swung away with the lazy, wicked ease that a turning shark shows."

None of these men had the technological tools now considered indispensable in journalism. Today's correspondent goes to war with the internet and a laptop computer and satellite phone. He files in real time or, as was the case in Afghanistan when I was laid low by a virulent bug, consults a GP in Sydney just to be sure about self-administering the correct drugs. Likewise, air travel and the ever-amazing preparedness of Afghani or Iraqi drivers to deliver us to the

Above In a series of swift raids in early June 1940, police closed businesses across Sydney and interned their Italian owners as "unnaturalised aliens" in response to Italy's entry into the war.

Above In early November 1943, dancers from the Tivoli Theatre, back from a tour of northern operational areas, do their bit to promote the Fourth Liberty Loan in Martin Place, complete with a Kittyhawk fighter as a backdrop. (Photo: Frederick Halmarick)

front line these days reduce travel to a matter of days — not weeks.

In 1940 the *Herald* cabled instructions for another of its correspondents, G. E. W. Harriott, to move from Cairo to London — but Harriott's nose told him that getting to Greece for the Italian invasion was a better bet. He performed brilliantly and heroically: he was mentioned in despatches and awarded the Greek Cross of Distinguished Merit.

Weeks later, following orders to head for Singapore, Harriott hitched a ride on an Australian ship carrying 400 Italian prisoners of war. It struck a mine and sank in less than 10 minutes. In an un-bylined despatch filed after he was fished from the Mediterranean — naked but for his wristwatch — Harriott wrote: "The water was full of prisoners completely crazed with fear. They were clutching at one another and screaming, over and over again: 'Madre, Madre — mother,

and erect, their helmets on their heads, their bayoneted rifles in their hands, 'sticking it out' to the bitter end."

Later, reporting from the Pacific, Harriott had to take control of a US landing barge when the officer in charge froze as the vessel ran aground on a reef during the invasion of Saipan. Mortars bounced around them, but the captain began reciting his rosary and it fell to the ever-resourceful Harriott to order the crew to abandon ship. They swam ashore, from where they watched the barge, with the skipper still at prayer, take a direct hit.

In 1943 Bill Mundy, an Australian who had cut his journalistic teeth in Fleet Street, became the *Herald's* man with the Allied invasion force in Italy. He followed American troops into Scafati, between Salerno and Naples, and was killed during the night when the Germans counterattacked. Macdonald, he of the African goose chase, was reassigned to step into Mundy's dead man's shoes in Italy. Seven months later, in May 1944, he too died, aged 32. He was running for cover with a British colleague during a German mortar barrage on Cassino when one of them trod on a mine. Both men died.

Today's reporters are amazed to see photographs of all but one of the *Herald's* World War II correspondents in full military uniform. Even today's "embeds"

Top German prisoners captured from as far away as North Africa arrive in Sydney in late August 1941. Australia held 1651 German POWs during World War II in camps in Victoria, South Australia and Western Australia.

Above Guy Edward Warre Harriott was 25 years old when he left with the second Australian convoy to the Middle East in January 1940. He witnessed the surrender of the Japanese at Singapore and in Malaya and the liberation of Allied POWs in Changi.

mother!' They drowned one another, and they drowned themselves, and but for desperate use of fists and boots they would have drowned me. I fought my way clear and looked back towards the ship. Her bow was canted high in the air, and Italians, too frightened to jump, were clinging to the rails and rigging. And then I saw something which I shall never forget: two Australian soldiers, evidently previously posted as sentries, standing on that reeling deck, still

Above Australian troops struggle through the mud of the Kokoda Trail in New Guinea in 1943. Japanese supply lines had been stretched to the limit but fighting was still fierce.

Right The *Herald* war correspondent Harry Summers types his story in the field on September 15, 1944, the day the Allies landed on the island of Morotai. The island was the stepping stone to the Philippines and paved the way for MacArthur's return in October of that year.

Above After liberation of Ambon in late September 1945, soldiers inspect the graves of Australian POWs executed by the Japanese on the island.

don't wear military clobber, and many resort to local dress, because they think it's cool. (The traditional roll-sided pakool hats looked silly but were very popular in Afghanistan, and a hunting vest with an Arab headscarf tied around the neck is de rigueur for many in the Middle East.) Some think it will disguise them (several female and even male reporters in Afghanistan, including the BBC's irascible John Simpson, thought they might evade the Taliban by wearing a tent-like burqa, apparently not appreciating that a good Afghan husband can recognise his burqa-clad wife at 100 paces). Or they hope it might confuse a sniper and result in just that extra few seconds' hesitation needed to get out of the line of fire; or to blind a would-be Iraqi hostage-taker to the fact that the keffiyeh-clad individual in the car next to him in Baghdad traffic is a trophy hostage.

By World War II, decades before the Pentagon coined the term for the contemporary manner in which reporters accompanied US-led forces in the March 2003 invasion of Iraq, the *Herald's* correspondents were deeply "embedded" with the military. And, as with their officers' epaulets and braid, they wore their patriotism on their sleeves — and often revealed it in their copy.

Compared with the more sophisticated media control devices used today, censorship during World War II was a horrendous

Above Australian internees and POWs from Hong Kong arrive in Sydney on September 22, 1945, aboard the Royal Naval Hospital Ship Oxfordshire. A report in *The Sydney Morning Herald* said that many of the men with beri-beri had responded to nursing and better food on the journey and had been "putting on a pound weight each day since boarding the hospital ship".

professional burden. But when G. E. W. Harriott compared the 1940s blue-pencil activity of the Australian, British and Greek armies, he concluded happily enough: "It was mainly a matter of common sense on both sides." In the New Guinea campaign, though, the *Herald* men began to discern a particularly hard-headed and narrow-minded Australian military view of what should be reported. One of the first recorded clashes between a *Herald* staffer and the military during World War II was in 1943 in the remote jungles of New Guinea. On the urging of the Australian Army Command, reporter Mel Pratt and photographer Gordon Short had trekked arduously over the mountains to report on the Aussie success in beating back the

Japanese. The army brass saw it as a "good news" assignment but Brigadier M. J. Moton, who apparently held a grudge against all correspondents, ordered that Pratt and Short be ejected from his camp. They had no choice but to comply. Heading down the valley and up the other side, the duo paused when level with Moton's outpost. Short gave vent to his frustration, calling out through the valley mist to a staff captain who had been deputed to convey Moton's order that they leave: "Hey, Cap, did you say you worked in a bank in O'Connell Street?"

"That's right, Shorty," the captain called back.

"The one with the fence of spears on the outside?"

"That's right."

"Well, you can do something for me when you get back to Sydney. You can take every one of those spears and …"

This military obstruction became even more unreasonable in Korea in the 1950s. A deeply frustrated Lawson Glassop wrote to his bosses at the *Herald*: "The story from Korea at the moment — it cannot be written — is one about the suffering and the low morale of the troops, including the Australian battalion, resulting from the intense cold. Our battalion, sitting in deep snow on a hillside in the front line, has suffered severely. It had 97 sickness casualties in 10 days a fortnight ago. There have been cases of self-inflicted wounds. When that happens morale has reached its lowest depth. The censorship and the winter stalemate have made it almost impossible to report the war… If the Australians fight a battle, I cannot say they were Australians."

Military obstruction was not too much of an issue in Vietnam — particularly as the *Herald* supported the war and decided not to send its own reporters to cover it, relying on the Melbourne *Herald's* Denis Warner, the Sydney *Sun's* Pat Burgess and *The Age's* Roy McCartney in Washington. Veteran *Herald* journalist Evan Whitton, writing in *The National Times* in 1975, revealed Australia's

role in urging Lyndon Johnson on to war in Vietnam in 1965 when the then US president was having serious second thoughts about such a venture. Equally, the Prime Minister, John Howard, and the Defence Minister, Robert Hill, were so enthusiastic about the 2003 invasion of Iraq that they seemed to declare war before George Bush did; theirs would have been a lonely military campaign had Bush changed his mind.

The willingness of Australian governments to help legitimise such wars by providing moral and troop support dictates that they must be closely covered for an Australian readership. Labor or Liberal, our prime ministers have been unable to resist being seen as "wartime leaders" strutting the international stage. However, the small

man-and-machine contributions they make do not match their "we're at war" rhetoric, and because of their minnow status in, say, the US-led "coalition of the willing" in Iraq, they have no capacity to influence events as they unfold. Conversely, when they sign on as a nation at war, or at least in name as an occupying "power", they do assume full moral and legal responsibilities on behalf of all Australians for conduct by their joint-venturers that would not be accepted at home — such as the abuse of prisoners at the Abu Ghraib prison, west of Baghdad; the denial of the rights of prisoners from the 2001 Afghanistan war who are being held at Guantanamo Bay in Cuba; and the hideous US practice of airlifting unconvicted terrorist suspects from democracies around the world

Above Families from suburban Sydney gather to welcome home an Australian soldier repatriated from Germany in January 1944. His group of 300 included members of the 5th Australian General Hospital, given protected status when they stayed behind to tend to the Allied wounded after the evacuation of Greece. They told of the devastating effects of Allied bombing on German cities.

Top The Japanese formal surrender on the battleship Missouri in Tokyo Bay on September 2, 1945. General MacArthur, behind the microphone, watches General Yoshijiro Umezu sign the surrender document. The Japanese foreign minister, Mamoru Shigemitsu, stands with hands on hips.

Above Home alert: a poster warns Australians to take the Japanese threat seriously.

where they have some rights and protections to undemocratic countries that engage in levels of torture and other abuses that would not be tolerated in the US or in Australia.

Only the media fringe-dwellers had attempted to report from the other side in Korea and Vietnam. But during the 1990–91 Gulf crisis, CNN broadcast from Baghdad throughout the US-led bombardment of the city and the rest of the country and, for a time, the likes of the BBC, ITN and the *Herald* reported from "behind enemy lines". Saddam was as adept at controlling the media as his foreign opponents were, but most of his efforts to limit what was reported collapsed in both the 1990–91 crisis and the 2003 invasion. In the first, some of my reports were tape-recorded at high speed, played down a telephone line to Sydney where they were again recorded at high speed, which was then slowed to be transcribed into legible copy. I smuggled others out of the country on mini-tapes hidden in the boots of some of the reporters leaving the country as war approached. In the lead-up to the 2003 invasion, Saddam banned the use of satellite phones, but I built a small platform which, under cover of darkness, I would push through a window at the Al Rasheed Hotel to position the dish so that it connected with a satellite orbiting over the Atlantic Ocean.

The art of the foreign correspondent is fourfold: get in; get the story; get it back to the foreign desk, either as a straight human account of war or as a setting in which to analyse the reasons for, or the impact of, the conflict; and, at all times, stay safe. But one of the weightiest decisions an editor makes is whether to put his staff at risk.

Faced with threats by the US of a "shock and awe" campaign and the possibility that Saddam or his henchmen might turn on any foreigners who remained in Baghdad, early in 2003 many editors around the world pulled their teams out of Iraq in the days

before the invasion. Even *The Washington Post* left.

We were all very jittery, but the *Herald* editors weighed the risks, listened to the arguments from those on the ground, and we stayed — as did about 100 other reporters, photographers and cameramen. I've been back regularly since the war, covering Iraq's first elections in more than 50 years and the post-invasion mess as Iraqis attempt the transition to a secure, prosperous and peaceable post-Saddam existence.

Herald correspondent Lindsay Murdoch remembers the relationship with the Australian forces during the 1999 East Timor crisis as "a reasonable deal": "They flew us in. They fed and watered us and offered pool positions as they fanned out across the island — there was tension, but not much contact with an enemy force."

Later Murdoch was embedded with the US military in the 2003 Iraq invasion, during which his movement was tightly restricted — he was warned if he so much as visited a

Above Australian troops formed part of the occupation force after Japan's surrender.

Above Australian soldiers advance through a village south of Pakchon, Korea, with US tanks in support, October 1950. (Photo: Laurie Shea)

village 500 metres from where his unit made camp, he would not be allowed to rejoin it. But he drew a disturbing comparison between his American minders in Iraq and the nervousness of the Australian officers in East Timor: "There was no censorship by the Americans. But the Australians have it rammed down their throats that journalists are the enemy."

Since East Timor the Australian defence establishment has dug in much more deeply,

practising censorship by withholding information and refusing access.

During the Iraq invasion, about 500 American reporters accompanied US forces as they moved on Baghdad, and the British media travelled with British forces — many of them reporting live. But the Australians would have none of that. Insurgency violence since the invasion has made Iraq so dangerous for reporters that often the only way they can move around is as an embed.

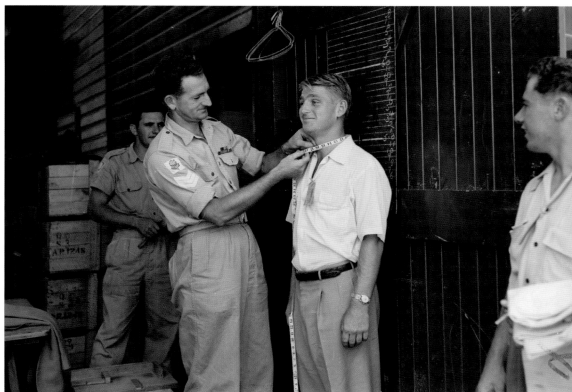

their arrival, the response was that this was "operational information" that could not be disclosed. It was as though the Federal Government believed that elements of the Iraqi insurgency needed the *Herald* to inform them that the Dutch were moving out and the Australians were coming in to Camp Smitty.

It was the same in Afghanistan early in 2002, when practised war correspondent and *Herald* stringer Craig Nelson, an American, was rudely escorted from a US base near Kandahar because he had reported that a unit of Australia's Special Air Service was there. Again, the Government seemed to know that Osama bin Laden read only the *Herald* or that his al-Qaeda terrorist network might make a targeting distinction between Americans and Australians sharing their base. Nelson wrote: "The absurdity is obvious. I had gone to the base for reaction to the first combat death of an Australian soldier since the Vietnam War — by any measure a momentous event. Now I was being escorted off the base in an effort to shore up the pretence that Australian forces weren't there in the first place. It is unclear who should feel sillier: the Australian Government for maintaining the charade or the Bush Administration for helping perpetrate it."

In terms of the freedom of the press and an obligation on politicians and top

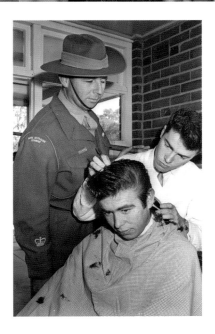

Top Tennis champion Lew Hoad has his neck measured at Ingleburn army camp on the outskirts of Sydney as he begins his national service in 1954.

Above Malcolm Corby, one of the first intake of National Service recruits for the Vietnam War, has his hair cut before training at Kapooka, near Wagga Wagga, in 1965. Between 1965 and 1972, 63,790 young men were called up for two years' service. Of the 17,424 "nashos" who served in Vietnam, 184 died. (Photo: Laurie Shea)

As it prepared to deploy in Al-Muthanna in 2005, the Australian military relented only slightly on its refusal to accommodate the media — it would let reporters visit its base at Camp Smitty, but a 48-hour limit was proof of its enduring wish to choreograph the coverage.

When a *Herald* reporter asked on a not-for-publication basis for rough dates for the planned deployment in April 2005, so that he could be in the region to cover

Above Roy Fluke, who served in New Guinea during World War II, on Anzac Day, 1987. He lost his leg to a sniper's bullet in 1945. Australia Post used this image for a postage stamp commemorating the 75th anniversary of the Gallipoli landings. (Photo: Rick Stevens)

Right Lest we forget: Ted Matthews was the last surviving veteran who landed on that first day of the Gallipoli campaign, April 25, 1915. He died in 1997, aged 101. (Photo: Steven Siewert)

Far right The remains of an unknown World War I Australian soldier are lowered into their final resting place in the Hall of Memory at the Australian War Memorial, Canberra, in 1993. The remains came from the Adelaide cemetery, near Amiens. He is unknown and unknowable yet, as Paul Keating said, he is "one of us". (Photo: Mike Bowers)

Above Veterans from every war and most peacekeeping missions since World War I gather in 2004. Left to right, back: Rowan Tink (Afghanistan), Barry Billing (Vietnam), Doug Mackinlay (East Timor), Bill Young (WWII), Ray Seaver (Korea), Brendan Jackson (Gulf War I), Harry Kirkman (Indonesian confrontation, Borneo), Paul Copeland (Cambodia, Sinai, Tonga, Vanuatu, Israel). Front: Lionel "Bluey" Jackson (Malayan emergency), Marcel Caux (WWI), Linda Baulch (Iraq). (Photo: Marco Del Grande)

military officials to allow the media to report on the Australian military, *The Australian* reported a more disturbing incident in April 2005. Nine servicemen and women had died in the crash of an RAN Sea King helicopter while engaged in humanitarian relief after an earthquake on the Indonesian island of Nias. Ten Australian journalists aboard HMAS Kanimbla, from which the downed chopper operated, were told there had been an incident. The journalists were not to leave the room and were not to contact their news desks.

This was no war zone; it was a relief operation gone wrong, but the journalists had effectively been imprisoned. The next morning the ship's captain, George McGuire, gave the reporters an emotional interview, but his officers told the reporters that they had received orders from Canberra that the interview with McGuire could not be aired. *The Australian's* Martin Chulov had reason to be furious. The *Herald's* Connie Levett was not on board the Kanimbla — she was back at her hotel, already writing a moving account of the crash based on graphic interviews with local people who had seen it all.

We'll never get it absolutely right. How war is reported will always lead to tension. Both *The New York Times* and *The Washington Post* have apologised to their readers for the manner in which they were

fooled by Washington and Co in the lead-up to the 2003 Iraq invasion — much of their now discredited reporting was reproduced in Australia and it informed local debate and commentary.

Governments desperately want people to suspend their critical faculties when they declare war, too often demanding that there not be serious analysis and debate on the reasons for, and the conduct of, war because it's unfair on the troops. And — too often these days — they have the slavish support of a chorus of hometown media commentators

and columnists who report courageously from their armchairs as they rehash what the government feeds them.

War correspondents are often presented as misguided vultures and the bearers of gloom. But a good working relationship should be possible between the media and the military — the Australian press is not bent on publishing material that would jeopardise the lives of Australian servicemen and women, and few among the military brass could fail to understand the public response to a story that was well told.

There will always be a need to sift and analyse what is being said and alleged as a justification for war — when Australia goes to war, better than the best is demanded of reporters on the beat in Canberra, correspondents in the power capitals of the world and their colleagues in the war zones, unilateralists and embeds alike. The media might have erred from time to time, mostly by accident or external manipulation. But the track record of governments, politicians and generals shows that they err much more often — usually deliberately.

Above Workers clean anti-war graffiti off the Sydney Opera House in 2003 shortly before the Prime Minister, John Howard, announced that Australians would join the US coalition in Iraq. Two men were sentenced to nine months' weekend detention and fined $151,000. (Photo: Rick Stevens)

Above Australian soldiers display a hard-won Japanese flag after their jungle-war victory, 1945.

The region

When Australians reached out to countries devastated by the Boxing Day tsunami of 2004 it took the nation nearer to the end of a long, painful journey.

For the first century or so of white settlement, Australians feared that the great powers of the old world, such as France, Russia and Germany, or upstarts like the rebellious United States, would invade to gain a staging post in the south. When there was no invasion, Australians developed another nightmare centred on their own neighbourhood.

Fortress Australia became more than a defence policy against the Asian hordes. For many Australians, it became a state of mind. The White Australia barriers went up and the sparse colony fought to attract immigrants made of the right stuff — the English, or, if pushed, Dutch or Finns.

World War II changed the nation forever. In a dramatic coming of age, Australia defied Winston Churchill's Britain and recalled troops to fight off the enemy at the door. Suddenly, Australians looked like accidental tourists in their own region and, in defending themselves against Japanese Asians, became defenders of other Asians. In Timor and Papua New Guinea, native populations fought by our side.

And the near nations had changed. New leaders and movements had risen in separate struggles. Soekarno in Indonesia was prepared to press on to keep the Dutch from reclaiming their colonial rule. By the late 1940s, Chinese-brand communism brought unrest in French Indochina (Vietnam), Malaysia, Indonesia and the Philippines.

Australia's significant military expeditions — until the events set in train by September 11, 2001 — were now in our wider region. Australian soldiers, sailors and air force personnel joined the occupation force to secure and stabilise Japan. In May and June 1950 Britain asked for and received help from Australia in the fight against communist insurgents in Malaya. The United States asked for and received help in the Korean War.

Above Australian troops of the 1st Battalion prepare to board US helicopters at Bien Hoa Airbase north of Saigon, South Vietnam, in June 1965. (Photo: Stuart MacGladrie)

But Vietnam brought Australia's biggest commitment beyond the two world wars, and 504 more deaths on the battlefields. More recently Australia has played a key role in setting the East Timorese on the path to independence as well as peacekeeping in Pacific nations, including the Solomons and Papua New Guinea.

It has been a hard lesson in geography, but it reshaped the way Australians saw the world. Increased trade came first, then nation-to-nation "dialogue", a trickle and then a flood of tourism to and from Asia, and finally a controlled but ever-increasing flow of immigrants.

Terrorism and disaster have tested these bright new ties in the first years of this century. The tsunami brought an outpouring of aid and personal involvement. Although the bombers of the Bali nightclubs had targeted Australians, we were knowing enough to avoid blaming the Balinese or the wider Indonesian population. The Dutch-inspired Indonesian justice system tested understanding during the Schapelle Corby drug trial, but xenophobia has not run riot.

Australia is still learning to live with its neighbours after more than 200 years of ignorance and suspicion. The welcome mat eventually put out for the boat people of Vietnam was withdrawn for other nationals in leaky boats in an alert and increasingly alarmed world. But a shared future in the region is inevitable. Only the terms of the relationships remain to be hammered out.

Above Troops scatter as soldiers loyal to president Ferdinand Marcos open fire in Manila during the "People's Power" uprising in the Philippines in 1986. (Photo: Peter Morris)

Right Rioting swept through the Tahitian capital of Papeete after France resumed nuclear testing and detonated a bomb at Mururoa in 1995. (Photo: Andrew Meares)

Above A member of the Moge people in the western highlands of PNG waits to vote in 1997. (Photo: Palani Mohan)

Top left The personal bodyguard of sacked PNG general, Jerry Singirok, questions the loyalty of a soldier during the PNG defence force's military coup, which was triggered by prime minister Julius Chan hiring a mercenary force to use on Bougainville in 1997. (Photo: Mike Bowers)

Bottom left Australian troops spread out across the Timorese capital of Dili on September 24, 1999 – the first week of the Australian-led mission to restore order in the strife-torn province. (Photo: Jason South)

Right The Prime Minister, John Howard, inspects surrendered weapons in Honiara, the Solomon Islands, in 2003. Operation Helpim Frens helped restore law. (Photo: Paul Harris)

Far right SAS soldiers board the container ship Tampa off Christmas Island in 2001 after Captain Arne Rinnan took 438 asylum seekers on board. (Photo: Mike Bowers)

Below Children at Honiara beach in 2003 as HMAS Manoora sits off Guadalcanal, the Solomon Islands. (Photo: Kate Geraghty)

Bottom Australian police forensic experts search for clues in what remains of Paddy's Bar in Kuta, Bali, after the bombings of 2002. (Photo: Craig Abraham)

Right A makeshift shrine outside the Australian consulate in Bali in memory of the victims of the Bali bombings. (Photo: Rick Stevens)

Far right Australian Navy personnel rescue asylum seekers from a sinking boat off Christmas Island in 2001.

Following pages

Top This panoramic photograph, comprised of 18 individual images, shows the devastation caused when a tsunami struck Banda Aceh on Boxing Day, 2004. (Photo: Mike Bowers)

Bottom left RAAF Hercules evacuates refugees from Banda Aceh after the tsunami. (Photo: Nick Moir)

Centre right More than a month after the tsunami, survivors were still struggling to clean up Banda Aceh. (Photo: Jason South)

Bottom right A soldier of the Free Aceh Movement. (Photo: Mike Bowers)

The two Vietnam wars

Above A smiling sergeant at Marrickville army depot with some of the 720 national servicemen who began their regular army duty in July 1965. Many went to Vietnam.

Top centre Sister Mary Colomba of Strathfield Dominican Convent farewells her brother, Private John Holst, 20, before he embarked on HMAS Sydney for Vietnam in 1967. (Photo: George Lipman)

Top far right Three potential conscripts burn their national service registration cards in protest against compulsory service in 1966.

Right Demonstrators outside Marrickville army depot protest against conscription and Australia's involvement in Vietnam.

When Australia committed troops to the Vietnam War in 1965, it had nearly 25 years of continuous jungle fighting behind it — from New Guinea and Borneo in World War II to the Malayan Emergency and confrontation with Indonesia after the creation of Malaysia in 1963. It was a record none of its traditional allies could match, and tributes to the fighting Australian echoed those after Gallipoli and the Somme. The US commander in Vietnam, General William Westmoreland, spoke of "good old-fashioned Australian courage", and declared in 1965: "I have never fought with a finer group of soldiers."

But Vietnam split Australia in a way no other war had. At a return home parade in Sydney on June 8, 1966, one year after deployment in Vietnam, march leaders had their uniforms smeared with the red paint worn by a lone woman protester who emerged from the showering confetti. Fined

$6 the next day for offensive behaviour, the 21-year-old said she did not belong to any organisation and her real target was not the soldiers but "complacency and apathy", adding: "I know Australians are very brave physically but I think they should show more intellectual and moral bravery."

A small group of Australian military counter-insurgency and jungle warfare experts had been in Vietnam since 1962, but the introduction of the National Service Act in late 1964 provided a catalyst. Conscription had divided the nation during World War I, when it was rejected twice by referendum, but this time there had been no referendum. The first demonstrations were small — mostly organised by groups of young people with no alliance other than their eligibility to be called up, and by equally non-political groups of mothers carrying placards opposing the call-up and wearing sashes reading S.O.S. — Save Our Sons.

Above A South Vietnamese soldier takes a break during a combined "search and destroy" operation with Australian and American troops in 1965. (Photo: Stuart MacGladrie)

Right A wounded soldier of the 1st Battalion is lifted into a medivac helicopter after a grenade accident in 1965 which killed three Australians and wounded 11 others. (Photo: Stuart MacGladrie)

Most Australians supported the war in its early years. The prime minister, Harold Holt, told the US president, Lyndon B. Johnson, that Australia was "all the way with LBJ". Johnson visited Australia in October 1966 and Holt easily won the election in November. However, as the death toll grew and front-line images came to the lounge rooms of the nation — Vietnam was the first "TV war" — the demonstrations became bigger and better organised. By 1970, when moratorium march organisers were claiming turnouts of up to 150,000 protesters across the capital cities, public sentiment had

turned. The prime minister, John Gorton, announced in November that Australian forces in Vietnam would be reduced.

Soldiers have always returned from war with mental and physical scars, but Australia's Vietnam veterans were denied the balm of the heroes' welcome. They were abused and lectured and not invited to join Anzac Day marches. Additional problems brought on by exposure to chemical defoliants were scoffed at. The Anzac Day welcome home march of 1987 and the jargon of "healing process" were too late for the men claimed by suicide and

illness. Now there is evidence that their children have inherited physical and mental burdens.

The debate about Australia's intervention in Vietnam continues. General Peter Cosgrove, after assuming command of Australia's defence forces in 2002, said he believed in retrospect that "we probably shouldn't have gone". In the same year, before his appointment as governor-general, Major General Michael Jeffery disagreed, saying the war had provided "breathing space" in the region at an important time. Both men served in Vietnam.

Above Colonel A. V. Preece of the 1st Battalion takes the salute during a march through Sydney. A female protester smeared him with red paint. The photographer Noel Stubbs won a Walkley award for best news picture in 1966.

Right All the way with LBJ. President Johnson's motorcade receives a ticker-tape welcome in Sydney in October 1966. (Photo: George Lipman)

Far right Demonstrators attempt to throw themselves in front of the US president's motorcade. (Photo: Vic Sumner)

Above Vietnam veteran Ross Mengano gets
a helping hand during the official "welcome
home" parade in Sydney on October 3, 1987.
(Photo: Brendan Read)

Left Joyful Australian soldiers kissing the
tarmac at Mascot on their return from Vietnam
in 1966.

Far left The 5th Battalion, known as the
Tigers, return to Sydney in 1970 on HMAS
Sydney – 5RAR had lost 25 men but it was
claimed they had killed 353 enemy soldiers.
(Photo: Stuart MacGladrie)

CHAPTER TEN

Sport Mad

Passions that unite, loyalties that divide

BY ROY MASTERS AND PHIL WILKINS

For countless Australians sport holds an enduring fascination, inspiring heartfelt passions. "Sport to many Australians is life and the rest a shadow," Donald Horne wrote in *The Lucky Country*. D. H. Lawrence wrote that Australians played sport as if their lives depended on it.

The passions can mobilise millions of people behind their national team or an individual on an international stage. Back home, they can divide people tribally between favourite teams, bringing weekend war without bullets. Success at the highest levels is underpinned by high participation among schoolchildren and adults, with huge numbers playing tennis, netball and lawn bowls. The step from playground to professionalism, from spectator to star performer, can happen almost overnight. Lew Hoad and Ken Rosewall were teenage Davis Cup heroes; schoolgirl and schoolboy swimmers break world records.

When Australia II won the America's Cup in 1983, the *Herald* described the day as Australia's greatest since victory in World War II. It went on to say the prime minister, Bob Hawke, had been lucky — with the breaking of the drought, a strengthening US economy and, now, a possible spinnaker-led economic recovery.

Australia's longest, most unforgettable, minute came on the night of September 25, 2000, when Cathy Freeman won the Olympic 400-metre title, Australia's 100th Olympic gold medal. The 112,524 people in the stadium would never forget it, that minute when millions of Australians focused their will and good wishes on one young woman doing what she loved best. Michael Wilbon wrote in *The Washington Post*: "It's a halting thing in any walk of life when people are confronted with surreal expectations and meet them. Freeman doesn't see it that way. People who can move the culture rarely do."

The nation's mood is reflected through its sportspeople, just as sport reflected the growth of colonial confidence in the 19th century. Ned Trickett became Australia's first world champion when the sculler defeated the Englishman Joseph Sadler on the Thames in 1876.

The first *Herald* sport report, in 1831, covered a horse-race meeting and began with the public wearing "light hearts and heavy pockets" and ended with "heavy hearts and light pockets". The paper paid scant attention

Above These walkers in an 1879 race, illustrated in *The Sydney Mail*, were serious about their sport.

Centre Camaraderie follows conflict: Norm Provan, of St George, and Wests' Arthur Summons leave the Sydney Cricket Ground together after the 1963 rugby league grand final, won by Saints. (Photo: John O'Gready)

Top right Cathy Freeman after winning the 400 metres at the 2000 Olympics – Australia's 100th Olympic gold medal and an unforgettable sporting moment. (Photo: Craig Golding)

Bottom right Wheelchair athletes compete in a 10-kilometre road race on Australia Day. The Paralympic champion, Louise Sauvage, won. (Photo: Tim Clayton)

Previous pages Competitors take on the water jump in the men's 3000-metre steeplechase at the 2000 Olympics in front of a packed stadium. Reuben Kosgei of Kenya won the gold medal. (Photo: Tim Clayton)

to the first Melbourne Cup in 1861, won by Archer. Now Melbourne Cup day is almost a national holiday.

Australia claimed its first Olympic victory when Edwin Flack won the 800 and 1500 metres in Athens in 1896, but the *Herald* described the Games as a farce and gross anachronism. The 1956 Olympic

Right The Great White Shark had a long drive and, occasionally, a short temper. Despite this outburst after a bad chip shot, Greg Norman wins his first Australian Open at The Lakes course, Sydney, in 1980. (Photo: Peter Morris)

Top right French rider Jean Michel Bayle's world turned upside down with this fall from grace during the 250cc Grand Prix at Eastern Creek. (Photo: Quentin Jones)

Below American Gene Sarazen – acclaimed the world's best golfer – was beaten by Bill Bolger at the Australian Open at Royal Sydney in 1934. Sarazen took the title two years later. (Photo: Harry Martin)

Bottom centre Jack Brabham won the Formula One drivers' world championship in 1959 and 1960. Then, in 1966, he won it again – the only driver ever to do so in a car of his own construction.

Bottom far right Rowing has had a loyal following since colonial days, most notably at the Head of the River, won in 2003 by Shore. (Photo: Tamara Dean)

Games in Melbourne put sport on the front page regularly. The paper also underrated the future of rugby league, saying about 100 years ago: "When professionalism comes in, fair play goes out the window." It paid little heed to boxing, perhaps because bare-knuckle fighting was illegal in NSW, but took notice in 1908 when Jack Johnson, fighting in Sydney, became the world's first black boxing champion. The *Herald's* attitude to champion boxer Les Darcy was cool because the paper had adopted patriotism in World War I and Darcy had gone to America to fight for a living while other young Australians were fighting in France.

In a way, it's all about patriotism. That's why Australians remember Heather McKay for having won 16 consecutive world squash titles. That's why Kay Cottee was on the front page in 1983 when she became the first around-the-world, non-stop woman sailor. In another way, though, it's definitely about having fun.

Top far left Schoolgirls welcome Liz Ellis, Marianne Murphy and the victorious Australian netball team in 1995. (Photo: Dean Sewell)

Bottom far left Adam Meinershagen is on the mound for the Sydney Blues at Parramatta in 1995. (Photo: Tim Clayton)

Left Australians lapped up the successes of Andrew "Boy" Charlton, an Olympic gold medallist in the 1500m freestyle in Paris in 1924.

Below Shirley Strickland (third from foreground) leads the 80-metre hurdles in a 1957 meeting at Moore Park. Strickland, Marjorie Jackson and Betty Cuthbert shone in Australian athletics in the 1950s and 1960s.

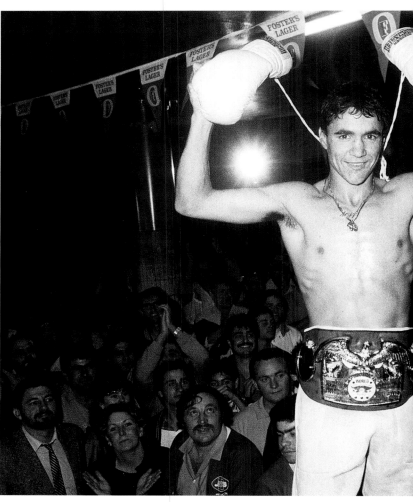

Above Lew Hoad (rear) and Ken Rosewall practise at Kooyong before their Davis Cup final in 1953. Coach Harry Hopman watches from the sidelines. Australia won the cup 3-2. (Photo: R. L. Stewart)

Left Ken Rosewall, 19, helps out in his parents' grocery store in Sydney in 1953, the year he helped Australia win the Davis Cup.

Top far left Dave Sands knocks out Henry Brimm at Sydney Stadium in 1950. Sands, ranked No. 2 for Raging Bull Jake La Motta's world middleweight title, died in a road accident. (Photo: Kenneth Issitt)

Bottom far left Ginger Honey takes off at Canterbury races in 1980. Jockey Neil Crothers ended up on the turf. The horse was withdrawn from the race. (Photo: Barry Stevens)

Centre Jeff Fenech returns in triumph to the Marrickville Hotel with his world championship belt in 1985. (Photo: Stephen Holland)

Team spirit

BY ROY MASTERS

If Rome is a soccer city and New York a baseball town, Sydney is the world capital of sport hobbyists. Our harbour, abundant playing fields and mild climate offer choice; not passionate commitment to one code.

No single sport unifies Sydney. The football fanatics of NSW are diffused among rugby league, rugby union, Aussie rules and soccer. If a fan's league team is doing badly, he might follow the Swans, a fashionable Sydney AFL label — provided they're competitive.

By contrast, Melbourne is an Aussie rules city. The code attracts all, from business to academia to politics to the arts. To follow an Aussie rules team does not diminish one's cachet but enhance it. The game is a religion, transcending social divisions. Sydney, however, is geographically divided between rugby union, popular in the city's northern and eastern suburbs, and rugby league, which is the No. 1 sport everywhere else, especially in the vast west.

Nor do Sydney families remain generationally glued to the same team. Season tickets don't work: we may or may not go to the game — it depends what the weather is like. Eminent Sydneysiders — unlike eminent Melburnians — don't queue to become chairmen of footy clubs. Football is simply not that serious to the people of NSW.

State of Origin rugby league, a three-game annual exercise in bad blood and good football played by the best athletes in NSW and Queensland, demonstrates this. The first game was staged in 1980 at Brisbane's Lang Park, nicknamed "the Cauldron", with players drawn mainly from Sydney clubs and chosen on the basis of the state where they learnt their football. The Queensland captain, Arthur Beetson, struck his Parramatta clubmate, the gentlemanly Michael Cronin, with a fierce blow, igniting a brawl and thereby guaranteeing the concept instant success because "state versus state" finally involved

"mate versus mate". The Maroons, starved of success because previous state teams were chosen on a residential basis, won easily.

The series regularly features in the year's top 10 most watched television programs and the Maroons' early domination had Queenslanders glued to their sets. Queenslanders think of themselves as outsiders — they barely voted for Federation and still speak of it as a mistake. Their players cry out "Queenslander" as they walk down the tunnel onto the field; but it would seem weird were the Blues to chant "New South Welshman".

New Zealand-born footballers who have grown up in Queensland, such as the Brisbane Broncos' spectacularly talented

Above Australians pride themselves on playing running rugby. It doesn't always work that way, as Rob Egerton found when playing for Sydney University against Parramatta in 1986. (Photo: Brendan Read)

fullback Karmichael Hunt, elect to play for the Maroons rather than the Kiwis. However, transplanted Kiwis living in NSW choose to play for New Zealand.

This is not to say sports followers in Sydney and NSW cannot mobilise and galvanise support for their city or state when the world demands it. Sydney is essentially a can-do city. Witness the spectacular success of the 2000 Olympic Games and the Paralympics which followed.

Despite gloomy predictions of traffic-choked roads, vast queues and double-booked seats, our Games remain the standard by which all future ones are set.

Sydney's army of volunteers, drawn from all over Australia but mainly local residents,

set the tone. Compliment their equivalents, as I did in Salt Lake City at the 2002 winter Olympics, or in Athens at the 2004 summer Olympics, and they say, "Ah, but if we can do half as good a job as your people, we will be very proud."

Similarly, the 2003 Rugby World Cup set stellar standards for organisation and cohesion. While matches were played all over Australia, Sydney was host for the big-ticket ones, including the final played at the Olympic Stadium at Homebush. This was the scene of the greatest night of track and field when Cathy Freeman won a gold medal in the 400 metres.

Freeman's triumph was but a morsel of an athletic feast, including a three-hour

Above State of Origin football, first played in 1980, reinvigorated rugby league, drawing in new fans and huge television audiences for the annual NSW-Queensland series. It took NSW five years to claim bragging rights, under captain Steve Mortimer. (Photo: Peter Morris)

Above George Gregan, who was to play more than 100 Test matches, made his name with a single tackle. As All Blacks winger Jeff Wilson – in the final seconds of the game – dived for the try that would win the Bledisloe Cup for New Zealand in 1995, Gregan leapt and jolted the ball free. Australia won 20-16. (Photo: Tim Clayton)

duel between the USA's Stacy Dragila and Australia's Tatiana Grigorieva in the women's pole vault. Grigorieva, who had emigrated from the old USSR, and Freeman, an Aborigine, were cheered by a national TV audience of 9 million who appreciated their representation of new and old Australia. The crowd also watched Cuba's Anier Garcia hold off the might of the United States in the men's 110-metre hurdles; saw Britain's Jonathan Edwards win the triple jump at his fourth Olympics; marvelled as the majestic American 400-metre runner, Michael Johnson, earned his fourth gold medal, equalling Jesse Owens's haul in 1936. If a blink of the eye equals one-hundredth of a second, there were only nine blinks separating the first- and second-placegetters in the 25-lap men's 10,000 metres, won by Ethiopian Haile Gebrselassie over Kenya's Paul Tergat. In the women's 5000 metres, only a quarter of a second separated first and second.

Sydney also hosted the 1938 Empire Games, a feat in itself considering the world was poised for war. Nor was Sydney intimidated about staging a world heavyweight title fight in 1908 between Americans Jack Johnson and Tommy Burns at the "old tin shed" at Rushcutters Bay. It was a world event because Sydney alone was willing to take a risk on a black American beating a white one. He did, and his success began a long line of black Americans holding the heavyweight belt.

Yet the people of NSW don't beat their chests and proclaim home-grown heroes as proof of superiority over the rest of Australia. Perhaps this explains the unusual mix of down-to-earth humility and gritty independence of many of its champions, particularly its women. Balmain-born Dawn Fraser, voted the greatest female Olympian ever, won three successive gold medals in the 100-metre freestyle at the Melbourne, Rome

The response to the announcement was muted but it is wrong to conclude that Sydney sports followers ignore the past. After all, on October 10, 1999, a crowd estimated at 80,000 marched on Sydney Town Hall in protest against a decision by the NRL to exclude Souths from the competition. The NRL had dumped the Rabbitohs in a rationalisation process, following a peace deal which ended a three-year, $1 billion war over pay TV rights, waged by rival billionaires Rupert Murdoch and Kerry Packer. While many marched in protest at the culling of the club called "the pride of the league", supporters from other NRL clubs objected to News Ltd's power to reduce the number of teams to suit its TV interests. When the Federal Court upheld the Rabbitohs' appeal against the NRL, News Ltd welcomed the club back to the competition. Although the High Court reversed the decision, News Ltd refused to act against Souths, having witnessed Sydney's can-doism and a campaign against News Ltd papers and subscriptions to its pay TV network.

The world game, soccer, has never caught hold in Sydney or NSW, despite early interest in the coalfields of the Hunter Valley and Wollongong. While British migrants helped popularise the game, post-1945 waves of Europeans have embraced rugby league. Lebanese and Greeks have taken to league with the same curious enthusiasm with which Irish teaching brothers adopted it when they arrived at Sydney's parish schools. League's hegemony over union was boosted in 1926 when the Marist Brothers announced their affiliation with the professional code.

The new game had split from union in 1908 after a demand for compensation for injured players. It is sometimes argued rugby league gained its impetus during World War I when the amateur code suspended its competition while the professional code played on. However, its crowds had already overtaken rugby union by the outbreak of war. In 1914, union crowds in the two Tests against New Zealand totalled 15,000, while league attracted 130,000 in three Tests.

and Tokyo Olympics. Barred for life for her undisciplined behaviour — which included stealing a flag from the emperor's palace — at the 1964 Olympics, she reinvented herself as a NSW parliamentarian and won a seat on the board of rugby league club Wests Tigers, the only woman on a club board in Sydney. Marjorie Jackson, fondly known as "The Lithgow Flash", won gold medals for athletics at the 1952 Helsinki Olympics after training on a track at Lithgow, illuminated by the lights of cars circling the oval. She later became governor of South Australia.

Because pragmatic Sydney has often been preoccupied with the bottom line, it is frequently accused of neglecting tradition. The South Sydney Rabbitohs, the city's oldest and most successful rugby league club, announced in 2005 that it would abandon its inner-city base of almost a century to relocate to the Olympic venue — for a guarantee of nearly $100,000 a game.

Top Souths' Dennis Pittard outlasts Manly's Fred Jones to score under the posts. Rugby league has thrived for almost 100 years on suburban rivalries. In the late 1960s it was Souths and Manly. (Photo: John O'Gready)

Above For five years after News Ltd launched a rival competition, rugby league was fought in the courts as vigorously as on the grounds. Tears flowed when Souths was tipped out in 2000. But the Redfern-based club fought its way back to the fold two years later. (Photo: Robert Pearce)

Top Swans midfielder Daniel Macpherson. (Photo: Adam Pretty)

Above The Socceroos' Harry Kewell after Iran ended Australia's World Cup hopes in 1997. (Photo: Vince Caligiuri)

Top right Barbara Elias with her son, Benny, after a match in 1992. (Photo: Craig Golding)

Bottom right John Hopoate and Paul Harragon in a 1995 league semi-final. (Photo: Craig Golding)

Working-class folk in NSW were becoming more confident, boosted by Justice Higgins's Harvester judgement in 1907, which established a basic wage. They probably thought history was on their side and the dairy and cane towns of northern NSW quickly affiliated with the new code. Although the then elitist *Herald* predicted the new code would fail because money destroyed sport, it did report the first games played at grounds such as Birchgrove Oval. Bush leagues soon followed.

The fickleness of many Sydneysiders with their sport — following the Swans in Australian rules, or the rugby Super 12 team, the Waratahs, when on winning streaks — reflects the city's ecumenicalism. The Swans came to Sydney in 1982, enjoyed most support when they made the 1996 grand final, and their membership base had slowly grown to 28,000 by 2005. By contrast, the NRL team the Storm was established in Melbourne in 1998, won the premiership the following year, but has been largely shunned by a Melbourne media desperate not to offend the AFL.

Aussie rules is sometimes referred to as "aerial ping-pong" and "cross-country

wrestling" in parts of NSW, but not with the venom Victorians refer to "thugby league". Their definition of a scrum as "one man pushing two men up three men's arseholes" is more a comment on what Victorians think of Sydney than on the rugby codes.

Sydney's generosity of spirit towards new sporting codes was evident as early as August 6, 1881, when the first important football match of any kind was played at what is now the SCG. It was an Aussie rules game between NSW and Victoria, the first inter-colonial match of any kind at the ground.

Support for boxing has ranged from apathy to high excitement, largely linked to the international success of home-grown champions. Maitland-born Les Darcy, and Sydneysiders Vic Patrick, Jimmy Carruthers, George Barnes, Rocky Gattelari and Jeff Fenech have all attracted big crowds when contending for, or holding, world belts. Overweight lards and aged has-beens are booed, whether the venue has been the long-demolished Rushcutters Bay stadium or modern facilities such as the Sydney Entertainment Centre.

Sydneysiders have an inbuilt radar when it comes to detecting duplicity —

a sham, a fix or a ring-in. Harness racing, or trotting, was dubbed the "red hots" when punters sniffed a fix. Two of the biggest rorts in thoroughbred racing were masterminded in Sydney and then exposed by NSW authorities. The Bold Personality/ Fine Cotton substitution took place at Eagle Farm, Brisbane, in August 1984, but punters at Sydney's Warwick Farm knew it was a ring-in, knew the real identity of the runner and fingered the organisers, all before the horse had returned to the enclosure. When Big Philou, the favourite for the 1969 Melbourne Cup, was sick half an hour before the race, Sydney punters quickly identified the Sydney men responsible.

NSW racing can also be inventive in a positive sense. The rest of the world said a sprint between two-year-olds would never be successful. Yet Sydney hosted the Golden Slipper in 1957, when Todman won, and it is now the world's richest two-year-old race. Melbourne, which scoffed at the notion that two-year-olds can be glorified, followed with the Blue Diamond. Sydney does not have an equivalent to Melbourne's spring racing carnival, with the Melbourne Cup and 100,000 crowds, but the success of the Golden

Slipper changed the breeding industry with a switch to sprinting six-furlong horses.

A shared emotional cosmology is important to Victorians, whether it is being packed together at Flemington or the MCG. Sydney does not take itself so seriously. When Sir William McKell, a former NSW premier, was governor-general of Australia, he visited the SCG with a member of the British House of Lords. Approaching the partly deaf secretary of the NSW Rugby League, Harold (Jersey) Flegg, he said: "Jerse, I'd like to introduce you to Lord McDonald." Flegg replied: "Pleased to meet you, Claude." McKell, hastily: "No, Jerse, Lord, not Claude." Flegg, dismissively: "This is Australia. We don't go in for all that bullshit here."

Sport's passions can mobilise millions of Australians behind their cricket team, any national team, or an individual on an international stage. But when it comes to club teams, if Sydney is the city of the one-night stand, Melbourne is the home of the painfully durable marriage. Sydney people drift between codes and teams.

Booker prize-winning author Tom Keneally, a resident of Sydney's northern beaches, admits he is a typical example: a football version of the English clergyman, the Vicar of Bray, whose zeal for each form of religion changed with every reign from Charles I to George I. Keneally began life as a rugby league follower, barracking for Western Suburbs, before shifting allegiance to St George during the Dragons' record 11 successive premierships from 1956 to 1966. He is now No. 1 ticket-holder of the Manly Sea Eagles. He chose Manly because his daughter's physical education teacher was Stephen Knight, a Sea Eagle centre. A biography of Des Hasler, the Manly and Australian player who went on to coach the Eagles, is now part of Keneally's formidable oeuvre of fiction and non-fiction. Keneally has even flirted with the Swans, and admits to watching the Waratahs, who attract a private school following of lawyers, doctors and other professionals.

Above When Australia faced England for the Ashes-deciding rugby league match in 1950, the Sydney Cricket Ground was so wet 40 tons of sand was spread on it before play could begin. Here, players exchange jumpers after Australia won 5-2. (Photo: Harry Martin)

"I get the ridiculous question: 'How can you be interested in Oz culture and follow that thuggish code?'" Keneally said of those who ask him about his allegiance to the Sea Eagles. "I like a good game of rugby union but, by God, it's hard to achieve. There are many people in NSW who actually think there's something intellectually superior in body contact in rugby union that's not there in body contact in rugby league."

Sydney is a city of sport hobbyists. While Melburnians are cosmologists, explaining Australia and the universe through their game, what happens to NSW teams is less a matter of inter-planetary significance.

Whereas Victoria was the only state in Australia that supported a republic and has its own locally invented game, Australia's oldest city unites only when the national team plays Great Britain. Playing Pommy games, such as cricket, rugby union and rugby league, "better than the Pommies" is our go. It's Gallipoli all over again. When it comes to sport, we are reactive patriots.

Left Souths, with 20, has won more Sydney rugby league premierships than any other club. But it's been a long time between drinks. Captain John Sattler, his jaw broken and teeth smashed, is chaired off the Sydney Cricket Ground by teammates in 1970 after the club's last grand final victory. (Photo: John O'Gready)

Below Australian rules football was a southern eccentricity until the Swans came to Sydney in 1981. Although the premiership has been elusive, one record was claimed proudly: in June 1999 star forward Tony Lockett kicked his 1300th goal to break one of the game's most famous records. (Photo: Steve Christo)

Right The Matraville High factor: the Ella brothers – Glen, Gary and Mark – changed rugby union with their audacious play. Even in the under-16s their talent was obvious. (Photo: Kevin Berry)

Below With victory in 2002, Lleyton Hewitt claimed Wimbledon, only the second Australian man to do so in 30 years. (Photo: Steve Christo)

Above right John Eales holds aloft the Bledisloe Cup for rugby union in 2002. Regarded by Kiwis as national property, Australia had won the cup for the fifth year in succession. (Photo: Craig Golding)

Right With more grit than grace, Allan Border held Australia together as the side struggled through the 1980s. His reward was to regain the Ashes in 1989, a feat acknowledged by a ticker-tape parade in Sydney. (Photo: Jack Atley)

Right Duelling champions: by the end of the Athens Games in 2004 the career tally for Grant Hackett (left) and Ian Thorpe was 14 Olympic medals, eight of them gold. Both were hoping to swim in Beijing in 2008. (Photo: Craig Golding)

The summer game BY PHIL WILKINS

When Arthur Phillip hoisted the Union Jack in Sydney Cove he was unaware of the stowaway he brought with him among the colonisers, convicts and soldiers. He had no idea that he had carried within his human cargo a spiritual import in the form of a barely recognised national sport.

In 1788 the Marylebone Cricket Club was a year old and cricket was no longer the simplistic pastime of bored shepherds, using as stumps the wicket gate through which they drove their flocks and applying the branch of a tree to a rounded hunk of wood as bat on ball. Cricket had evolved from "club ball", an outdoors activity in Kent and Sussex, dating as far back as the 13th century.

As Britain built an empire to empty its overcrowded prisons, capitalise on the raw materials of its dominions and find worldwide trading markets, one of the exports was cricket. The game went to Australia, New Zealand, South Africa, the West Indies, India and Sri Lanka. Initially introduced to entertain and humour what passed for the ruling aristocracy, governmental bureaucracy and soldiery, the game's popularity led to its expansion to the people.

Cricket's acceptance was one thing, but integration within the game was gradual and painfully protracted in some regions. The bitter opposition within South Africa to

Far left When Dawn swam, Australia won – or so it seemed – during a career that spanned three Olympic and two Commonwealth Games. She won 11 medals, all but one of them gold.

Left Just a little kid from the country: the talent of tennis player Evonne Goolagong (left) was already obvious in 1964. Seven years later she won Wimbledon. (Photo: R. L. Stewart)

Above left Schoolgirl and world champ. Shane Gould heads off to class the day after setting another world record in 1971. (Photo: Ton Linsen)

Above Australians were unaware taekwondo was an Olympic sport but not after Lauren Burns won gold in Sydney in 2000. (Photo: Phil Carrick)

Left The Opals contest the basket while going down to the USA in the Olympic Games of 2000. In 2004 they ran second again. (Photo: Steve Christo)

Centre Sydney had already guaranteed a great Olympics by the time of the women's 400 metres on day 10. All that it needed was a champion. Step up, Cathy Freeman. (Photo: Tim Clayton)

22 men. Yorkshireman Roger Iddison said on returning home: "Well, oi doan't think mooch o' their play, but they're a wonderful lot o' drinkin' men." Sydney hosted its first official inter-colonial match in 1857, when NSW beat Victoria by 65 runs, led by the round-arm deliveries of Captain Edward Ward, custodian of the Sydney Mint. Fifteen thousand people watched the second day's play — the estimated population of the city and suburbs in 1856 was only 69,000.

The legendary England batsman, Dr William Gilbert Grace, led a team to Australia in 1873–74, enduring "a wretched trip" to Sydney which coincided with a loss to a combined NSW–Victorian side of 15 players. Emotions often ran high in such representative games. Gambling was intense with bookmakers' stands scattered through the pavilions. In an up-country game, the publican apologised to Grace: "Sorry we can't fix you up like they do in the cities, Doc. No bloody baths, you know!" W. G. replied: "That's all right, my man. We Graces are no bloody water spaniels." When Lord Harris's team visited Australia in 1878–79, spectators stormed the field in protest against the dismissal of a NSW batsman, and His Lordship was struck with a stick by an invader. The game was abandoned for the day after two more crowd invasions. It was claimed that two of the Englishmen insulted spectators by describing them as "nothing but the sons of convicts".

The "sons of convicts" had seen equality dawn on Australian cricket in March 1877, when Dave Gregory led a colonial — essentially Victorian — team in an 11-a-side challenge match against James Lillywhite's tourists, more a band of mercenaries than a team of gentlemanly amateurs. Gregory's Australian XI beat England by 45 runs at the Melbourne Cricket Ground, thanks to Charles Bannerman's 165 retired hurt and the fact that the Englishmen had arrived from New Zealand the previous day, still afflicted by sea sickness. The *Herald* recorded: "There was great excitement at the

the coloured and black populations playing with and against white civilians lasted a century. However widespread and popular the game in the Caribbean, the West Indies were always captained by a white cricketer until the Barbadian Frank Worrell led his magnificent team to Australia to play against Richie Benaud's side as recently as 1960–61.

The earliest documented cricket match in Sydney took place in 1834 — three years after the first *Herald* — and the first officially recognised tour by an English side, led by Heathfield Harman Stephenson, the Surrey captain, in the season of 1861–62. The standard of local cricket was such that the tourists played against sides of 15 to

Top The country boy made good: Doug Walters, from Dungog, was determined never to let the game of cricket get in the way of the rest of his life.

Above Jason "Dizzy" Gillespie, one of Australia's leading fast bowlers, strives to beat New Zealand batsmen with speed during a one-day match at the SCG in 2004. (Photo: Tim Clayton)

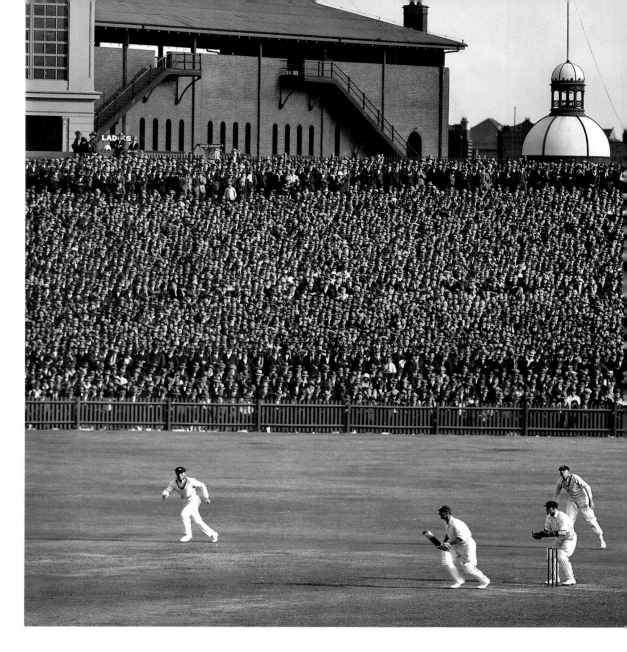

Right The England opener, Jack Hobbs, plays forward before a huge crowd at the second Test at the SCG in December 1928. Clarrie Grimmett dismissed Hobbs but England won the Test and series 4-1. (Photo: H. H. Fishwick)

Above Neil Harvey, 19, is greeted by an admirer on his Test debut at Adelaide Oval against India in the 1947-48 series. He became one of Bradman's "Invincibles'" soon after.

close, and vociferous cheering." The match became recognised as the first Test.

Historically, Sydney's first Test match took place five years later, in February 1882, although it was not categorised then as a "Test". It was said the Englishmen were pitted against the "Combined Colonies". Australia won by five wickets, thanks to the medium-fast spin bowling of George "Joey" Palmer and his match haul of 11–165.

In 1894–95, it appeared Australia was impregnably placed when Syd Gregory made 201 and George Giffen 161 of Australia's massive 596 in the first Sydney Test. Bowled out for 325, England followed on and was again dismissed, leaving Australia 177 to win. Overnight, rain turned the unprotected SCG wicket into a bog but the Englishmen, having anticipated comprehensive defeat, went out on the town and came home late, heavily intoxicated. Their left-arm spinner, Bobby Peel, was so drunk the Englishmen had to push him under a cold shower to sober him

up. Peel confounded everyone by taking 6–67 on the gluepot pitch, and England won an astonishing victory by 10 runs.

If the Lord Harris affair was regarded as infamous, it was nothing compared with the international furore which greeted the Bodyline series of 1932–33 when Douglas Jardine led England to Australia. With Don Bradman in full flight on the 1930 tour of England, and with Bill Woodfull's side having reclaimed the Ashes, the arrogant, authoritarian Jardine brought with him two fast bowlers from Nottinghamshire: Harold Larwood and Bill Voce.

In the first Test in Sydney, with Bradman absent due to ill health, Larwood claimed 10–124, despite a remarkable 187 not out by Mosman's Stan McCabe. Bodyline was born and Australia lost by 10 wickets. The word "bodyline" was condensed by the journalist Hugh Buggy from a report by another cricket writer, R. E. W. Wilmont, that the English bowling attack was concentrating

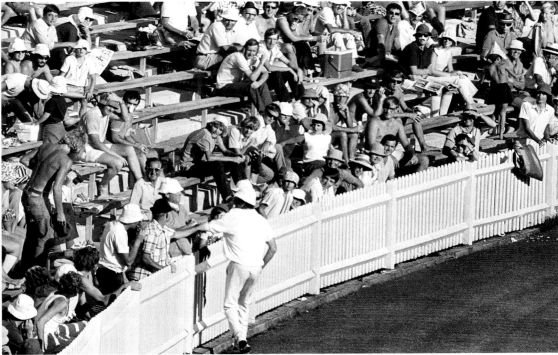

"on the line of the body". By the second Test in Melbourne, the nation and its players, still suffering the effects of the Great Depression, were seething over England's strategy, which they considered little better than thuggish. It wasn't cricket, they thought. Radio cricket commentaries, then in their infancy, were being broadcast around the nation, adding to the drama. Bradman's first-ball dismissal for a duck only inflamed opinion. He made 103 in the second innings, and 10 teammates mustered only another 79 runs. Australia won by 111 runs, with leg-spinner Bill O'Reilly taking five wickets in each innings.

The third Test in Adelaide brought the differences to unprecedented hostility. Four hundred policemen assembled around the boundary fence and another 400 mounted police waited outside. After Larwood struck Woodfull on the chest with a vicious bouncer, Jardine flagrantly strengthened his Bodyline field to six short legs with two men deeper at square leg and the last fieldsman at midwicket for any attempted pull shot. The crowd screamed its outrage. Woodfull was struck twice and wicketkeeper Bert Oldfield deflected a Larwood ball into his face. Australia was crushed by 338 runs. England's team managers, Pelham "Plum" Warner and R. C. N. Palmer, went to the Australian dressing room to sympathise with Woodfull, who replied: "I don't want to see you, Mr Warner. There are two teams out there. One is trying to play cricket and the other is not. The game is too good to be spoilt. It is time some people got out of it."

The Australian Board of Control sent a cable to its England counterpart claiming: "Bodyline bowling has assumed such proportions as to menace the best interests of the game, making protection of the body by the batsman the main consideration. This is causing intensely bitter feeling between the players, as well as injury. In our opinion it is unsportsmanlike. Unless stopped at once, it is likely to upset the friendly relations existing between Australia and England." The English deplored the cable but added that if the Australians wanted to propose a new cricket rule "it shall receive our careful consideration in due course".

Jardine and his team were so angered by the charge of unfair play that they threatened not to play the Brisbane Test unless the claim was retracted. It was, and England won by six wickets, thus regaining the Ashes 3–1. With England under pressure in the final Test in Sydney, Larwood scored an aggressive 98 to

Top They play for mythical Ashes but passions flare when Australia meets England. At the SCG in 1971 John Snow is manhandled by an Australian fan. (Photo: John O'Gready)

Above Shane Warne, never quite as loveable as his talent deserved, rejuvenated leg spin bowling, claiming more than 600 Test wickets. (Photo: Tim Clayton)

Above A breath of fresh air: Michael Clarke celebrates his first Test century in Australia, three months after a debut Test hundred in India. (Photo: Craig Golding)

give his side an advantage. He left the SCG to a resounding ovation from the capacity crowd. The Australian public did not blame him for the antipathy.

Bradman's "invincibles"', who toured England in 1948, helped rebuild postwar morale in the two nations. The Australians won comfortably but Justice Sir Norman Birkett, who had presided at the Nuremberg war crimes trials, wrote that the welcome given the tourists "was in some measure a thanksgiving that one of the great institutions of our common life has been restored".

In 1970–71, having seen six series against Australia pass without England winning the Ashes, the resolute Yorkshireman Ray Illingworth brought another team, including the powerful, obdurate fast bowler John Snow, and an even more obdurate opening batsman, Geoffrey Boycott. In Sydney, Snow bowled a bouncer into the head of leg spinner Terry Jenner and then fielded defiantly against the fence below the Paddington Hill where an inebriated — although anything but hostile — spectator reached over and seized him.

Spectators pelted the ground with rubbish. Illingworth led his players from the SCG until informed they would forfeit the Test unless they returned.

England won the series 2–0 and held the Ashes until Ian Chappell's mighty Australian attack of Dennis Lillee, Jeff Thomson, Gary Gilmour, Max Walker and Ashley Mallett destroyed Mike Denness's side in 1974–75. In the wonderful Ashes Centenary Test in Melbourne between Greg Chappell's Australians and Tony Greig's Englishmen, Rodney Marsh made an unbeaten century and David Hookes struck Greig's spinners for five successive boundaries in an innings of 56. The incomparable Lillee claimed 6–26 and then 5–139 and, by glorious chance, Australia won the Test by 45 runs, the identical result to that reached between the nations a century before.

In 1983–84, Australia's clash with Pakistan in the Sydney Test produced declarations on three successive mornings that Greg Chappell, Dennis Lillee and Rodney Marsh were retiring from cricket. It was the drum roll announcing Australia's decline in Test cricket which ended only when Allan Border's team won the 1987 World Cup in India. Chappell departed with an innings of 182, completing his career with a century in his first and last Tests and surpassing Bradman's 6996 Test runs.

Spectator rage might have been greater during Bodyline, and the crowds' day-long thunder as Lillee and Thommo ran in to bowl in 1974–75 might have been louder, but for personal achievement nothing could have surpassed the century by Stephen Waugh in the gloaming of the Sydney Test against England in 2003. Despite having won four successive Tests and with the Ashes in Australia's keeping, skipper Waugh was under enormous pressure to retain his position in the side when he came out to bat before his home crowd in the first innings. Waugh might rate his double-century in Jamaica, when Australia regained the Frank Worrell Trophy in 1995, as his

finest moment, but for those at the SCG one performance will live forever.

Careering towards his 29th Test century, Waugh faced England's off spinner Richard Dawson in the last over of the day, requiring five runs for his hundred.

Waugh took three runs from the fourth ball and needed two from the final delivery. Displaying uncanny nerve and conviction that it was his evening, Waugh crashed the delivery through the covers to the boundary, dancing in full circle as the crowd exploded with joy.

Test cricket had long proved to be one of the most enduring of sports. Yet, while it endured, cricket itself was changing. Limited-over cricket began in England in 1963 but Australian authorities were slow to follow suit. It was not until Kerry Packer bought two teams of leading Australian cricketers and established World Series Cricket in 1977 that the popularity of day–night cricket was recognised. Fifty thousand people streamed through the SCG gates to see Ian Chappell's team play Clive Lloyd's West Indians the next season. With

the Australian Cricket Board all but on its financial knees, Packer's Nine Network won television rights and the hatchet was buried.

Women's cricket has never received the recognition, status and publicity it considered its due. Yet the national women's team has results as impressive in its own way as the men's team, and the number of active women cricketers has risen in keeping with the international success. From a mere 5000 participants in 1984, the number had risen to more than 50,000 in 2005.

The first official English touring team arrived in 1934, captained by the redoubtable Betty Archdale, who subsequently migrated to Australia and became principal of Abbotsleigh School for Girls. The women's game commanded more attention from the 1970s, with the first World Cup in 1973. Australia has won five of the eight World Cup tournaments: in India in 1978, New Zealand in 1982, Australia — appropriately — in the bicentenary year of 1988, India in 1997 and South Africa in 2005, when Belinda Clark's team beat India by 98 runs.

Above Australian Test captain for five years, Steve Waugh led the side to a world record 16 consecutive victories. Packed SCG stands salute him when he retired in January 2004. (Photo: Steve Christo)

Top left Dennis Lillee, among the greatest Australian bowlers, on the rampage for Western Australia against NSW at the SCG in 1989. (Photo: Robert Pearce)

The Sydney Morning Herald

WEDNESDAY, MAY 1, 1996 — No. 49,504 FIRST PUBLISHED 1831 58 PAGES 80c*

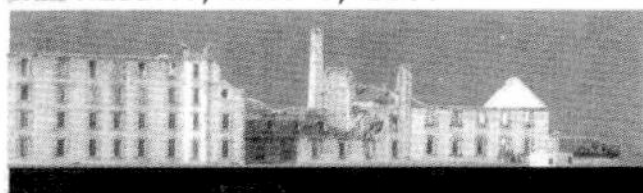

PORT ARTHUR MASSACRE

THE ANGER AND ANGUISH

They never had a chance

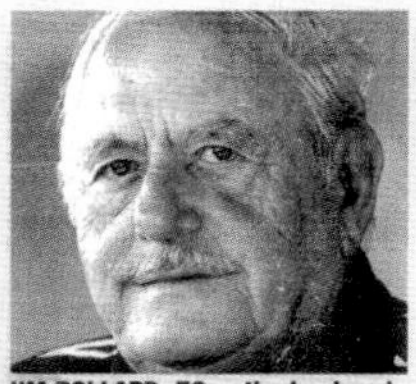
JIM POLLARD, 72, retired university administrator, Brunswick Heads, NSW. On holidays. Shot dead in car at tollbooth and body dragged into car park.

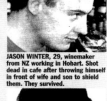

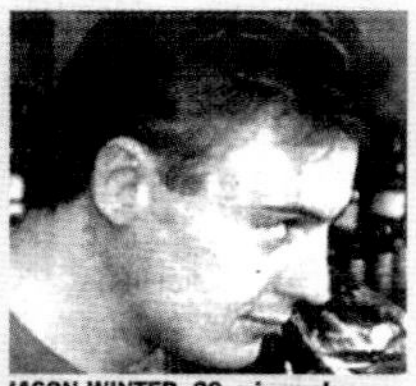
JASON WINTER, 29, winemaker from NZ working in Hobart. Shot dead in cafe after throwing himself in front of wife and son to shield them. They survived.

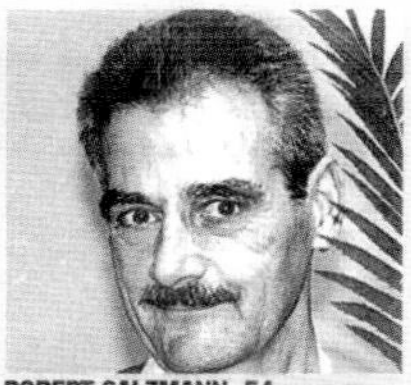
ROBERT SALZMANN, 54, carpenter, Ocean Shores, NSW. On holidays with wife. Shot dead in car at tollbooth and body dragged into car park.

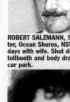

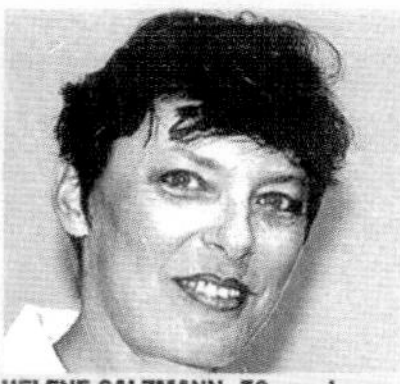
HELENE SALZMANN, 50, gardener, Ocean Shores, NSW. On holidays with husband. Shot dead in car at tollbooth and body dragged into car park.

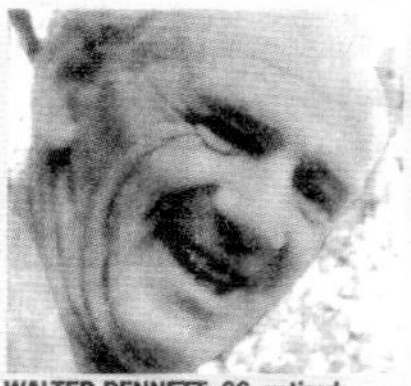
WALTER BENNETT: 66, retired, from Diamond Creek in Victoria. Holidaying with golfing friends from Kilmore. Shot in cafe as he sat with friends.

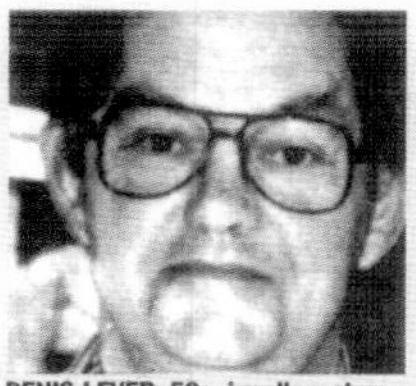
DENIS LEVER: 50s, jewellery store owner from Red Cliffs, near Mildura. On holiday with wife who survived. Shot in cafe after pushing wife under table.

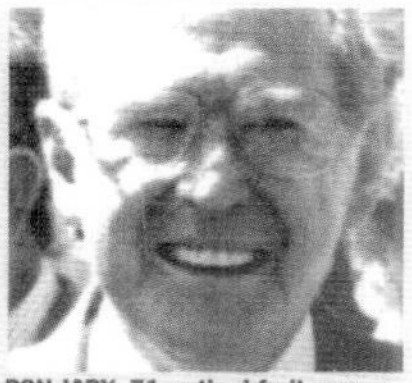
RON JARY: 71, retired fruit grower from Red Cliffs near Mildura. On holidays with wife. Shot in cafe while trying to push wife to safety.

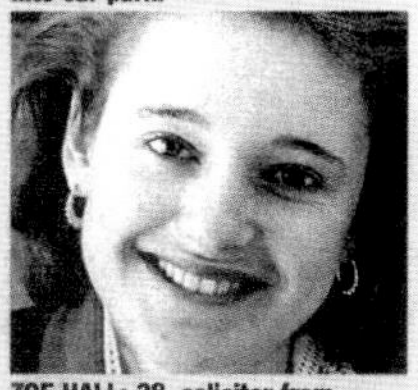
ZOE HALL: 28, solicitor from Kangaroo Point, Sydney. On holiday to attend 30th birthday party. Shot in car at service station.

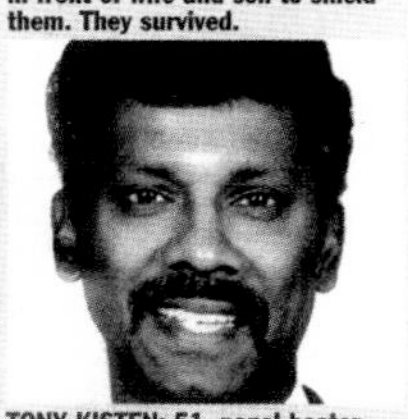
TONY KISTEN: 51, panel beater and Salvation Army member from Summer Hill, Sydney. On holidays. Shot dead at cafe, died in wife's arms.

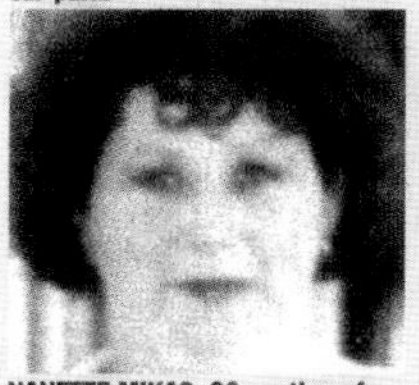
NANETTE MIKAC: 36, mother of two from Triabunna, Tasmania. Wife of local chemist. Shot dead while picnicking with daughters near tollgates.

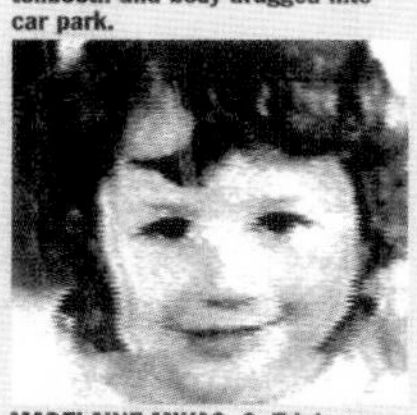
MADELAINE MIKAC: 3, Triabunna, Tasmania. Shot dead cradled in her mother's arms while picnicking at the tollgates.

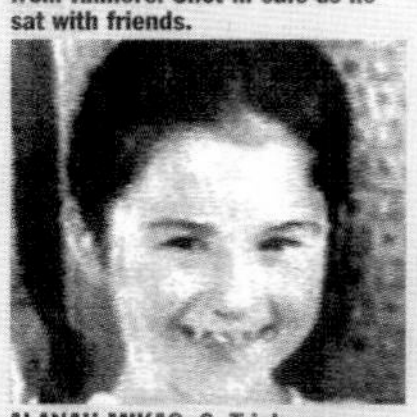
ALANAH MIKAC: 6, Triabunna, Tasmania. Picnicking with mother. Shot dead while trying to hide from gunman behind a tree.

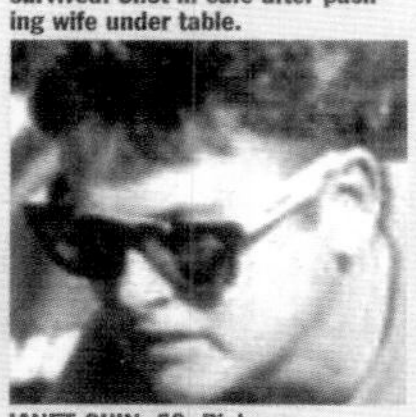
JANET QUIN: 50, Bicheno, Tasmania. Believed shot dead in Broad Arrow Cafe.

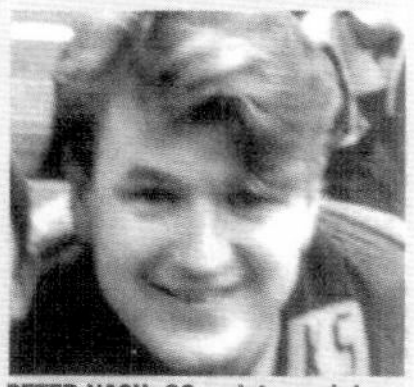
PETER NASH: 32, painter and decorator from Laverton, Victoria. On holiday with wife. Shot dead as shielded wife in cafe.

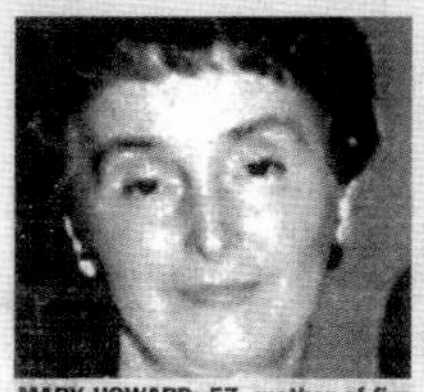
MARY HOWARD: 57, mother of five from Dunnstown near Ballarat, Victoria. On holiday with husband. Believed shot dead in cafe.

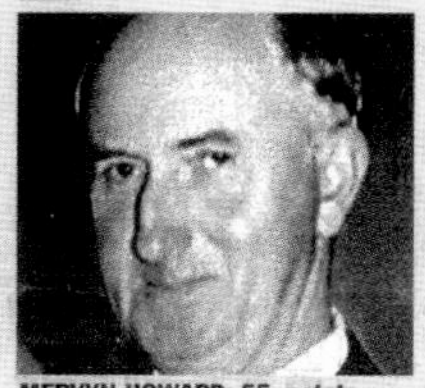
MERVYN HOWARD: 55, potato farmer from Dunnstown, near Ballarat, Victoria. On holiday with wife. Believed shot dead in cafe.

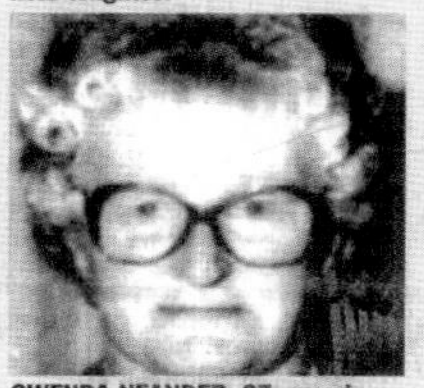
GWENDA NEANDER: 67, grandmother of 17 from Parafield, SA. On holiday with husband who survived. Believed shot dead in cafe.

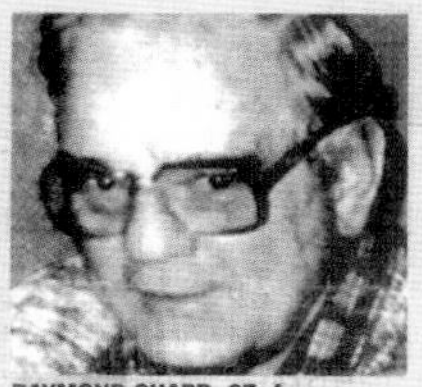
RAYMOND SHARP: 67, from Kilmore in Victoria. On holiday with members of golf club. Shot in cafe while trying to protect wife.

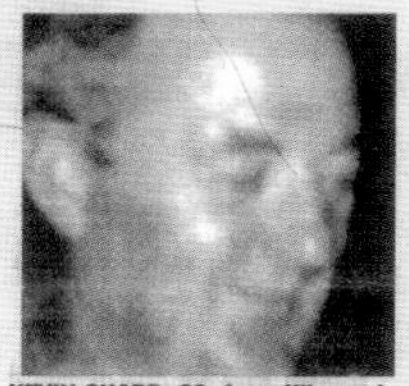
KEVIN SHARP: 69, from Kilmore in Victoria. On holiday with 12 members of local golf club. Shot in cafe while shielding wife.

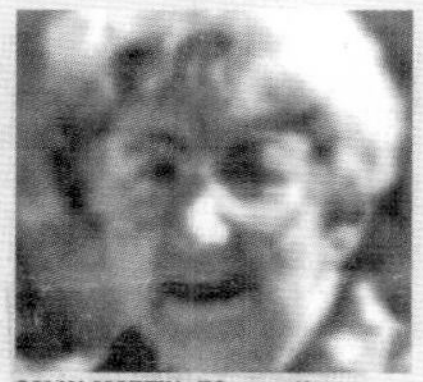
SALLY MARTIN: 70, guesthouse owner at Port Arthur. Taken hostage by gunman. Body in burnt-out house after gunman captured.

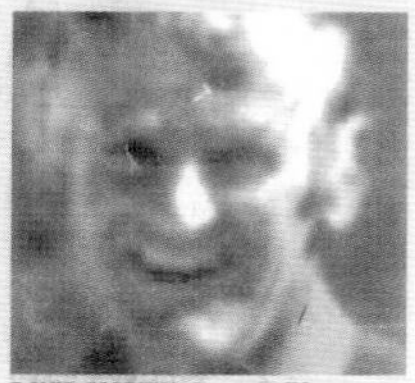
DAVID MARTIN: In early 70s, guesthouse owner at Port Arthur, also taken hostage. Body found in ashes after gunman captured.

– These are photographs of 21 of the 35 victims killed in the Port Arthur massacre

Campaign for national gun laws as man is charged at bedside

By STAFF REPORTERS

Pressure is building on the Federal Government to change the Constitution to give it the power to introduce uniform national guns laws as a response to the Port Arthur massacre.

The death toll in Australia's worst random shooting reached 35 yesterday with the discovery of third body in the burnt-out shell of the guesthouse where three hostages were held.

At a bedside hearing in the Royal Hobart Hospital, police charged Martin Bryant, 28, with the murder of one of the massacre victims, Kate Elizabeth Scott, 21, of the northern Perth suburb of Balga.

As community anger grew, the Tasmanian Government abandoned its opposition to tighter gun laws, announcing it would move as early as next week to ban military-style semi-automatic weapons.

The Federal Opposition last night backed calls from the NSW Premier, Mr Bob Carr, among others, for the Commonwealth to seek constitutional power to regulate the sale of guns and the licensing of shooters if it was unable to get the States to agree to uniform national laws. The Federal shadow ministry substantially toughened its stance on gun laws by supporting calls for a ban on all semi-automatic weapons other than for professional use.

The developments came as a *Herald* survey of Federal MPs and senators showed an overwhelming majority of respondents supported uniform national gun laws, a national register of all firearms and the banning of semi-automatic weapons other than for professional use.

However, doubts arose about the resolve of the National Party on these points, with the party Leader, Mr Tim Fischer, refusing to respond directly.

The survey also elicited a mixed response from State leaders with Mr Carr saying he would need to see concrete proposals before supporting a blanket ban on semi-automatic weapons.

The Queensland Police Minister, Mr Russell Cooper, opposed national registration of all firearms, saying this "simply created a new layer of bureaucracy".

In Parliament late yesterday, the Prime Minister, Mr John Howard, called for a bipartisan approach to tightening gun laws.

However, Mr Howard did not specifically call for uniform laws or express any view on the idea of the Commonwealth taking the power to act unilaterally to overcome State resistance.

He also declined to respond specifically to the *Herald's* questions. But the Opposition Leader, Mr Kim Beazley, used the Parliamentary debate to signal that the Labor Party would back any move by the Howard Government to take Federal powers by a referendum. The Australian Democrats took a similar stance.

Under the Constitution, any referendum to alter the Constitution must be held between two and six months after the legislation is cleared through Parliament.

Mr Beazley congratulated Mr Howard for his decision to bring forward the national police ministers' conference to consider ways of toughening the existing State guns laws.

He said he believed the pressure on State ministers to agree to uniform standards was so great that Mr Howard would probably succeed in getting agreement.

"If he does not I would ask him to contemplate the offer of the Premier of NSW to take upon ourselves Federal powers in this regard." Mr Beazley said.

Mr Beazley also supported comments by Mr Howard suggesting the need for a review of violence on television.

A spokesman for Mr Fischer said the issues raised in the survey would be addressed at the Commonwealth and State police ministers' meeting scheduled for Friday week and that Mr Howard had stated the Government's position.

There was a low level of response from National Party MPs, but a spokesman for the Queensland National Party MP Mr Bob Katter said that if a responsible person had been armed at Port Arthur the shooting spree might have been stopped earlier.

Mr Katter supported uniform national gun laws but said there should be a register of shooters rather than firearms and an exemption for farmers in rural areas in regard to any ban on semi-automatic weapons.

The Opposition's shadow Attorney-General, Senator Nick Bolkus, responded to the *Herald* survey with a letter on behalf of the 27-member shadow ministry supporting national gun licensing, a national firearms register and a ban on all semi-automatic weapons.

INSIDE

■ **BEDSIDE JUSTICE** Martin Bryant faces court in hospital room shared with attack victims – Page 5

■ **DEATH THREATS** How police turned a blind eye – Page 5

■ **MEDIA WARNED** Tasmania's fears about a fair trial – Page 5

■ **GUESTHOUSE COUPLE** They knew their killer – Page 6

■ **PLAYED DEAD** The cafe hero who saved two women – Page 7

■ **LAWYER SHOT** Sydney colleagues in mourning – Page 7

■ **GUN CONTROL** Where your MP stands – Page 8

■ **ME FIRST** Is the cult of the individual behind the rise in mass murders – Agenda, Page 13

■ **LETTERS** Readers have their say – Page 14

■ **OPINION** Gun laws and the ballot box – Page 15

Buying spree feared as shooters try to beat ban

By GREG ROBERTS and PHILIP CORNFORD

Fears of a rush to buy semi-automatic weapons were raised yesterday when a leading gun dealer revealed he had received many calls from potential buyers wanting to beat any ban on sale of military-style guns following the Port Arthur massacre.

"There's panic buying going on because people are worried they won't be able to buy them soon," said Mr Ron Owen, who owns two gun shops in the south-east Queensland town of Gympie.

Mr Owen received between 15 and 20 extra calls yesterday and on Monday from people wanting to beat the introduction of uniform firearm controls now being debated by the States.

"The calls started on Sunday afternoon as soon as the news was out," Mr Owen said. "The more publicity there is, the more people want to buy them."

Military style semi-automatics such as the AR-15 and SKS semi-automatics used to kill 35 people at Port Arthur are banned or heavily restricted in most States but are freely available in Queensland, the source of the great majority of mail order gun purchases in Australia.

Brisbane mail order dealer Mr David Auger said: "You've got the money and the licence, we'll sell you the gun.

But Mr Auger, of the Queensland Gun Exchange, and two other Brisbane mail order sellers all insisted they sold guns only within the law, checking interstate with police to make sure a buyer had the relevant licence.

"If you've got the right licence, we can get a gun to you in about a week," one dealer said.

The head of the Queensland Police Weapons Licensing Branch, Inspector John McCoomb, said the law was difficult to enforce, and an unknown number of mail order sales to unlicensed buyers were made.

Inspector McCoomb said: "It doesn't help that there are no restrictions of any kind on mail order advertising."

Queensland is also the base of several extreme right-wing organisations which are in the forefront of opposition to gun controls.

Mr Craig Lovejoy, of Silhouette Militaria and Frontline Firearms, had two SKS weapons for sale for $350 and $550 and two SKK sporting versions priced at $650 and $595.

Following a 1991 Federal ban on their importation, "they're hard to come by," said Mr Lovejoy.

Another dealer, who asked not to be named, said: "I've had two phone calls from Tasmania today from collectors who want to sell. You can guess why, and who can blame them. Ninety-nine per cent of our sales of military-format weapons are to Queenslanders who want them for shooting pigs or paper punching – target shooting."

In a statement yesterday, the Queensland-based Firearm Owners Association of Australia said: "A few hundred murdered by nut cases is infinitesimal in comparison to what Mao, Stalin . . . have committed."

COLUMN 8

A SCAM that could be nasty . . . On a train from Central to Bankstown the other morning, a man came through the carriage where Anne Merrick, of Rozelle, was sitting, announcing he was a ticket inspector. In his early 30s and dark-complexioned, he wore navy blue trousers, a grey jumper, sunglasses and a police-style cap with white and blue checks. The "inspector" found one young man without a ticket, and announced he was being booked. "You can pay $20 now, or $100 in court," he said. The young man paid $20. Anne sensibly challenged the "collector", asking for ID, which, of course, he didn't have, and he left. Anne was quite right, says the SRA. Its collectors wear suits, have big badges, and issue infringement notices. Police do not check tickets.

IT WAS Saturday night, and 20-year-old Allyson was off to a fancy dress party – but, as a police constable, her choice of gear was a little suss. She was one of Robin Hood's merry band, wearing a cutaway sack as a jerkin, tights, a cap and with a quiver of "arrows" over a shoulder. Driving along Erskine Park Road, St Marys, she came upon an accident, and stopped. And that's why, folks, if you had driven by, you would have seen a Sherwood Forester directing traffic around the site until her more conventionally uniformed colleagues arrived to take over.

GOOD to see the RAAF has a sense of humour. It's advertising in the *Port Stephens Examiner* for recruits . . .

So, if you are between 6 and 30 months of age, have sharp teeth, fur, and are a German Shepherd and have been desexed, then you are the dog for us . . .

MORE on what drivers do besides drive – Kylie Knox, of Randwick, nominates her most alarming motorist. At the wheel of a van weaving down Anzac Parade, Maroubra, with head tilted back and eyes closed, one hand on the wheel, he was trying to put in eye drops. Barbara Jools, of Neutral Bay, drove just ahead of a woman driver flossing her teeth – try that with one hand. Nancy French, of Cromer, while on the Newcastle expressway, saw a driver wrapping a large box in gift paper.

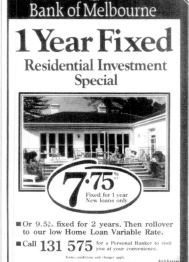

HOME DELIVERY (02) 282 3800

ISSN 0312-6315

9 770312 631032

WEATHER **TODAY Sydney** 15 to 20. Cloudy with a few showers. Light to moderate east to north-east winds. **Liverpool** 13 to 19. **Richmond** 12 to 19. **NSW:** Rain in the central and northern parts. Showers in the south. **Sunrise** 6.30 am **Sunset** 5.14 pm.

TOMORROW Sydney Showers with an expected maximum of 21. **NSW:** Rain or showers along the coast and central and northern inland. Fine in the south-west. **FULL DETAILS** Page 23.

INSIDE

		Classified Index	46	Opinion	15
		Crosswords	23	Personal Notices	31
Agenda	13	Editorials	14	Sport	42-46
Amusements	20-23	Law Notices	42	Stay In Touch	24
Arts	16,17	$2 Lottery 5948	M 12	Television	24
Business	25-30	Obituaries	31	World	11,12

PHONE

Editorial 282 2822
Classifieds 282 1122
General 282 2833

Left Martin Bryant's victims were chosen at random but the consequences of his rampage were immediate and enduring. Walter Mikac, one year on from the shootings, at the spot where his wife and two daughters died. (Photo: Jason South)

Below Port Arthur already had a horrible past when Bryant arrived on a Sunday afternoon in April 1996 with an SKS assault rifle and a stash of ammunition. When he was finally captured – and taken to hospital – the next morning 35 people were dead and the nation got serious about gun control. (Photo: Andrew Freeman)

MASS MURDERERS Australia has had many mass killings, beginning with the slaughter of Aborigines, but none has shocked the nation to the extent of Martin Bryant's murderous rampage at Port Arthur on April 28, 1996.

Bryant, 29, a well-off but angry loner, chose the Broad Arrow Cafe at the old convict settlement as his killing ground. There were plenty of targets — 60 people were gathered. He killed 20 and wounded 12. Then he went on a walkabout, shooting anyone he saw, including a mother holding an infant who was rushing towards him hoping he might help. He killed both with one bullet, and then a second child sheltering behind a tree, leaving the father to cry: "Couldn't you have left just one of them for me?" After killing 35 people and setting fire to a guesthouse, Bryant was arrested. His actions prompted a national outcry and gun law reform.

On Christmas Day in 1975, Reginald John Little set fire to the Savoy Hotel in Kings Cross because his boyfriend had not turned up. He killed 15.

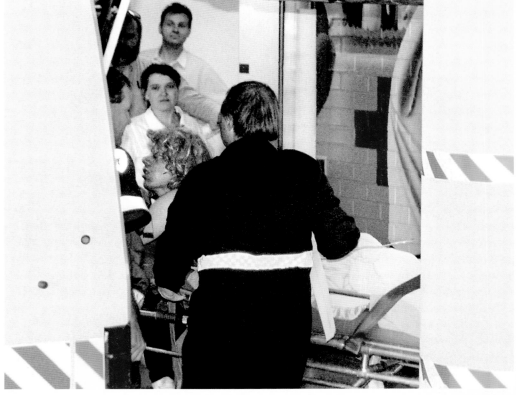

Right A man lies over his dead brother after the 1984 Fathers' Day massacre in Milperra. A thousand people were in the Viking Tavern car park for a bike swap meet when a war broke out between the Bandido and Comanchero gangs. Nine bikies were charged with murder and 21 with manslaughter. (Photo: Bruce Miller)

Below Wade Frankum lies dead after a mass murder in Strathfield Plaza in 1991. Frankum tried to flee by carjacking a shopper, but when the police arrived he left the car and turned the gun on himself. (Photo: Steve Christo)

Bottom A serial arsonist, Gregory Allan Brown, was convicted of setting fire to the Downunder backpackers hostel in Kings Cross in 1989. Six young travellers died.

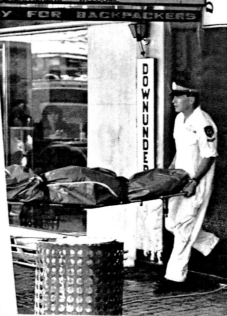

During the so-called "Fathers' Day massacre" in 1984 six bikies died, as did a 14-year-old girl, who had been caught in crossfire between the motorcycle gangs.

Young men taking out their frustrations against society in general began, at least in the modern era, with Julian Knight, a failed Duntroon cadet who, armed with two rifles and a shotgun, cut loose in August 1987 in Melbourne's Hoddle Street, Clifton Hill. By the time he was cornered and meekly surrendered to police, Knight had killed six and wounded 18, one of whom later died. His legal representative told the court that Knight had "for a long time harboured fantasies of being in a war zone".

In August 1991 Wade Frankum, a taxi driver and failed private schoolboy, went on a rampage with a rifle, initially at a railway station, then at the Strathfield shopping centre. He sat in a cafe, the Coffee Pot, and drank four cups of coffee. Then he lunged with a knife and killed a patron, before shooting other patrons and the cafe proprietor. With his own suicide at the end of the rampage, Frankum's tally was eight dead and six wounded. A psychiatrist, Dr Rod Milton, told the coroner's hearing that although Frankum was unhappy and had "accumulated much envy, resentment and anger", there was nothing in his background to explain the murders. He added: "I believe societal factors promoting violence exist now which did not exist previously, and it was these which tipped the balance for Wade Frankum."

SERIAL KILLERS In the Depression era, the Narromine area in the central west of NSW was terrorised by Albert Andrew Moss, a tramp with ferocious strength who waylaid drifters, robbed and killed them, burnt their bodies and threw their remains into waterways. Brought to trial in 1939, he said he had killed "a baker's dozen". For decades afterwards his legend was told and retold in the area, particularly to generations of Boy Scouts, who were too terrified to leave their tents at night.

John Wayne Glover, a British migrant whom a police officer said in his youth had the makings of a future sex offender, sought out elderly women and killed six of them on Sydney's north shore and the northern beaches during 1989–90, returning home each night to express his fears to his wife and daughters about how such a monster could operate. He was arrested on March 19, 1990, and had been under surveillance as a suspect at the time of his last murder.

Ivan Milat was a some-time roadworker who lived in the Liverpool area of Sydney. His targets were backpackers hitchhiking south on the Hume Highway. Just how he got them off guard, or whether he had any help, is unknown. One body was discovered in the Belanglo State Forest, near Bowral in the Southern Tablelands. The discovery of a second body in the same area sparked a search of the forest which eventually offered up six more. They had all been stabbed. The hunt was on. Milat's fundamental error was unsuccessfully attacking a British

backpacker, Paul Onions, who later identified him. When he was arrested in 1994, some of the victims' possessions were found on his premises.

In May 1999 police broke into a disused bank vault at Snowtown, 160 kilometres north of Adelaide, and found eight mutilated bodies stuffed into barrels. They had been murdered by people who knew them and who had then assumed their identities in order to collect social security benefits. Most of the dead had been transported to Snowtown, but two were buried in north Adelaide suburbs. Four men were arrested and convicted.

Above The bodies of seven missing backpackers were eventually found buried in the Belanglo State Forest. The discoveries were made over the course of six months' searching. (Photo: Dean Sewell)

Top left Ivan Milat, shown leaving an unsuccessful appeal hearing, was given a life sentence for the backpacker murders. (Photo: Adam Pretty)

Top right Albert Andrew Moss, known as Herbie, probably Australia's worst serial killer.

Above Unbowed by death threats and a bullet fired through the window of his Cabramatta electorate office, politician John Newman was eventually killed in a conspiracy that had been masterminded by a political rival, Phuong Ngo.

HIGH-PROFILE KILLINGS The first instance of an "assassination" attempt in Australia was the shooting of Prince Alfred at Clontarf in Sydney on March 12, 1868.

Then on March 22, 1921, a deranged Russian immigrant, Koorman Tomayeff, shot dead radical Labor MP Percy Brookfield at Riverton, South Australia. Brookfield had been a powerful supporter of the Soviet Union. Tomayeff, an anti-communist, told police he had been paid to kill him. It was never confirmed there was a political motive.

On March 21, 1966, Peter Kocan tried to kill the then leader of the federal opposition, Arthur Calwell. Kocan, sentenced to life and released after 10 years, said he had done it because he did not want to be a "nobody".

The killing of John Newman, state ALP MP for Cabramatta, on September 5, 1994, was a full-blooded political assassination. Newman had been in conflict with Fairfield City councillor, Phuong Canh Ngo, who in 2001 was sentenced to life imprisonment.

The bomb that exploded outside the Hilton Hotel in Sydney early on February 13, 1978, killing three, ushered in a new era of international terrorism. Hundreds of armed servicemen were mobilised to strengthen security for the 12 world leaders attending the Commonwealth Heads of Government Meeting at the hotel and the country retreat at Bowral. Evan Dunstan Pederick was convicted of the bombing and imprisoned. He has since been released.

Above David Carty's funeral in Parkes in 1997: the young officer is one of at least 248 police killed on duty in NSW. (Photo: Nick Moir)

Top left A bomb exploded outside the Hilton Hotel, Sydney, in February 1978. The prime minister, Malcolm Fraser, and 11 other leaders attending the Commonwealth Heads of Government Meeting were inside. Two council workers and a policeman died.

Left A bungled kidnapping attempt in 1991 took the life of Victor Chang, one of Australia's leading heart surgeons. Anne Chang, with daughter Vanessa and son Marcus, at Chang's funeral. (Photo: Robert Pearce)

Above Police and citizens comb the sands of Wanda beach after two 15-year-old girls, Christine Sharrock and Marianne Schmidt, were found murdered there on January 11, 1965. The case was never closed and early in 2005 detectives interviewed Victoria's longest-serving prisoner, child killer Derek Ernest Percy, about the crime.

Right Bodies, clues, titillating revelations: the Bogle-Chandler murder case had it all. Everything but the cause of the deaths and an arrest. The coroner, J. J. Loomes, and investigating police at the Lane Cove River site where the physicist and his lover were found dead at dawn on New Year's Day, 1963. (Photo: N. Herfort)

Below Margaret Chandler in the year before her death.

THE UNSOLVED The disappearance of Azaria Chamberlain, not quite 10 weeks old, at Uluru on August 17, 1980, drew out some of the best and much of the worst in the Australian psyche. The claim by Azaria's mother, Lindy, then 32, that a dingo had snatched the baby from the family tent created immediate scepticism. Discussion about the seemingly odd behaviour of Lindy and her husband, Michael, then 36, combined with ignorance about their religion, developed into a national frenzy. Lindy was charged with murder and Michael with being an accessory after the fact. Much of the Crown evidence at two coroners' inquests and at the trial was later shown to be inept. But Lindy was convicted on October 29, 1982, and sentenced to life imprisonment. Michael received a bond. Their supporters continued accumulating evidence pointing to innocence.

Top The improbable claim that a dingo had taken her baby provoked years of speculation, interrogation and, eventually, jail for Lindy Chamberlain. The disappearance of baby Azaria from a camping ground at the base of Uluru in 1980 forced Lindy and her husband, Michael, in front of the cameras for many years. (Photo: Russell McPhedran)

Left Lindy Chamberlain was released from jail after Azaria's jacket was found at the base of the rock six years after her disappearance, but the couple never really left the public gaze.

Above Despite the discovery of her jacket, Azaria's death has not been solved.

Lindy was released on February 7, 1986, and a royal commission under Justice Trevor Morling exonerated the Chamberlains. Their convictions were expunged and both were compensated. No trace was ever found of Azaria's body. A disclosure in 2004 by Melbourne man Frank Cole that he and his mates had shot the dingo that took Azaria and had disposed of her body could not be backed up by evidence. Lindy, long divorced from Michael, said: "Let it rest."

On New Year's Day, 1963, the bodies of Dr Gilbert Bogle, 38, a CSIRO physicist, and Margaret Chandler, 29, were found in bushland on the banks of the Lane Cove River. The couple had been at a New Year's Eve party. Dr Bogle's near-naked body was covered with a piece of carpet and his neatly draped coat and trousers. The body of Ms Chandler, wife of scientist Geoffrey Chandler, was covered with three flattened beer cartons. A coroner's inquest concluded the two had suffered gastric attacks and then acute heart failure. But the cause of death has never been established. One theory was it was a non-detectable poison. NSW police engaged the services of Scotland Yard and the FBI. Geoffrey Chandler was a suspect but nothing was ever established against him, a point he reaffirmed in his 1970 book, *So You Think I Did It?*. Other theories were that the two had died of LSD poisoning, or that someone had spiked their drinks. Twenty-five years later, forensic pathologist Dr Geoffrey Oettle said he believed the two had died of an overdose of LSD, a popular party drug in the social set the couple frequented, and the techniques were not available at the time to identify it. But who had laid the items on the bodies?

Above Samantha Knight's 1986 disappearance was not solved until 2002.

Top left Ken Marslew (centre) whose son Michael was shot dead at Jannali Pizza Hut in 1994, with Peter Simpson (left), Garry Lynch (right), and Chris Simpson (far right), outside Darlinghurst court in 1995. The Simpsons, whose daughter Ebony was murdered, formed the Homicide Victims Support Group with Garry and Grace Lynch, Anita Cobby's parents.

Right Anita Cobby after winning the Miss Western Suburbs title in 1979. "We can't ever forgive these five [convicted of murder] for what they did," Anita's mother Grace Lynch told reporters, "but we must stop hating them or that hatred will destroy us."

Top right The search party for Graeme Thorne trawls the streets of Bondi. Graeme was the victim of Australia's first kidnapping for ransom.

ABDUCTION AND MURDER The annals of Australian police are full of murders and missing persons entries.

Sometimes a body has been found, as with Sydney boy Graeme Thorne, 8, in 1960. His kidnapper, Stephen Bradley, fled the country but was intercepted in Colombo on a boat to London. Or the offender has been caught but the body not found, as with Samantha Knight, 9, who disappeared in Bondi on August 19, 1986. Sex offender Michael Guider pleaded guilty in June 2002 to her manslaughter but refused to say what

he had done with the body. On July 15, 1977, Griffith anti-drugs campaigner Donald McKay disappeared after shots were fired. James Frederick Bazley was convicted, but McKay's body was never found. The body of heiress, publisher and anti-redevelopment campaigner Juanita Nielsen, who disappeared in July 1975, the apparent victim of a professional hit ordered by business interests affected by her publication, was never found and nobody has been convicted of her murder.

On November 13, 1973, Kevin Gary Crump and Allan Baker went to the isolated home of a grazier near Collarenebri, in NSW's far west, and abducted Virginia Gai Morse, who was alone in the house. They committed atrocities and shot her dead. Arrested after a police chase in the Hunter Valley, the two were convicted of Mrs Morse's murder and that of a motorist, Ian James Lamb, from whom they had intended to steal petrol.

On February 2, 1986, Anita Cobby, 26, a nursing sister and a former Miss Western Suburbs, was abducted and raped by a gang roving in Blacktown. The men were led by John Raymond Travers, an abattoir worker. Police traced the gang through a witness's description of their car and Travers, brothers Michael, Gary and Leslie Murphy, and Michael James Murdoch were convicted and sentenced to life imprisonment.

The threat of life imprisonment did not deter a gang of four, led by Stephen "Shorty" Jamieson, 22, from abducting and raping Janine Balding, a young bank clerk, as she was getting into her car at Sutherland station in Sydney's south in 1988. The abduction was spotted but by the time police arrived the gang had left with Ms Balding, who was drowned in a dam at Minchinbury, in Sydney's outer west. The case saw DNA evidence presented for the first time at a Supreme Court hearing in NSW.

Above The anti-drugs campaigner Donald Mackay disappeared from outside the Griffith Hotel on July 15, 1977.

Left Juanita Nielsen had been campaigning against the eviction of Kings Cross residents by developers when she disappeared on a rainy day in 1975. (Photo: Nigel McNeil)

CHAPTER ELEVEN

Reaching Out

Meeting the challenges

BY TONY STEPHENS

John Arthur Passmore was one of many clever Australians whose lives are unsung in their own land. On the international stage his books, including *Man's Responsibility for Nature*, made him a pioneer in applying philosophy to such everyday subjects as the environment, the arts, science and politics.

Passmore, who died in 2004, accepted that most humans had average talents but that co-operation could harness those talents to benefit everyone. He rejected offers of chairs from foreign universities, preferring the Australian, communitarian, way. Rejecting both Margaret Thatcher's notion that there is no such thing as society and the communist view that society is above all, Passmore wrote: "We are always being told about the virtues of competition, but seldom about the virtues of co-operation. Yet Australia is in this respect very strong, whether in war or peace, in team sports, in tennis doubles, in filmmaking, in opera, in scientific research. If, in spite of the anxieties, the overwork, the unemployment, the pollution, the average length of life is not getting shorter — as it may nevertheless do in the near future — we can thank co-operative medical research for this."

He might have had in mind Howard Florey, who shared the Nobel prize for physiology and medicine in 1945. Florey brought to the world the miracle drug penicillin, thereby saving the lives of 50 million or so people. He led the march to the age of antibiotics, among the greatest adventures in science history. No Australian can have contributed more to the wellbeing of humankind.

No one can dispute Australians are an inventive people, capable of cleverness at the highest levels. And with the shocks of the new millennium they will need to draw increasingly on those qualities.

The deadly strikes against the United States on September 11, 2001, sent a shudder throughout Australia. Nearer home, the Tampa's rescue of refugees in the Indian Ocean in 2001, coupled with the

storming of the vessel by Australian special forces, and controversy over the detention of asylum seekers, including children, created a national divide. Then came the deadly bombing in Bali in 2002 and the realisation that holidaying Australians had been deliberately targeted. In May 2005 the agonised face of Schapelle Corby, on trial for her life in a foreign courtroom, captured the front pages, as did the kidnapping of Australian Douglas Wood in Iraq. His release 47 days later lifted the nation's spirits momentarily, coming just three weeks after Corby had been sentenced to 20 years in an Indonesian jail for drug trafficking. Again we were anxious, confused and divided.

The self-confidence of such occasions as the 2000 Olympic Games in Sydney was rocked. Doubts clouded the notion that a mature and tolerant Australia could become an enlightened 21st century democracy, showing the world the virtues of cultural pluralism. No one questioned the need to keep security as a national priority, but insecurity was rubbing the shine off the

Above The philosopher John Passmore was born in 1914, grew up in working-class Manly and was influenced at the University of Sydney by the fiery Scottish philosopher John Anderson.

Centre right Cleaning up Erskine Street in The Rocks during the bubonic plague in 1900. John Ashburton Thompson, the NSW chief medical officer, urged the government to clean up its slums and adopt simple hygiene as the best way to prevent the plague's spread.

Previous pages Sydneysiders send their love to, and empty their pockets for, victims of the 2004 Boxing Day tsunami at a concert outside the Opera House. Australians donated millions of dollars to the appeal through charities, collection tins on shop counters and fundraisers. (Photo: Janie Barrett)

nation's sunny confidence. It brought a similar anxiety to that caused by the "downward thrust" of communism in the 1960s, or Chinese immigration in the 19th century.

In our daily lives, rapid change was testing the team-spirited, egalitarian Australia that Passmore admired. Most people had never been so well off as in 2005. Even the poor were not quite so poor. But the gap between rich and poor was blowing out. What's more, Clive Hamilton and Richard Denniss wrote in their 2005 book *Affluenza* that Australians were richer but unhappier, working longer to enjoy less. Hamilton and Denniss say Australians have been infected by affluenza, an unhealthy preoccupation with money and material things. They say: "The richer we become as a society the more unwilling we are to sympathise with those at the bottom of the heap." Hamilton said in an interview: "People have always wanted to keep up with the Joneses. But now we want to crush and defeat the Joneses ..." These divisions no doubt played a part in the street riots at Redfern in 2004 and Macquarie Fields

Above An Aboriginal woman dances near the Trans-Australia Railway line before a crowd of passengers in South Australia, 1924. (Photo: H. H. Fishwick)

Top right Amanda Jane Mikokajs and Phong Tran acted in the film *Fish Sauce Breath*, which examined the culturally fraught relationship between two young people from different backgrounds. It was screened at Sydney's first ethnic short-film festival in 2003.

in 2005, factors in the growing incidence of depression in the community.

In the midst of all this, Australians continue to face smouldering issues of nationhood. Chief among these is reconciliation between the first Australians and the rest. The historian John La Nauze wrote in 1959 that Aborigines had appeared in Australian history only as "a melancholy anthropological footnote". But the 1967 referendum, including indigenes in the census, brought bright hopes. So did the High Court's Mabo decision in 1992, overturning the legal fiction that Australia was unoccupied before European settlement,

and the reconciliation walk by about 200,000 people across the Sydney Harbour Bridge in 2000. The three events proved false dawns. Pat Dodson, the indigenous leader, said in 2005: "Aboriginal people will continue to occupy that place deep within the national psyche that prevents this nation attaining true maturity … Do we have the courage and leadership to gift our children a truly reconciled and just future in one nation?"

The environment, both built and natural, remains an issue. The harbour is cleaner than in decades but traffic chokes the roads. Trade-union green bans saved some of the better buildings and spaces, but the green

belt around the city has been bulldozed to cater for all the people wanting to live in one of the world's most desirable cities.

"Sydney has been sequentially demolishing itself since the early 19th century," Elizabeth Ellis of the Mitchell Library said in 2005. Governor Macquarie began the process by introducing planning and building codes and knocking down the settlement's wattle and daub huts. The growing town began to develop its sandstone style in the 1830s and later built more elaborate Victorian architecture in great warehouses, banks and commercial buildings. A variety of styles blossomed in

the 20th century: Edwardian, beaux arts, art deco and, from the 1930s, functionalism. Sydney became an international city, with less of a British imperial look. And it grew vertically, the suburbs horizontally. Although Sydney's record on preserving buildings has improved, we're not so good at the big picture: streetscapes, precincts, historic landscapes, the skyline. In the city centre, commercial buildings have virtually obliterated glimpses of the harbour that once took the breath away.

Even the cleverest Australians can do little about the weather. But they might address the drying dams and other effects of

Above After school, a bus carries asylum-seeker children back behind the wire of the Baxter detention centre in 2003. Children sewed their mouths shut, drank shampoo, cut themselves with razors and threatened suicide in protest against their detention. The Federal Government decided to release children from detention in 2005 after lobbying from its back bench. (Photo: Bryan Charlton)

Above Anti-logging protesters cling to a 7-metre tripod in Chaelundi State Forest, near Dorrigo in northern NSW, in 1991. Others crouched in concrete pipes embedded in the road and buried themselves up to their necks to block access to the park for roadworks and logging vehicles. (Photo: Rick Stevens)

Right Teenagers burn a mattress during four nights of riots at Macquarie Fields in 2005. The violence began when two teenage residents of the suburb were killed during a police chase. The 20-year-old driver of the stolen vehicle survived but spent 12 nights on the run before surrendering. (Photo: Nick Moir)

drought. According to the National Climate Centre, the drought that lasted well into 2005 was the third worst recorded, after the Federation drought from 1895 to 1902 and the 1940–47 drought.

Sydney's — and the nation's — ability to provide services to the public is an issue again. Governments, terrified of going into debt to replace, expand or maintain water storage and delivery, drains and sewers, trains, buses and ferries, ports and airports, are again under pressure. Returning to the fray in a tradition dating back to its beginnings, in 2005 the *Herald* demanded an end to rhetoric on Sydney's needs. A page-one editorial set the priorities: "It needs a transport system capable of moving people quickly, safely and reliably; it needs to collect at least as much water as it sensibly uses; it needs to curb its obsessions with polluting cars and energy-hungry appliances; and it needs to provide homes that are pleasant to live in, easy to get to, and possible to pay for."

The republic will return as an issue: will Australians want King Charles III as their head of state? And long-term geopolitical trends will grow. Chief among these will be the rise of China and any strategic competition between China and the United States, the great power on which we have depended for over half a century.

The challenges are huge, but the record shows we have the compassion and commitment to do great things. This is the Australia that welcomed masses of refugees from Europe after World War II and hundreds of thousands from Indochina in the 1970s. When the Boxing Day tsunami struck South-East Asia in 2004, Australians were first to help. Once again the nation

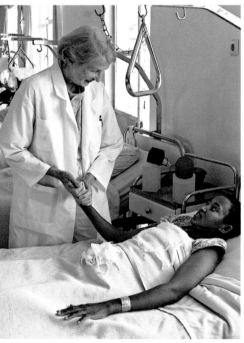

Above Dr Catherine Hamlin holds the hand of Tege Kassane, 18, at her Addis Ababa hospital in 2000. Women in their thousands make the trip to the Ethiopian hospital to seek treatment for fistulas – damage caused in prolonged or difficult childbirth. The condition causes chronic incontinence and regularly makes village outcasts of child brides.

appeared friendly and formidable, throwing off its old anxiety, reaching out and drawing in, making the best of East and West.

The record also shows that we are well equipped to find solutions. After all, Peter Doherty won a Nobel prize in 1996 for research into the body's immune defence system; Fiona Wood developed a revolutionary treatment for burns victims; Catherine Hamlin, by 2005, had spent 44 years performing and teaching surgery to help African women overcome childbirth injuries; Fred Hollows found ways to restore the eyesight of the world's poor people.

At the turn of the last century, NSW's chief medical officer, Dr John Ashburton Thompson, showed irrefutably that the bubonic plague was carried from infected rats to humans by fleas. His findings allowed effective control measures for a disease known and feared since medieval times as the "Black Death". The original heart pacemaker came in 1926 from a Sydney doctor. Neil Moore, of Sydney University, carried out the first frozen embryo transfers, in sheep, in 1960. Monash University scientists reported the first in vitro fertilisation pregnancy in 1973. Professor

Graeme Clark was responsible for the bionic ear, first implanted in 1978.

This nation was forged courageously out of adversity. Mistakes have been made but we can be proud of the achievements. In 1951 Charles Bean, who first encouraged Australians to look at themselves in the light of the warriors of Anzac, wrote about the meaning of Australia Day and broadened his original legend to include the clever Australians: "Equally striking was the way in which engineers, scientists, technicians, managers answered the test, especially in World War II. In the greatest crisis in our history, with their improvised blueprints, alloys and methods, they produced results previously undreamed of."

And from the time of the Korean War and the communist spectre comes his message for today's equally anxious world: "Perhaps the Australian, intensely loyal to family and mates, has less conception of his wider duty to the community. But that can be overcome by leadership, example and education; and so long as freedom remains its guiding star, the nation will avoid the one danger which is fatal to nations: the loss of its soul."

Above You can't keep young Australians at bay for long: the new Paddy's Bar in Kuta, Bali, 10 months after the first bar was destroyed by a bomb on October 12, 2002. (Photo: Rick Stevens)

Left A Bali bombing victim, Kristie Webster, at the Australians Together tribute at the Sydney Domain in 2002. She placed flowers at the remembrance shrine in memory of her mother, Robyn. (Photo: Andrew Meares)

Top far left Ratee Cewchan and her daughter Nongrak in the Bang Maruen refugee camp. Their fishing village, Nam Khem in Thailand, was hit by the 2004 Boxing Day tsunami. (Photo: Tamara Dean)

Bottom left An Australian volunteer, Jesse Maulder, a year into her medicine degree at Monash University, helped with the tsunami recovery operation at the temporary morgue in the Thai city of Krabi. (Photo: Andrew Taylor)

Notes on contributors

PETER FITZSIMONS played seven Tests for the Wallabies and has been a journalist for the *Herald* since 1989. He has written about Kokoda and is preparing an account of Tobruk. His biographies include works on Kim Beazley, John Eales, Steve Waugh, Nick Farr-Jones and Nancy Wake. He is a contributor to the *International Herald Tribune* and London's *Daily Telegraph*, and appears on both Channel Nine and Fox Sports.

ROSS GITTINS is economics editor of *The Sydney Morning Herald* and an economic columnist for *The Age*, Melbourne. His journalistic experience includes editorial writing and stints in the parliamentary press galleries in Sydney and Canberra. Before joining the *Herald*, he worked as an auditor with the national chartered accounting firm Touche Ross & Co. In 1993 he won the Citibank Pan Asia award for excellence in finance journalism, and has written or contributed to various books and periodicals.

JOHN HUXLEY is an associate editor of *The Sydney Morning Herald*. He was born in England and worked as a senior editor on *The Times* and *Sunday Times* in London before moving to Australia in 1988 as business editor of the *Times on Sunday*. He has edited the *Herald's* sports section and *Good Weekend* magazine, and has written books on the British oil industry and the Australian cricket team, as well as a piece of crime fiction.

VALERIE LAWSON is a senior feature writer with *The Sydney Morning Herald*. For John Fairfax Publications, she has been a writer on media and marketing for *The Australian Financial Review*, the editor of its Friday magazine pages, a Saturday features and sections editor for the *Herald*, foundation editor of *Good Weekend*, editor

of the *Times on Sunday* and arts editor of the *Herald*. She is the author of three books and is a Walkley award-winner for arts criticism.

DAVID MARR is the biographer of Patrick White and Sir Garfield Barwick. He joined *The National Times* in 1976 and his career since has been spent working for Fairfax newspapers, broadcasting for the ABC and writing books. Before his return to the *Herald* in 2005, he was presenter of ABC TV's *Media Watch* for three years.

ROY MASTERS was a first-grade rugby league coach for 10 years, winning the Coach of the Year award three times. He joined the *Herald* in 1988 and is an inaugural board member of the Australian Sports Commission. Although covering nine Olympics, he persists with rugby league, or, as the high-brow detractors of Masters and the code would say, returns to it like a dog to its vomit.

PAUL McGEOUGH, a former editor of the *Herald*, has been writer-at-large for the paper since 2001. He has been a reporter for almost 30 years, covering international conflicts since the 1990–91 Gulf War. McGeough has won Walkley awards for international journalism and for journalistic leadership, and was twice named Graham Perkin Journalist of the Year. In 2003 he published two books: *Manhattan to Baghdad: Despatches from the frontline in the war on terrorism* and *In Baghdad: A reporter's war*.

ANDREW STEVENSON has been a journalist for more than 20 years and has worked for a number of publications, including *The Daily Telegraph* and *The Sydney Morning Herald*. He has written on a variety of topics and spent two years as the *Herald's* rural reporter.

Above From inkwells to plasma screens: in between, the typewriter reigned supreme.

Right A male domain: the *Herald* reporters' room, about 1930.

The editors

PHIL WILKINS's career in journalism spans six decades. He began as a copyboy with John Fairfax in 1958 and, despite retiring in 2004, continues to contribute to the *Herald*. His experience in covering both cricket and rugby union is without peer and he was honoured in 2004 with a Walkley award for his outstanding contribution to journalism.

SUSAN WYNDHAM is a senior writer on books and culture for *The Sydney Morning Herald*. She began her career in journalism as a *Herald* cadet and has been a news reporter, feature writer, *Good Weekend* editor, literary editor and deputy editor (features/arts). She has been New York correspondent for *The Australian* and has contributed to several books.

MAX PRISK has worked as a newspaper journalist for more than 40 years, with stints in country NSW and Queensland before joining *The Canberra Times*. In 1977 he moved to *The Sydney Morning Herald* where he has held various senior positions. He was the editor of the *Herald* from 1988 to 1993.

TONY STEPHENS has been a journalist in Australia and England since 1961, after graduating in arts from Sydney University. He has worked at *The Sun-Herald* and *The Sydney Morning Herald* since 1979, writing on subjects from politics to sport, with a particular interest in history. His awards include a Walkley. His books include *The Last Anzacs* and *Sir William Deane: The things that matter*.

MICHAEL BOWERS worked at the Australian War Memorial, before embarking on a photographic career, during which he has worked for most major media organisations in Australia. A multi-award-winning photographer whose work has been widely exhibited, Bowers is managing editor, photographic, Herald Publications. He is co-editor of the book *Gallipoli: Untold stories*.

Acknowledgements

After the then *Herald* editor Robert Whitehead signalled his enthusiastic go-ahead for this book, we received encouragement and support from many quarters within John Fairfax Publications.

Our "book bunker" was set up on the library floor of our offices in Sussex Street, Sydney, and we salute the information services manager, Dean Leith, the head reference librarian, Sandra Arthur, and her team — Helen Bayliss, Chris Berry, Deborah Brown, Kathy Georgiou, Lyn MacCallum, Jemima McDonald, Brigitte Mahler-Mills, Lorine Marsh, Natarsha Norton, Amanda Peacock and Susan Walton — for their help and encouragement in the face of a considerable lack of decorum.

The picture library came under particular pressure, responding diligently to the many obscure and seemingly impossible requests. Many thanks to Harry Hollinsworth and his team: Sarah Drayton, Bonnie Prior, Marianna Papadakis, Ellen Fitzgerald, Zoe Slater and Joanna Vintiner. Additional dedicated work in preparing and cataloguing countless negatives and prints for loading into our electronic archive came from Sasha Woolley, Matthew Rushton and James Brickwood.

Graphic reproduction for the endless flow of prints and negatives was provided by Fairfax Imaging, led by Jeff Smith, and Michael Sykes of Fairfax Magazine Operations. Team members Kristen Greaves, Will Mottram and Paul Borderi did sterling work.

Various *Herald* journalists with specialist knowledge were patient and helpful when accosted in lifts or at their desks for key bits of information. Special thanks to Jennifer Cooke for details on early health issues, particularly the plague and Spanish flu period. We also thank John Sinclair, a senior *Herald* subeditor, who cast his practised eye over many of the first proofs.

Above George Bell was the first *Herald* photographer. His heavy, full-plate camera was an added challenge on outback assignments.

Centre right Bringing you the news: the *Herald* team, Darling Park headquarters, Sussex Street, 2004.

SELECT BIBLIOGRAPHY

Adam-Smith, Patsy. *The Anzacs*, Penguin, 2002.

Barnard, Marjorie. *A History of Australia*, Angus and Robertson, 1962.

Barton, G. B. *Literature in New South Wales*, NSW Government Printer, 1866.

Bateson, Charles. *Gold Fleet for California*, Ure Smith, 1963.

Bean, C. E. W. *Anzac to Amiens*, Australian War Memorial, 1946.

Bean, C. E. W. *On the Wool Track*, Angus and Robertson, 1963.

Blainey, Geoffrey. *A Land Half Won*, Macmillan, 1980.

Blainey, Geoffrey. *The Tyranny of Distance: How distance shaped Australia's history*, Macmillan, revised 1982.

Brett, Judith. *Robert Menzies' Forgotten People*, Macmillan, 1992.

Brunton, Paul (ed). *The Diaries of Miles Franklin*, Allen & Unwin, 2004.

Cannon, Michael. *Australia in the Victorian Age: Life in the country*, Penguin, 1988.

Carlyon, Les. *Gallipoli*, Macmillan, 2001.

Clark, C. M. H. *A History of Australia*, 6 vols, Melbourne University Press, 1962–87.

Clark, C. M. H. *Select Documents in Australian History*, 2 vols, Angus and Robertson, 1950–55.

Coman, Brian. *Tooth and Nail: The story of the rabbit in Australia*, Text, 1999.

Connell, John. *Sydney: The Emergence of a World City*, Oxford University Press, 2000.

Davison, Graeme. "Sydney and the Bush", in *Historical Studies*, vol 18, No 71, October 1978.

Day, David. *John Curtin: A life*, HarperCollins, 1999.

Dennis, Peter; Grey, Jeffrey; Morris, Ewan; Prior, Robin. *The Oxford Companion to Australian Military History*, Oxford University Press, 1995.

Freudenberg, Graham. *A Certain Grandeur: Gough Whitlam in politics*, Macmillan, 1977.

Gilbert, Alan D.; Inglis, K. S. (ed), *Australians: A historical library*, 5 vols, Fairfax, Syme and Weldon Associates, 1987.

Greenwood, Gordon. *Australia: A social and political history*, Angus and Robertson, 1974.

Greer, Germaine. *The Female Eunuch*, MacGibbon & Kee, 1970.

Hains, Brigid. *The Ice and the Inland: Mawson, Flynn and the myth of the frontier*, Melbourne University Press, 2002.

Hall, Richard (ed). *Sydney: An Oxford anthology*, Oxford University Press, 2000.

Hamilton, Clive and Denniss, Richard. *Affluenza: When too much is never enough*, Allen & Unwin, 2005.

Higgins, Matthew. *Journal of the Royal Australian Historical Society*, vol 68, pt 4, March 1983.

Hodge, Brian. *Valleys of Gold*, Cambaroora Star Publications, 1976.

Horne, Donald. *The Lucky Country: Australia in the sixties*, Penguin, 1964.

Inglis, K.S. *Sacred Places: War Memorials in the Australian Landscape*, Melbourne University Press, 1998.

Jahn, Graham. *Sydney Architecture*, The Watermark Press, 1997.

Jupp, James (ed). *The Australian People: An encyclopedia of the nation, its people and their origins*, Cambridge University Press, 2001.

Kelly, Paul. *The End of Certainty: The story of the 1980s*, Allen & Unwin, 1992.

Kennedy, Paul. *The Rise and Fall of the Great Powers: Economic change and military conflict from 1500 to 2000*, Unwin Hyman, 1988.

Kent, Jacqueline. *A Certain Style: Beatrice Davis, A literary life*, Viking, 2001.

Knightley, Phillip. *The First Casualty: The war correspondent as hero, propagandist, and myth maker from the Crimea to Vietnam*, Andre Deutsch, 1975.

Lawson, Valerie. *Connie Sweetheart: The story of Connie Robertson*, William Heinemann Australia, 1990.

Macintyre, Stuart. *A Concise History of Australia*, Cambridge University Press, 2004.

McGeough, Paul. *In Baghdad: A reporter's war*, Allen & Unwin, 2003.

McGeough, Paul. *Manhattan to Baghdad: Despatches from the frontline in the war on terrorism*, Allen & Unwin, 2003.

McKernan, Michael. *This War Never Ends: The pain of separation and return*, University of Queensland Press, 2001.

McMullin, Ross. *Pompey Elliott*, Scribe Publications, 2002.

McPhee, Margaret. *The Dictionary of Australian Inventions and Discoveries*, Allen & Unwin, 1993.

McQueen, Humphrey. *Social Sketches of Australia 1888–2001*, University of Queensland Press, 2004.

Molony, John. *The Native-Born: The first white Australians*, Melbourne University Press, 2000.

Moorhouse, Geoffrey. *Sydney*, Allen & Unwin, 1999.

Odgers, George. *100 Years of Australians at War*, Ken Fin Books, Melbourne 2000.

Official Year Book of NSW, Government Printer.

Official Year Book of the Commonwealth of Australia, Government Printer.

Park, Ruth. *The Harp in the South*, Angus and Robertson, Sydney, 1948.

Park, Ruth. *Fishing in the Styx*, Viking, 1993.

Park, Ruth, and Champion, Rafe. *Ruth Park's Sydney* (revised edition of *The Companion Guide to Sydney*), Duffy & Snellgrove, 1999.

Review of Marketing and Agricultural Economics, NSW Department of

Agriculture, vol 17, no 1, March 1949.

Reynolds, Henry. *Frontier: Aborigines, Settlers and Land*, Allen & Unwin, 1987.

Seal, Graham. *Inventing Anzac: The digger and national mythology*, University of Queensland Press, 2004.

Sexton, Michael. *War for the Asking: How Australia invited itself to Vietnam*, New Holland, 2002.

Sitelines: Aspects of Sydney Harbour, Sydney Harbour Federation Trust, 2005.

Souter, Gavin. *A Company of Heralds*, Melbourne University Press, 1981.

Souter, Gavin. *Heralds and Angels: The house of Fairfax 1841–1990*, Melbourne University Press, 1991.

Souter, Gavin. *Lion and Kangaroo: The initiation of Australia*, Text Publishing, 2000.

Spearritt, Peter. *Sydney's Century: A history*, UNSW Press, 2000.

Spender, Dale (ed). *The Penguin Anthology of Australian Women's Writing*, Penguin Books, 1988 (for the play *Call Up Your Ghosts* by Miles Franklin and Dymphna Cusack)

Stanner, W. E. H. *White Man Got No Dreaming: Essays, 1938–1973*, Australian National University Press, 1979.

Tritton, H. P. *Time Means Tucker*, Akron Press, 1984.

Walker, Robin. *From Scarcity to Surfeit*, NSW University Press, 1988.

Watson, Don. *Keating, Memoirs of a bleeding heart*, Random House, 2002.

Wealth and Progress of New South Wales, Government Printer.

Wood, Beverley (ed). *Tucker in Australia*, Hill of Content, 1977.

Wright, Judith. *The Generations of Men*, Oxford University Press, 1959.

A NOTE ON IMAGE SOURCES

The editors deliberately set out to source most of the images from the archives of *The Sydney Morning Herald*, which also include the work of photographers and artists on former mastheads, including *The Sydney Mail*, which began as the *Herald's* weekly digest for the country in 1860 and continued into the late 1930s, the afternoon *Sun* and *The National Times*. Some images came from associated mastheads, including *The Sun-Herald*, *The Herald*, Newcastle, the *Illawarra Mercury*, *The Australian Financial Review* and *The Age*, Melbourne.

A number of early images clearly come from old photo studio presentation albums and the great public archives the *Herald* has worked with since their beginnings, including the Mitchell Library, the NSW Government Printing Office and the Australian War Memorial. We seek forgiveness where we have not been able to pin down the source for attribution. The NSW Department of Commerce helped with photographs originally from the NSW Government Printing Office. In some cases we found that images held in public collections came originally from Fairfax publications.

Thanks go to Alan Davies, the curator of photographs at the State Library of NSW, James Logan, archivist and associate lecturer, Charles Sturt University, for help in providing background on the Reg Sharpless photograph "The Bog" in Chapter Four, and to Caroline Merrylees, archivist, Hay Historical Society, for providing details of the World War I contingent setting off from Hay in Chapter Nine.

Prints of all Fairfax images used in *The Big Picture* can be purchased. Go to www.fairfaxphotos.com for details.

Every effort has been made to correctly identify all images. If you can provide more information about photographs used — either the photographer's details or the people who feature in them — please write to The Big Picture, GPO Box 506, Sydney NSW 2001.

CONVERSIONS

We have chosen to retain original currency and measurements throughout the book, in order to maintain authenticity.

Australia converted from pounds, shillings and pence to decimal currency in 1966, and from imperial units of measure to metric in 1973.

Currency
A£1 = A$2
1 shilling = 10 cents

Weights
1 ounce = 28.3 grams
1 pound (16 ounces) = 0.45 kilograms
1 stone (14 pounds) = 6.4 kilograms
1 ton = 1.02 tonnes

Measures
1 inch = 2.54 centimetres
1 foot = 30.5 centimetres
1 yard = 0.9 metres
1 mile = 1.6 kilometres

1 acre = 0.4 hectares

1 pint = 0.6 litres
1 gallon (8 pints) = 4.5 litres

70°F = 21°C
100°F = 38°C

Index